James Joyce

JAMES JOYCE

Texts and Contexts

Len Platt

continuum

Continuum International Publishing Group

The Tower Building
11 York Road
London SE1 7NX

80 Maiden Lane
Suite 704
New York, NY 10038

www.continuumbooks.com

© Len Platt 2011

British Library Cataloguing-in-Publication Data
A catalogue record for this book is available from the British Library.

ISBN: 978-1-4411-9761-0 (paperback)
    978-1-4411-1333-7 (hardcover)

Library of Congress Cataloging-in-Publication Data
A catalog record for this book is available from the Library of Congress

Typeset by Newgen Imaging Systems Pvt Ltd, Chennai, India
Printed and bound in India

Ireland, a small nation, is nonetheless, large enough to contain all the complexities of the twentieth century.

Thomas Kettle, 1913

Contents

Acknowledgements

This introduction was helped along by a number of people, especially by Michael Peake who helped with editorial matters and the members of the *Finnegans Wake* research seminar at the Institute of English Studies, University of London. In particular, Finn Fordham helped with some ideas around the issue of introducing *Finnegans Wake* and Andrew Gibson assisted in the formulation of some thoughts about scoping an introduction to Joyce and the sort of problematics with which such a project might engage. Other members of this lively and engaging group had a less direct influence, but would certainly have informed my thinking on this book in all sorts of indirect ways.

My thanks are also extended to Cambridge University Press for permission to reproduce some material from my earlier book *Joyce, Race and Finnegans Wake*, notably the section on eugenics in Chapter 6 of *Texts and Contexts*, and to the *James Joyce Quarterly* who published a fuller version of the material on the *Wake* and the *Encyclopaedia Britannica*, also included here as part of Chapter 6. Carol Kealiher, managing editor of the *JJQ*, also kindly helped me locate some material on recent Joyce conferences, produced here as part of Chapter 7.

Abbreviations

Works by James Joyce

D	*Dubliners*, the corrected text with an explanatory note by Robert Scholes and fifteen drawings by Robin Jacques (London: Jonathan Cape, 1967).
E	*Exiles* with the author's own notes and an introduction by Padraic Colum (London: Jonathan Cape, 1952).
Letters I	*Letters of James Joyce*, edited by Stuart Gilbert (New York: Viking Press, 1957).
Letters II	*Letters of James Joyce*, edited by Richard Ellmann, vol. 2 (London: Faber and Faber, 1966).
Letters III	*Letters of James Joyce*, edited by Richard Ellmann, vol. 3 (London: Faber and Faber, 1966).
FW	*Finnegans Wake* (London: Faber and Faber, 1964).
JAA	Michael Groden (gen.ed.), *The James Joyce Archive* (New York and London: Garland, 1977). In this referencing system VI.B refers to the notebook series. The numbers following refer to volume and page number respectively.
OCPW	*Occasional, Critical and Political Writing*, edited with an introduction and notes by Kevin Barry; translated from the Italian by Conor Deane (Oxford: Oxford University Press, 2000).
P	*A Portrait of the Artist as a Young Man*, edited with an introduction and notes by Jeri Johnson (Oxford: Oxford University Press, 2000).
U	*Ulysses*, the corrected text, ed. Hans Walter Gabler, et al (New York and London: Garland, 1984, 1986).

Others

Annotations	Roland McHugh, *Annotations to 'Finnegans Wake'* (1980; Baltimore and London: Johns Hopkins University Press, 1991).
CH	Robert H. Deming (ed.), *James Joyce: The Critical Heritage* (2 vols., London: Routledge and Kegan Paul, 1970).

EB11	*Encyclopaedia Britannica* 11th edition (Cambridge: Cambridge University Press, 1910–11). This text will be cited by volume and page number. Where helpful the indexing principle of EB11 will be adopted. Here the letters a, b, c and d signify, respectively, the upper and lower halves of the first and second columns of the text
JA	Don Gifford, *Joyce Annotated: Notes for 'Dubliners' and 'A Portrait of the Artist as a Young Man'*, second edition revised and enlarged (Berkeley: University of California Press, 1982).
JJ	Richard Ellmann, *James Joyce*, new and revised edition (Oxford: Oxford University Press, 1982).
JJQ	*James Joyce Quarterly* (Tulsa: University of Tulsa, est. 1964).
MBK	Stanislaus Joyce, *My Brother's Keeper*, edited and with an introduction by Richard Ellmann with a preface by T. S. Eliot (London: Faber and Faber, 1958).
MU	Frank Budgen, *James Joyce and The Making of Ulysses and other writings* with an introduction by Clive Hart (1934; London and Oxford: Oxford University Press, 1972).
N	Brenda Maddox, *Nora: a Biography of Nora Joyce* (London: Hamish Hamilton, 1988).
NBB	Vincent Deane, Daniel Ferrer and Geert Lernout (gen. eds), *The 'Finnegans Wake' Notebooks at Buffalo* (Turnhout: Brepols, 2001–). In the referencing system used for this and other editions of Joyce's notebooks, 'VI.B' refers to the notebook series. The numbers following refer to volume and page number, with *NBB* using a letter for a line number.
Ulysses	Cited in the text by episode number followed by line number. Episode numbers correspond to Homeric titles as follows: 1 — Telemachus, 2 — Nestor, 3 — Proteus, 4 — Calypso, 5 — Lotuseaters, 6 — Hades, 7 — Aeolus, 8 — Lestrygonians, 9 — Scylla and Charybdis, 10 — Wandering Rocks, 11 — Sirens, 12 — Cyclops, 13 — Nausicaa, 14 — Oxen of the Sun, 15 — Circe, 16 — Eumaeus, 17 — Ithaca, 18 — Penelope.
Finnegans Wake	Cited in the text by page number followed by line number and referred to by book and part number. Book One has eight parts; Books Two and Three each has four parts and Book Four has one part.

CHAPTER 1

Introduction to a 'Biografiend'

'The house of Atreox is fallen indeedust' . . .

To begin at a beginning, James Joyce was born on 2 February 1882 at 41 Brighton Square, West Rathgar – a respectable seaside suburb of Dublin. He was the eldest surviving son of John Stanislaus Joyce and Mary (May) Jane Joyce (née Murray). Both families had advanced in trade. John Murray was a corn agent, and the Joyces had once been builders. By 1882, the latter were successful property owners and beneficiaries of the more general rise of nineteenth-century Catholic society in Ireland. They also had some notable connections with radical politics. John Joyce's grandfather, another James, had been a Whiteboy[1] and was sentenced to death at a special assize set up in Cork after the armed insurrection of 1822 (see *P*, 31). He was later reprieved by a government concerned about the spread of civil disaffection. John's mother, daughter of John O'Connell, was related to Daniel O'Connell, the leader of the Catholic emancipation movement, and John Joyce himself had been involved with Cork Fenians in 1871 following the release of prisoners from the rising of 1865.[2] He later became an active supporter of the Irish Nationalist Party under Charles Stewart Parnell and saw the rise and fall of his own fortunes as being intimately bound up with those of the 'Chief'.

It was in part the O'Connell connection that led to James Joyce being sent to Clongowes Wood School in 1888, one of the most prestigious Catholic schools in Ireland. Daniel O'Connell had sent his sons there to be educated by the Jesuits and John Joyce was keen to emulate that tradition – in *A Portrait of the Artist as a Young Man* (1914) Simon Dedalus tells his son he will be no stranger at Clongowes 'because his granduncle had presented an address to the liberator [i.e. Daniel O'Connell] there fifty years before' (*P*, 21). John Joyce had done well out of Irish nationalism and, ironically enough, the 'British connection', both of which accompanied the development of a substantial Catholic middle class over the nineteenth century. From the early 1890s, however, the fortunes of John Joyce began to decline. He was made redundant from a quite privileged post in the Collector's General office, which in 1892 was taken over by the Dublin Corporation. There were concerns about his political activities in support of Parnell and suspicions about his professional life – it was known that he had sold off some of his Cork properties, probably at the Collector General's insistence, to make up for deficiencies in the rates he had collected. Under these circumstances he was initially retired without pension, although following his wife's intervention he was eventually awarded the £134 2s 4d per annum allowance standard for someone in his position. John Joyce was 42 and according to Richard Ellmann, author of the standard James Joyce biography, from then on

> trapped. He was too accustomed to high living to subsist on his low income; in none of the ill-paid jobs that were sometimes available to him could he hope for the erratic hours of the Collector General's office. He blamed his misfortunes on imaginary 'enemies' and turned on his family, rancorous because their support curtailed his consumption of alcohol, though it did not do so very much. To himself he was never a poor man, always a rich man who had suffered reverses.
>
> (*JJ*, 34)

Unable to meet the school fees even before his redundancy, John was forced to withdraw his son from Clongowes in 1891, the year of Parnell's death. After a short period attending the Christian Brothers School in North Richmond Street, an episode to which he never referred in later life, James Joyce, in April 1893, was given a place at Belvedere College, a Jesuit day school.[3] The place was free of charge, courtesy of the then prefect of studies Father John Conmee, later fictionalized by Joyce as the rector of Clongowes in *A Portrait* and as the superior of the residence at the Jesuit College of St Francis Xavier in *Ulysses* (1922), both posts that Conmee held in reality. Joyce entered the matriculation (preparatory) course of University College, Dublin in 1899, studying Latin, French, English, Mathematics and Philosophy in the first year and graduating in September 1902.

By this time Joyce was already known on the Dublin literary scene, in part for his conspicuous poverty – his sister Eva recalled how as a student 'he prided himself that lice would not live on his flesh', a product of an antipathy for 'soap and water' (*JJ*, 65). More substantially he had an early literary success. Astonishingly for an undergraduate, his essay on Ibsen's *When We Dead Awaken*, entitled 'Ibsen's New Drama' (1900), had been accepted for publication by the prestigious *Fortnightly Review*.

He was much involved in contemporary debates concerning cultural nationalism in general and the idea of a national drama in particular. Before he was 20, Joyce had met many of the leading Irish revivalists, including W. B. Yeats and George Russell (AE), and surprised them by his arrogance – although Yeats, a Protestant, was not so surprised that a young Catholic intellectual from University College, not fully chartered until 1908, should think that 'everything has been settled by Thomas Aquinas' (*JJ*, 102). Between 19 December 1902 and 1903 Joyce made two trips to Paris, initially intending to study medicine but informing Yeats in December 1902 of his intention to make a career in literature.

First 'turf aside' – Joyce, Yeats, Revivalism

Almost any of the details in the above brief account of Joyce's early life is worth elaboration. All have a bearing on his fiction and most appear in it in some shape or form, some fundamentally so. When his father died towards the end of 1931, for example, a grief stricken Joyce wrote how 'Hundreds of pages and scores of characters in my books came from him' (*Letters* I, 312). Quite apart from his role in the shaping of the Simon Dedalus character – 'A medical student, an oarsman, a tenor, an amateur actor, a shouting politician, a small landlord, a small investor, a drinker, a good fellow, a storyteller, somebody's secretary, something in a distillery, a taxgatherer, a bankrupt and at present a praiser of his own past' (*P*, 203) – John Joyce figures largely behind the HCE figure and his monumental fall from grace in *Finnegans Wake*. The relationship between Joyce and Yeats is a further case in point, less obviously pervasive perhaps, but nonetheless figuring everywhere in Joyce's fiction and at an intriguing range of levels.

In one sense they were fellow Irish writers, mutually supportive to the extent that Yeats admired Joyce's talent, in the early days supporting his application for a Royal Literary Fund grant. His initial reaction to *Ulysses*, that it was a 'mad book!', was later revised. 'I have made a terrible mistake', he confided to L. A. G. Strong. 'It is a work perhaps of genius. I now perceive its coherence' (see *JJ*, 530). For his part, Joyce fully understood that Yeats was central to modern Irish literature. From a quite early age he had committed many of Yeats's poems to memory; Stephen Dedalus puts 'Who Goes with Fergus' to music and sings it to his dying mother in *Ulysses* (see *U* 1.249–53). On Yeats's own death, Joyce apparently paid the poet the supreme compliment of conceding that Yeats was a greater writer than he (see *JJ*, 660n). Perhaps this was a moment of highly uncharacteristic sentimentality – there is no record of Joyce ever repeating the comment – but there can be no doubt that Joyce fully accepted the importance of Yeats.

At the same time their relationship was, to put it mildly, fractious – especially on Joyce's side but by no means exclusively so. At one stage Yeats dismissed Joyce as a mere esthete. He rejected Joyce's translations of Hauptmann's plays, *Before Dawn* and *Michael Kramer*, on behalf of the Abbey Theatre, and, later Joyce's own play *Exiles*. For his part, Joyce, in February 1907, described Yeats as 'a tiresome idiot quite out of touch with the Irish people' (*Letters* II, 211). He made similar criticisms of many revivalists, gloating over George Moore's 'Damn stupid' ignorance over factual details in *The Untilled Field* (see *Letters* II, 71) and later claiming that James Stephens's 'knowledge of Irish life was non-Catholic and so, non-existent' (*JJ*, 333). But Yeats held a special place in this engagement with turn-of-the-century Irish writing and writers. He was not just one of the 'mumming company' excoriated in the broadside 'The Holy Office', but symptomatic of the whole 'motley crew' – this being Joyce's collective term for the neo-revivalist romantics then attempting to make a national literature out of fragmentary remnants of Celtic antiquity. Here the future writer of intensely realistic urban fictions, just about to make his departure from Ireland, takes the opportunity to ridicule people like George Russell, the mystic, ('who once when snug abed/Saw Jesus Christ without his head'); John Eglinton, the aristocratic essayist, (he, 'who will his hat unfix/Neither to malt or crucifix/ But show to all that poor-dressed be/ His high Castilian courtesy'), and, above all, Yeats, the architect of literary revivalism at the *fin de siècle*. These were important figures in contemporary Irish culture, joined in a common agenda to rejuvenate the country through a highly specified version of cultural nationalism. But in Joyce's account they become little more than out-of-touch idealists, dreamers of 'dreamy dreams' and figures decisively lacking in moral courage. In the poem, written two months before Joyce left Dublin in 1904, Joyce reserves for himself the demeaning role of manservant carrying off the 'waste' the revivalists refuse to deal with – 'a vicar-general' who relieves 'their timid arses' in performance of his 'office of Katharsis/My scarlet leaves them white as wool/Through me they purge a bellyful'.

The venom expressed in this invective, which has Yeats appeasing 'his giddy dames' frivolities/While they console him when he whinges/ With gold-embroidered Celtic fringes'[4] was suggestive of deep animosities. The tensions of a new generation defining itself against the old were hugely aggravated by even more powerful dynamics around issues of class, culture and nation.[5] From Joyce's perspective, Yeats, like many revivalist leaders before, was crucially identified by the Protestant landed traditions of his family background.[6] The importance of that identity for Joyce was confirmed by Yeats's politics. Whereas Joyce in these early days claimed to be a socialist and, later an anarchist, Yeats was a conservative, not least in terms of the revivalist agenda that constructed Ireland in landlordist terms as a paternalistic 'Unity of Culture' – the syncretic whole which, conveniently from Joyce's point of view, smoothed out a long history of Anglo–Irish hegemony in Ireland.

At this point an identity gap of some considerable significance opens up to become suggestive of the aesthetic differences between Joyce's work and revivalist culture. His fictions appear not merely fortuitously different to revivalism but, at almost every point, in precise and explicit antithesis. They present a version of Ireland completely at odds with that presented in revivalist literature. The Revival's restoration of Celtic myth is displaced in Joyce by the wilful intervention that places Homer at the centre of an 'Irish' epic of modernity; the Literary Revival's celebration of an aristocratic culture of heroism ousted by Joyce's celebration of the culture of Dublin's streets, his mock-heroic. Against the neo-Platonic aesthetic of Yeats and Russell, Joyce plays out his own concoction of Aristotle and Aquinas; against the revivalists' evocation of a timeless idyllic rurality are Joyce's excessively time-specific urban fictions. His realism counters their mysticism; just as, at a very different level, his Leopold Bloom who eats 'with relish the inner organs of beast and fowls' (*U* 4.1–2) responds to the Revival's 'Windandwatery' vegetarianism (*U* 7.537). The reverse side to Joyce's classical detachment is the emotionally charged temper of romanticism which he ascribed to the Revival. While the Revival often stressed the unconscious, 'spiritual' element in art-manufacture, Joyce's fictions contains the most intricate designs and patterns. He saw a parallel in this respect between *Ulysses* and the complex decorative art of *The Book of Kells*, an art 'at which the ancient Irish excelled' (*OCPW*, 114), a parallel which, significantly, takes place across a pre-plantation history from which Anglo–Ireland was excluded.[7]

The Joyce and Yeats relationship, then, was far from just 'personal'. It extended out into the difficult area of Joyce and nationalism. Ultimately it connected up with the question of Joyce's politics and has substantial bearing on the imagining of a potential solidarity of Irish culture placed under postcolonial pressure – an issue fundamental to some of the most central critical debates on Joyce and Ireland that have taken place over recent years. For now though, it is enough to say that biography has a tendency to spin out, notably so in the case of Joyce, not just into the fictions but also into wider cultural history – and to register also that while it is indisputable that Joyce was making ready to leave his country of birth in 1904, a great deal of it would be going with him in very particular forms. It would be travelling not as baggage stored way for later nostalgic indulgence, but rather as the active constituent in Joyce's critical engagement with the world.

'. . . but deeds bound going arise again'

To return to the biographical outline – in June 1904 Joyce left home for
Europe once more; as it turned out, for the last time. He never returned
to live in Ireland. The departure was perceived by Joyce as a great sundering, partly a product of his being somehow 'betrayed', but also an
affirmation of his radicalism, a wholesale rejection, Joyce said at the
time, of the 'whole present social order and Christianity . . . I left the
Catholic Church', he continued, 'hating it most fervently . . . I make
open war upon it by what I write and say and do'. As for his home 'it was
simply a middle-class affair ruined by spendthrift habits which I have
inherited . . . We are seventeen in family. My brothers and sisters', he
claimed, 'are nothing to me' (*Letters* II, 48).

A good deal of this self-dramatizing vigour was shaped by the fact
that this time he was not leaving alone. A forceful young woman from
Galway had agreed to go with him – indeed, as far as leaving Ireland
was concerned she appeared to be as keen, if not more so, than Joyce
himself. For his part, much of what he was doing, Joyce claimed, was for
possession of Nora or, more accurately, he constructed his sexual desire
in terms of his intellectual rebellion – 'When I was waiting for you last
night', he wrote . . . It seemed to me that I was fighting a battle with every
religious and social force in Ireland for you' (*Letters* II, 53). In October
1904, Joyce and Nora Barnacle left Dublin for Zurich, travelling via
Paris, never to return except for a few business trips and holidays, some
of them abortive and with Nora after her trip home to the new republic
in 1922 hardly having 'a good word to say about Ireland' (*N*, 264).

According to a family friend quoted by the biographer Brenda
Maddox, Nora Barnacle, hugely important to Joyce for many reasons,
became not least Joyce's 'portable Ireland', 'that little bit of Ireland Joyce
always had to have with him', although she grew up in traditions quite
at odds with the Catholic nationalism which surrounded Joyce at home
and at University College (*N*, 341). The Healys on Nora's mother's side,
especially her uncle, Michael Healy 'with his Civil Service position, were
lifelong supporters of the British Crown. It was a loyalty Nora retained'
(*N*, 24). Throughout her life the woman that Joyce imagined as being
crucially connected with his ambition to become the 'poet of . . . [his]
race' remained a reader of the *Daily Mail* (*Letters* II, 248) and favoured
holidays in England as opposed to 'her native dunghill' (*N*, 264).[8]

Between 1904 and 1913, this modern unmarried couple lived in
Pola, Rome, and for much the longest period, in Trieste. During that
time, Joyce published very little. *Chamber Music*, the short collection
of love poems which Joyce later thought 'poor and trivial' (*Letters* II,
182) appeared in May 1907, with Irish reviewers commenting on how

far removed the poems were from the cultural nationalism so much a feature of contemporary Irish writing. Writing in the *Freeman's Journal* (1907), Joyce's college contemporary, Thomas Kettle, noted that there was 'no trace of the folklore, folk dialect, or even national feeling that have coloured the work of practically every writer in contemporary Ireland' (*CH*, 37). Apart from *Chamber Music*, Joyce's only publications in this period were the nine articles he wrote for the Triestine newspaper *Il Piccolo della Sera*, most of them about Irish politics and cultural history.

For all the limited success in publishing terms however, this was a time of great creativity with most of *Dubliners* (1914) being written between 1904 and 1906, at the same time that the *Stephen Hero* manuscript was being worked on. The second draft of the latter project, now entitled *A Portrait of the Artist as a Young Man*, was completed across the same period and revised for serial publication in the *Egoist*, which started in the February 1914 edition. *Dubliners* appeared in the same year in an edition of 1250 copies published by Grant Richards. By the end of 1915 Joyce was building a small but enthusiastic and prestigious following. He was championed with particular force by Ezra Pound as a masculinist modern writer capable of producing hard, clean, prose. No less a figure than H. G. Wells was advising J. B. Pinker, the London literary agent, to act for Joyce and, at Pound's instigation, the Royal Literary Fund awarded Joyce a £75 grant. He had also completed the play, *Exiles* (1918), which was Ibsenite in many ways, but at the same time rehearsed many of the themes of exile and betrayal that were becoming characteristically Joycean. On top of that, in 16 June 1915, the day that was to become known as 'Bloomsday', Joyce informed his long-suffering brother, Stanislaus, that the first chapter of *Ulysses* had been written.[9] Later that month the Joyces moved to Zurich.

Placed against the Celticism of the Irish Literary Revival, *Dubliners* looked to be a stunning appropriation of European realism and *A Portrait* an innovative intervention into the *bildungsroman* tradition, but neither of these texts could fully prepare the world for *Ulysses*. Epic in scale, mock epic in substance, *Ulysses* was nothing less than a reinvention of the novel. For all the emphasis it received in the early reception, the radical application of interior monologue, or stream-of-conscious, was only part of the book's innovation, as was the ironic application of a myth 'structure'. Even more substantially, *Ulysses* was an astonishingly bold reproduction of the world in the realist tradition and at the same time a thoroughgoing and often hilarious deconstruction of that very same tradition, an anti-novel. It incorporated as narrative technique, the style of romantic novelese; the format of newspapers; a fantastic 'hallucinatory' play; a version of romantic Irish revivalism and street slang colliding together in the very same episode; science discourse and what appeared to be scientific method.[10] One episode adopted music for the purposes of formal structure; another was a jangling amalgam of commonplace bourgeois idiom. Yet another appeared to be narrated through a history, or sampler, of the novel tradition, at the same time as incorporating into its fabric the stages of foetal development. *Ulysses* was a comic novel on a vast scale, although for early readers the targets of its comedy were often far from obvious or, for some, too close to home. Richard Aldington writing in the *English Review* in 1922 found *Ulysses* 'more bitter, more sordid, more ferociously satirical than anything Mr Joyce has yet written . . . There is a laughter in *Ulysses*', he continued, 'but it is a harsh, sneering kind, very different from the *gros rire* of Rabelais' (*CH*, 188). By the time of its full publication by Sylvia Beach's Shakespeare and Company in 1922, *Ulysses* had been suppressed no less than three times, twice burned and once successfully prosecuted for obscenity. Its author was on the verge of becoming a celebrity, in some circles at least.

'Whispering another aside' – Joyce, the Modern, Europe?

While nothing in the above account of Joyce's life in Europe between 1904 and 1921 is knowingly false, far from all of it is uncontroversial and the general tone could be taken to contradict what was implied earlier in this introduction about the importance of Ireland to Joyce and his fictions. In this exilic, émigré version of things – a version much sustained by the Ellmann biography – Joyce's life story has a tendency to become metaphorical for his Europeanization. Here the 'paralysis' he apparently experienced in Ireland and later anatomized as the Irish condition is firmly responded to by what appears to be a heroic escape into Continental artistic freedom. That release from 'the old country', characterized in those stark ways, is far from innocent. Potentially it sets up a whole series of deeply politicized oppositions that once dominated Joyce criticism, but which have unravelled over the last fifty years or so, largely as a result of paradigmatic shifts in intellectual culture.

In the exile formulation of the biography, Ireland becomes stultifying to the young James Joyce; Europe liberating. The latter, to which Joyce is delivered, becomes by extension a literal and figurative centre characterized by its modernity, rationality and cultured sophistication. The former, Ireland, gets reduced to the status of a borderland or outpost – primitive, conservative, superstitious and backward looking. Joyce is not now merely living in Europe. He is transformed by the courageous act of will and imagination that extricates him from a stultifying Irish 'background'. As the author of classic modernist texts he then gets fully incorporated into a 'European' pantheon of cultural genius, an elevation asserted influentially by the French critic and early Joyce admirer Valery Larbaud who claimed in 1922 that with *Ulysses* Ireland would make 'a sensational re-entrance into high European literature' (*CH*, 253) – a statement no less controversial for being largely true. For in such formulations Joyce remains in some sense 'Irish', but it is the stimulation of the European context and, above all, the sheer cultural authority of the tradition he transforms that most fully throws his prodigious creative powers into gear. Under these conditions, Joyce's achievement appears to become absorbed into Western tradition at a fundamental level.

Not surprisingly, that version of things has been challenged, not least by an Irish academy which can point with justification to the real Dublin of the early-twentieth century as a modern centre of lively intellectual life – 'indescribably brilliant' according to one of Joyce's contemporaries, Arthur Cleary, with the UCD student body being 'highly politicised . . . entering into and sometimes instigating debates on many of the leading issues of the day: Home Rule, the Irish language and women's suffrage'. Another of those controversies was the university question itself and University College 'stood at the heart of a prolonged debate about the establishment of a university that would be acceptable to the Catholic hierarchy and successive Britain governments'.[11]

But this relatively straightforward historiographical challenge problematises only the fact of Joyce's highly critical reproduction of the Irish intellectual culture of his day. The postcolonial perspective which has sometimes accompanied such objections, however, is a more fundamental contestation of the Western intellectual tradition itself, which now struggles to maintain itself as an authorised history, figuring instead as a highly politicised 'appropriation' of the very concept of the modern world. Supported by a great body of theoretical work, much of which is derived from French philosophical traditions – 'deconstruction' in particular – postcolonialism typically attempts to topple the modern from its former privileged Western foundations. Here 'modernity', always a difficult concept, becomes detached from the 'metanarratives' of its progressivist history, now returned as Western ideology, and with that simple move is rendered profoundly problematic. Former binaries across tradition and progress, centre and margin, conservative and radical are subverted, sometimes dissolved altogether. One result is that the cultivated modern self, and its former antithesis – the primitive other – become repositioned as necessary opposite sides of the same coin, interdependent constructions that, again, perform in obviously ideological ways. To paraphrase Yeats, under these conditions the 'centre' finds itself unfolding, waking up to condemn the lies of progressivism because its history, as well as implicating the invention of the steam engine and the spread of welfarism, also incorporates the Holocaust, now firmly understood not as an mindless aberration but, rather, as a horrific culmination of scientism and modern bureaucratic 'efficiency'.

All of which has had a deep impact on Joyce studies. However much we may be considered to be beyond the postcolonial moment, fundamental questions raised by its intervention remain. Joyce's position as a modernist cannot be seriously challenged, but does that render his account of the world radically liberating or somehow conservatively tied to a defunct masculinist order of reason and rationality? The facts of Joyce's Europeanisation can hardly be disputed, but does that make his fictions now less 'Irish' or more so? How about the critique of early twentieth-century Ireland that his fictions are often seen to effect? Is this a product of naïve or mischievous misreading or is Joyce himself a 'gay betrayer' of his country or, at least, of some nationalist versions of it? These are some of the central questions with which Joyce criticism now engages, hardly answerable in this interval between Joyce climbing the mountain of European intellectual culture and arriving triumphant at its peak; the substantive point, however, should be clear. Biography, like fiction, is not as innocent as it sometimes looks – an especially appropriate reminder as it turns out, not just in terms of the biographical material that preceded this second aside but also in terms of the narrative which follows it – a necessarily guarded account of some of the immediate 'European' conditions that informed the writing of *Finnegans Wake*.

'The chaosmos of alle'

Again as a product of Pound's intervention, the Joyces had moved to Paris in 1920 and here, especially with the publication of *Ulysses* in 1922, their social life underwent 'intensification'. Paris was 'the crossroads to everywhere' (*N*, 241) – which meant that Irish and English friends like Frank Budgen and Arthur Power could visit easily – and Joyce was famous. Friendly with Pound, Ford Madox Ford, T. S. Eliot, Wyndham Lewis, and a younger generation of writers including Ernest Hemingway, he was also a cult hero to figures such as the American writer Robert Almon and celebrated as the leading European modernist by the critical avant garde, including the influential Larbaud. 'Fame', as Maddox puts its, 'was lifting all four Joyces [James and Nora and their children, Lucia and Georgio] to the circles of international café society'. If they often appeared surprisingly ordinary in the company of more extravagant figures like Gertrude Stein, Djuna Barnes and Nancy Cunard, it nevertheless seemed natural enough that they should, in March 1922, attend the society wedding of 'Laurence Vail, a dashing young American writer and Peggy Guggenheim, the New York heiress' (*N*, 255).

The Parisian background was not an insignificant part of the context that produced Joyce's last important work, *Finnegans Wake* (1939) – hardly a society book, but a text which, in its astonishing complexity, alienated many of Joyce's readers to the extent that even his most loyal supporters, his brother Stanislaus for example, and his benefactress Harriet Shaw Weaver, had great difficulty in accommodating it. Indeed to some it seemed that with this extraordinary production Joyce had finally lost his wits, a view that he may have partly encouraged as his daughter's mental illness worsened with the composition of the *Wake* and Joyce tried to console himself with the idea that Lucia's increasingly alarming condition was somehow aligned to the creative faculties she clearly possessed. The fact that many saw the *Wake* as a 'book of the night', a fantastic reproduction of 'dreamwork' and psychodynamic processes no doubt fuelled that fantasy.

Dream or not, the *Wake* had no discernible narrative – although it seemed to revolve around dozens of tiny narratives repeated over and over. Reading across the *Wake* from 1.i to 4.i, it was impossible, however, to recover a single, reliable narrative dynamic. The ending famously joined up with the beginning, which implied that it was possible to enter the *Wake* at any stage with no loss to understanding, or misunderstanding. There were characters of a kind, but these merged into each other and multiplied out into hundreds of parallel identities. The language of the *Wake* was more than simply 'difficult'. For most readers it was virtually unreadable, not because it had no meaning but, on the contrary, because it seemed to allow all or any meaning. Even more than *Ulysses*, it seemed to imply, as Joyce well understood, a new kind of devotee, one with endless time at his or her disposal and a preparedness not just to read his text but somehow study it.[12] For unlike *Ulysses*, the *Wake* was comprised not of many styles but, rather, of one extremely dense, tongue-twisting *Wake* style. This was based on English vocabulary and syntax but, at the same time, self-consciously designed as a machine that systematically appeared to resist any singularity of meaning. The *Wake* announced a new 'revolution of the word' – a powerfully resonant cultural practice involving not exactly a new language, but a new *kind* of language, one that worked not to stabilize the world in meaning, but, rather, to unfix it in an apparently wild diversity of possible or potential meaning. One early reader raised the problematic issue of 'whether or not a public can ever be trained to absorb this kind of thing'.[13]

It is easy to imagine how a work such as this may have been specifically steered towards the Paris avant garde and the small-scale institutions set up precisely for the reception of modernist art at this time.[14] Certainly the *Wake* initially needed support from such quarters, which it received in the earlier stages from *transition*, the journal that between 1927 and 1938 printed no fewer than seventeen instalments of *Work in Progress*, the working title of the *Wake*, as well as several critical interpretations. *Work in Progress* was at the centre of *transition*. Eugene Jolas – who with the American novelist Elliot Paul founded the journal – wrote of Joyce as 'our bellwether in the neologistic pilgrimage'.[15] Although, as one of the key collaborators in both the production and reception of the *Work in Progress*, Stuart Gilbert, pointed out with some degree of pique, the dynamic worked in both directions. 'One sometimes hears it said that *Work in Progress* "made" *Transition*', he wrote, – 'but, in some respects, the converse is equally true'.[16] Whatever, the intimacy was evident in the manifesto formulated by *transition* and brought to life by *Work in Progress*, although, true to form, Joyce himself never signed the manifesto.[17] Here the artist 'TIRED OF THE SPECTACLE OF SHORT STORIES, NOVELS, POEMS AND PLAYS STILL UNDER THE HEGEMONY OF THE BANAL WORD, MONOTONOUS SYNTAX, STATIC PSYCHOLOGY [and] DESCRIPTIVE NATURALISM' becomes free TO USE WORDS OF HIS OWN FASHIONING . . . WE ARE NOT CONCERNED', the manifesto went on, 'WITH THE PROPAGATION OF SOCIOLOGICAL IDEAS, EXCEPT TO EMANICIPATE THE CREATIVE ELEMENTS FROM THE PRESENT IDEOLOGY . . . THE PLAIN READER BE DAMNED'.[18]

Joyce died on 13 January 1941 from a perforated duodenal ulcer, but with these two astonishing texts, *Ulysses* and the *Wake*, he eventually joined not only the ranks of great twentieth-century Irish writers that included Yeats and Beckett but also the pantheon of high modernists that went beyond literature. Like Picasso, Freud and Nietzsche, Joyce became seemingly indispensable to the modern world and the ways in which it thought itself. In her introduction to the Oxford edition of *Ulysses*, Jeri Johnson registers the sheer spread of Joyce's influence in the context of reflecting on the question of where to begin reading this great work. For Joyceans, she writes, 'There is no possibility of beginning *Ulysses*, much less of finishing (with) it. Joyce's book has so colonised twentieth-century Anglophone culture that we can never now enter it for the first time'.[19] It is significant of his perceived importance that between his death in 1941 and 2012, while the popularity of his modernist contemporaries in the field of literature, and of modernism generally, has gone through considerable swings, Joyce's status has never suffered serious diminution. His work has sometimes been criticized as being elitist, as has the work of many 'classical' modernists, but it is peculiarly designed to counter, or at least wildly complicate, the making of that particular charge, not least by virtue of the care it takes over the everyday. Indeed it has a powerful capacity for resisting most charges, which is one reason why Joyce can remain so powerfully supported by large sections of the academy. Alone of Lewis's 'men of 1914', and the women he ignored, Joyce retains his full purchase against the deep shifts in critical tradition since the 1970s. The more challenging the 'turn to theory' has become, the more central *Ulysses* and the *Wake* appear to be as texts that keep their contemporaneity. For many these books are not, even now, historical culture at all but remain culture of our own times.

'The sameold gamebold adomic structure'

Texts and Contexts is styled as an introduction. It responds with enthusiasm to the idea that introductions to Joyce, and there are an increasing number available, are a serious and important part of what is sometimes disparagingly referred to as 'the Joyce industry'. For those who know the literature, this one pitches itself somewhere between the takeaway delights of Paul Strathern's *James Joyce in Ninety Minutes* (2005) and the fine-dining version of something like the *Cambridge Companion to James Joyce* (1990; 2004), which is really aimed at the Joyce expert rather than the 'ordinary reader'.

    Texts and Contexts also fully acknowledges that the Joyce text is now inextricable from the intellectual communities that formulate it so substantially and accepts our relative ignorance about who the ordinary reader is or how contemporary readers outside the academy receive a text like *Ulysses* or *Finnegans Wake*. Some will maintain that the latter should never seriously arise as an issue, because these texts, once described in the Australian press as 'cult object[s] worshipped with arcane rituals',[20] are often thought of as having no real life outside the academy. But this is certainly not the case. If the public response to the BBC's 'cheat's guide' to *Ulysses* (2004), one of the briefest synopses anywhere, is anything to go by, there is a more 'general' interest in the Joyce text than a proprietorial academy sometimes likes to imagine. At the very least, strong anecdotal evidence supports the view that '*Ulysses* . . . enjoys a popular life that would seem to belie its inaccessibility' – although whether this readership needs another introduction remains an issue.[21] As Julia Sloan Brannon puts it in her account of the so-called 'Joyce wars', *Who Reads Ulysses?* (2003)[22] – there is a truth 'long denied by the academy that its own agendas are not the only literary agenda . . . [moreover] the common reader does not necessarily need scholars to tell them what to read – or how'.[23]

    For all such complexities, an introduction must operate under the premise that there is a point to opening out its subject and imagine a common language for so doing. The problematics of 'introducing' Joyce, however, do not end there. The everyday assumption might be that the readers of an introduction will, whatever else, be seeking ways of approaching the Joyce text – especially *Ulysses* and *Finnegans Wake*. But these are the texts that figure prominently as icons of modernist *unreadability*. They are specifically set up, some argue, to defeat the reader by multiplicity of meaning, if not sheer exhaustion – and not just 'the ordinary reader' or differently formulated 'uncultivated or half-cultivated reader' who, according to Larbaud, 'will throw *Ulysses* aside after a few pages' (*CH*, 253). The *biens cultural* and even the Joyce expert (Larbaud was one of the first) will also find *Ulysses* and *Finnegans Wake*, at the very least, highly resistant to 'conventional' literary understanding. The high-modernist literature these texts represent is often characterized as a particularly unfixed and unfixing culture that, by its nature, not only accommodates but often achieves a radical condition of contradiction and ambiguity. It is often ironically disposed, and at the same time famously decentred in terms of narrative positioning – it is typically 'multivocal' or 'dialogic'. Joyce's fictions, especially in the later incarnations, are highly illustrative of all these characteristics. Whether one views them as a reproduction of a 'multiplicity' and 'relativity' present in the modern world, at one time a standard position of Joyce criticism, or a postmodern performance of endless play, a more contemporary perspective, albeit one much on the wane, the Joyce text seems specifically designed to resist reading in the singular.

How is this multiplicity of meaning to be handled in an introduction to the Joyce text? For many readers there can be no default position hidden away in what are often perceived as 'open' texts, nor in the critical literature now so much part of the Joyce world. Here we have a related hurdle for an introduction of this kind – the multiplicity of accompanying readings and schools of readings produced in thousands of essays and monographs, the intimidating prospect of a huge body of extremely variable secondary material produced over a period of some ninety years. Certainly all approaches to Joyce will be informed by that body of work, in many different ways, but should not an introduction somehow familiarize the reader with the generalities of a history of this critical tradition? The material *could* certainly be so reduced down – some of it is here, in parts of this introduction and at the beginning of Chapter 4 for instance – but, as with all histories, there could be endless variations to the broad story across a range of approaches, each with their own specific agendas. In a project of this introductory kind the result could only be very limited.

There is a further complication in that the Joyce text has not just been the passive object of critical scrutiny. Especially since the 1960s, from structuralism through deconstruction and post-structuralism, Joyce's fictions have been much involved in the formation of highly controversial ideas about language and culture. Some of the key figures here – Gilles Deleuze, Jacques Lacan, Jacques Derrida, Julia Kristeva, Heléne Cixous – have addressed themselves directly to the Joyce text. This would seem to signify a further potential obligation on the introduction to Joyce – to provide an overview of how Joyce's fictions have been implicated in the development of contemporary intellectual life, a problematic ambition not least because of the complexities of this culture and the fact that distinctions between theoretical schools at its centre, structuralism and post-structuralism, are 'somewhat blurry', the confusion stemming 'from a tight interplay of similarities and differences between what these two fields now name'.[24]

Intellectual culture of the last sixty years, however, is only one of many contexts surrounding Joyce's fiction, often understood as being 'encyclopaedic' in its terms of reference. A 2009 publication, *James Joyce in Context*, for example, has no fewer than twenty chapters in its third part entitled 'Historical and Cultural Contexts', ranging from the Irish Revival to cinema and including the influence of places (Dublin, Paris, Trieste); cultural forms (newspapers, music, cinema and modernisms) and systems of knowledge and belief (philosophy, religion and science). All these categories and many more inform and at the same time are acted upon by the Joyce text. Which, if any, should be included in an 'introduction' is anyone's guess, or, to put it differently, it is entirely conceivable that a case could be made for the central importance of each and any of these contexts – or none depending on one's critical persuasion.

For most, however, one of the most important of these contexts must be the biographical. One pervasive critical cliché insists that Joyce's fiction is autobiographical to an unusual degree – Harry Levin in an early critical account (1959) set the tone in this respect, describing Joyce as 'the most self-centred of universal minds. Far more explicitly than most writers . . . he exploited his personal experience for purposes of literary documentation'.[25] Clearly something needs to be known about the life of Joyce, 'the first till last alshemist' who 'wrote over every square inch of the only foolscap available, his own body' (*FW* 185,34–6), which is one reason why this introductory chapter began with biographical material. At the same time, the version of the life story told above is by its nature sketchy and underdeveloped. It also carries with it an underlying assumption that there is an agreed Joyce identity that we can synthesize in a few pages of biographical information, which, as we have seen, is actually far from the truth. The Joyce biography is, again, highly contested at quite fundamental levels. In a recent account of the biographical state of play in Joyce studies, for example, Finn Fordham argues that the pervasiveness of the most celebrated version of Joyce's life, Ellmann's, is itself one of the greatest obstacles to the production of anything like a definitive life.[26]

Under these challenging and highly unstable circumstances *Texts and Contexts* adopts a necessarily pragmatic approach. Taking what is a hopefully not too wild a shot in the dark, it imagines a readership and pitches accordingly. It commandeers as full a range of scholarship as is helpful to the primary aim of 'introducing'. Trying to avoid over simplification, it develops a cavalier willingness to put all and any critical materials at the disposal of producing strategies for reading, aiming to provide an account of Joyce's writing, and the critical traditions that surround it, that will be of use to the interested – even at the risk of bringing together approaches that under different conditions would be better kept well apart.

That said, *Texts and Contexts* inevitably has its critical preferences and indeed goes so far as to insist on at least one critical rule of thumb. This is that the innovation of Joyce's work, often involving the kind of textual practice described above in terms of 'fluidity', 'ambiguity' and so on, is never *just* formalistic, playful or 'open' for the sake of it. Even where it looks most self-obsessed and/or most fascinated by epistemological uncertainty, the Joyce text always looks outward. In this sense the kind of critical strategy used to introduce Joyce here could be understood as taking issue with a range of formalistic approaches, but it is at the farthest move from the kind of Joyce criticism, from whatever critical school, which argues that these powerfully engaged texts are actually lost causes, where multiplicity of registration cancels out meaning to produce a labyrinth, for a reader who 'can never tell, any more than Joyce himself could tell, where Joyce was going'.[27]

Quite simply, this aimlessness does not exist in Joyce's writing. Restoring the Joyce text to its Irish dimensions, contemporary Joyce criticism has shown how Joyce's writing is not just a product of colonial history but also an active constituent in the transformation of postcolonial culture. Critics have also constructed his fictions as products of bourgeois decadence, as well as expressions of radical individualism. They have been read as critiques of modern scientific rationalism; commodified culture and political authoritarianism, addressing in these guises, and others – gender issues; sexual politics and the full range of controversies surrounding modern 'mass' culture and society. My own work also represents a broadly engaged Joyce – a writer responding not just to Irish issues and colonial politics but to a wider early-twentieth-century Europe, in the case of the *Wake* making a spectacular entry into the charged discourses of racism that were to culminate in Hitler's Final Solution.

The Joyce text introduced in *Texts and Contexts* is drawn from all these traditions. What Joyce produced here, then, is a long way removed from the international figure made central by American modernism as it was formulated in the 1950s and 1960s, as indeed are most contemporary responses to Joyce. The cosmopolitan genius who allegedly turned his back on Ireland in an act of heroic individualism to become the high-priest of modernism in a 'spiritual enterprise',[28] figures here as an Irish writer, radicalized by his formative years in Ireland, who became an internationalist engaging with the politics of modern and modernist cultures on the widest scale.

As part of its general perspective, *Texts and Contexts* makes an unusually firm distinction between *Ulysses* and *Finnegans Wake* and what are referred to here as the 'early' texts. This is not to deny the importance of the pre-*Ulysses* writings, but there is an intention to work against the drift of a critical tradition once familiar in an early structuralist mode and now returned to in recent years that has attempted to read *Dubliners* and *A Portraits of the Artist as a Young Man* as though they were earlier versions of *Ulysses* and the *Wake*.[29] It is in order to counter the blurring of what were actually transformations in Joyce's writing styles and artistic ambitions that *Texts and Contexts* draws quite strong distinctions between early and late Joyce, devoting more space than is usual in introductions of this kind to Joyce's last work, *Finnegans Wake*.

Chapter 2 focuses on these 'early' texts, which includes the critical and political writings, *Dubliners*, the fragment *Stephen Hero* (1944), *A Portrait of the Artist as a Young Man* and *Exiles*. To readers familiar with the modern and postmodern literary culture that Joyce was so instrumental in creating, especially those without significant exposure to late-nineteenth-century aesthetics, these pre-*Ulysses* texts may not now seem greatly challenging or innovative. That said, it clearly is the case that these earlier writings are crucial to any serious understanding of *Ulysses* and the *Wake*, as well as being more complex than they might initially appear. This chapter, then, works with the earlier texts, both in order to establish the terms of some of Joyce's characteristic cultural interventions and also to explore how aspects of the later aesthetic radicalism are prefigured in, for example, the combination of realism and literary architecture that characterizes *Dubliners* and *A Portrait* and in the narrative distancing of both these texts that is a precursor of the relativizing perspectives that make up *Ulysses*.

Chapter 3 gives an introductory overview to *Ulysses* drawing on some of the older critical traditions. It examines the growth of the text from the early sketches of 1914 to full publication in 1921, describing and analysing the development and the architectonics of this extraordinary novel. The chapter engages with the mythic structure of the book and other central features of its design – its symbolic structuring; its relation to organs of the human body and the arts, colours and 'technics' deployed in its eighteen episodes. The chapter also considers the realism of *Ulysses* and considers relationships between technique and meaning and the idea that the increasing technical experimentation and textual complexity of *Ulysses* represents a substantive movement away from traditional literary approaches. Here 'textuality' itself displaces the traditional literary engagement with 'character' and 'theme' to become the critical focal point of *Ulysses*. An alarmingly quality of the novel as it develops is that the characters, Stephen Dedalus and Leopold Bloom, become increasingly displaced by complexities of style – the play text and 'hallucinations' of 'Circe', for example, the clichés of 'Eumaeus' and the scientism of 'Ithaca'. This marks the true beginning of the 'revolution of the word' described by Jolas and taken up, much later, by Colin McCabe in *James Joyce and the Revolution of the Word* (1979) and contemporary theoretical perspectives. Chapter 3 begins to explore how such a 'revolution' might be read, a theme taken up in later chapters.

From the very earliest days of Joyce criticism, Ireland in general and Dublin in particular have been recognized as crucial contexts for understanding Joyce. All Joyce's texts are thoroughly loaded with Irish culture and history in many of its forms from the archaeological to musicological. They are also awash with the minutiae of everyday urban Irish life in the early part of the twentieth century – the popular songs, foods, fashions, street furniture and other aspects of the ordinary and commonplace. At the same time as lovingly reproducing the phenomenological Dublin in what many see as encyclopaedic proportions, the Joyce text is also a political engagement, saturated both with the experience of the colonized native, the 'paralysis' that strikes a keynote in *Dubliners*, and with a politics of radical egoism. In the romanticized form of the artistic identity, this fictionalized Irish rebellion seeks independence from what Stephen Dedalus understands in *A Portrait* as the 'nets' of nation, church and family (*P*, 208).

As Joyce criticism now appreciates, however, with the later fictions the imperative to reproduce the colonial experience realistically from 'native' perspectives of both conservative conformity and radical dissent takes new dramatic turns. After a brief account of the critical developments that accompanied this shift, Chapter 4, '*Ulysses*, Ireland and Empire', explores how the mimetic imperative is problematized in *Ulysses* and, to a large degree, displaced by a stylistic innovation centrally concerned with undermining and destabilizing English and a wider Western cultural and political authority. This chapter charts these astonishing developments in 'style' in terms of the politics and radicalism of the Joyce text.

The fifth chapter is concerned with *Finnegans Wake*. The materials which went into producing the *Wake*, the forty-eight notebooks and the sketches, drafts, typescripts and galley proofs, tell a story almost as incredible as the *Wake* narrative itself. Indeed, for many *Wake* critics working in the traditions of genetic scholarship, the meaning of the *Wake* is tightly bound up with the procedures of extension and expansion that governed its extraordinary genesis over seventeen years. Drawing on that scholarship, this chapter gives an overview of the *Wake*'s textual development. The chapter also serves as an introduction to reading the *Wake*. It is a practical guide, suggesting ways of approaching the *Wake* text, responding to its multiplicity of meaning and offering a brief critical consideration of the well-known interpretation of *Finnegans Wake* as a 'book of the dead', a night-time counterpart to Joyce's day book, *Ulysses*. Drawing on the long tradition of *Wake* exposition, the chapter explores strategies for responding to the *Wake*'s dispersal of 'character', considering its bizarre narratological complexity, and responding to what many regard as its linguistic chaos. Critical accounts of narrative 'events' in the *Wake* – useful, perhaps indispensable, as a guide – are considered here. At the same time, however, there are strong limitations to this kind of approach to the *Wake*. Guides, and 'keys' to *Finnegans Wake*, and there are many of them, by their very nature reduce the essential nature of the multi-layered and dialogic *Wake*. Above all, then, the aim of the chapter will be to open up the *Wake*, rather than reduce its complexity to an order it was never designed to express.

Repeating the pattern established in the *Ulysses* chapters, Chapter 6 draws on some of my earlier work to position *Finnegans Wake* in terms of a wider modernity. The aim is to articulate the significance of this hugely complex text in terms of some of the key formulations of the modern world in the 1920s and 1930s. It engages with the question of the epistemological in the *Wake*, showing how its slipperiness in terms of meaning engages with the post-Enlightenment crises that produced social Darwinism, eugenics and Aryanism as science-based forms of knowledge. The full scope of the nineteenth- and early-twentieth-century professional academy – including linguistics, biology, anthropology, palaeontology, sociology and history – was devoted to defining social and cultural order in terms of hierarchies and progressivism. In part by considering the intertextualities between the *Wake* and the classic text of modern epistemology in its populist form, the *Encyclopaedia Britannica*, this chapter sees the *Wake* as an engagement with modern knowledge and its formation. Through this route, Chapter 6 gets to the political *Wake*, showing how this text, positioned in the extremities of 1920s and 1930s politics, delivers a hilarious assault on scientific racism and fascism.

The concluding chapter, finally, is not a summary but an extension which returns to some of the issues raised here in this introduction about the problematics of writing an introduction, not least the problem of who such a project addresses. In the absence of empirical research on the 'ordinary' Joyce reader, Chapter 7 examines how Joyce and the Joyce text have been both adopted and updated by the contemporary world – in music, theatre, film, on the web and in tourist industries across the world. It makes the point with some emphasis that both Joyce and his writing, however, much contingent on the academy, have a much wider role in a larger world, a role which, just as much as the texts itself, deserves the courtesy of an 'introduction'– whatever the conceptual difficulties.

CHAPTER 2

Early Works

Critical and Political Writings (1890–1914)

Joyce's reviews, lectures, essays and other occasional writings were first published in 1959 in a collection edited by Ellsworth Mason and Richard Ellmann. A later version edited by Kevin Barry, including some previously unpublished pieces, appeared in 2000. In themselves, these essays, reviews and lectures have received relatively little critical attention; indeed, doubt has been cast on their value in recent years. A review of the 2009 Trieste Summer School, for example, dismisses the essay 'Island: Isle of Saints and Sages' as plagiarized and 'slapdash', posing more general 'questions as to just how seriously we as readers are supposed to take the lectures and screeds that make up the body of Joyce's heavily politicized Triestine journalism'.[1] More usually, however, critical accounts have successfully drawn on this fascinating material in order to illustrate particular perspectives on Joyce's fictional writing.

There are, in the Barry edition, fifty-two items dating from the 1880s to 1937, a significant number covering a long period although most belong to specific phases of Joyce's writing career and form coherent groupings. Twenty-three are reviews, most dating from the period 1903–1905, twenty-one of which were written for the *Daily Express*, the newspaper Gabriel Conroy writes for in 'The Dead' – much to the serio-mock displeasure of Molly Ivors, the revivalist. A further nine articles were written for the Trieste publication *Il Piccola della Sera*, which was 'nationalist in character' and rarely missed 'an opportunity to write about [. . . regions] which suffered under foreign domination and so the Irish question received a lot of coverage' (*OCPW*, 322) – Trieste itself was a sea port ruled by Austria, with Italians comprising seventy-five percent of its population. Six items are lectures, two of which were delivered to the Literary and Historical Society of University College, Dublin when Joyce was an undergraduate, the other four being delivered at the Università Popolare in Trieste, three of them in 1907 and the last in 1912.

The *Il Piccola della Sera* articles were at one point offered by Joyce to the Genoese left wing publisher, Angelo Fortunato Formiggini, with the proposal that they should together write a book on Ireland for Italian readers. In some ways these are the most interesting of the critical and political writings. Joyce shows in them a detailed and sophisticated knowledge of the then contemporary political relations between England and Ireland and of the complexities of Irish nationalism, albeit with some assistance from Arthur Griffith's editorials in *United Irishman* and *Sinn Féin*.[2] As Barry has shown, these provided material, especially statistical material, for such pieces as 'Fenianism: The Last Fenian' (1907) and 'Home Rule Comes of Age' (1907). In these, and in 'The Home Rule Comet' (1910) and 'The Shade of Parnell' (1910), Joyce expresses contempt for what he regarded as duplicitous Gladstonian liberalism and for the remnants of the Irish Parliamentary Party under John Redmond, which he saw as hopelessly weak and compromised – not least because it had conspired, along with the Catholic Church and Irish Press, in the betrayal of Parnell.

England and a conservative Ireland represented by the Church and parliamentary Irish nationalism, all three invariably seen by Joyce as being complicit, are targeted with consistency in these articles. Radical political Irish nationalism, the 'so-called physical force party', has, at the very least, a strategic advantage over the Irish nationalist party: 'They say (and history fully supports them in making such a claim) that any concession by England to Ireland has been granted unwillingly, at bayonet point, as the saying goes.'[3] As the poignant representation of a broken John O'Leary suggests, the 'last Fenian' returning to Ireland after 'years of studious exile in Paris', Fenianism also attracts Joyce's sympathy and produces some self-identification (*OCPW*, 138–40).

But, and despite the frosty objectivity typical of the style of these pieces, there is also frustration, ambiguity and contradiction here, not least because historically the radicals have been characterized by romantic gestures and nativism and rendered helpless by what Joyce sees as a cultural propensity for betrayal. 'In Ireland', he writes, 'just at the crucial moment, an informer appears' (*OCPW*, 139). The one moderately bright hope for Ireland's future, as Joyce represents it, is a new, pragmatic and modernizing 'Fenianism . . . regrouped in a party called 'ourselves alone' – this being Arthur Griffith's Sinn Féin.

They aim to make Ireland a bilingual republic, and, to this end, they have established a direct ferry link between Ireland and France. They boycott English goods, they refuse to become soldiers or swear an oath of allegiance to the British crown. They are attempting to develop the industry of the whole country and, rather than fork out one and a quarter millions each year to maintain the eighty deputies in the English Parliament, they want to institute a consular service in the principal world ports with the aim of merchandising industrial produce, without the intervention of England. From many points of view, this latest form of Fenianism may be the most formidable.

(OCPW, 140)

This degree of involvement with the detail of public politics is perhaps unexpected. But even more surprising for a writer still sometimes charged with 'having little concern for politics; his only interest was literature', is the degree to which Joyce's politics spill over into the engagement with cultural history and aesthetics in these writings.[4] Indeed, one of the main reasons why the critical and political essays and reviews remain important is that they offer such an early and compelling insight into what became a thorough entanglement of the literary with the political.

The lectures planned for delivery at the Università Popolare, for example, are highly suggestive here (there were originally three; only a small fragment, a paragraph, of the last of these, 'The Irish Literary Renaissance' is extant). The first to be delivered, 'Ireland: Island of Saints and Sages' (1907), enters the deeply controversial domain of Irish cultural history with an intervention that radically interrupts the historiographies constructed by Protestant cultural nationalism in its most familiar mid-to-late nineteenth-century revivalist forms. Dispensing in one sentence with pre-Christian Ireland, the so-called age of Celtic heroism that inspired revivalist literature, Joyce offers in its place a catalogue of early Irish Church achievement in art, philosophy, history and science. The effect here is to render Irish cultural achievement crucially contingent on Catholic scholasticism. At the same time, the association between cultural nationalism and a pre-Christian Celticism, central to a revivalism that had strong roots in landlordist culture, becomes undermined:

Even in the first century of Christianity under the apostolate of St Peter we find the Irishman, Mansuetus, later canonized, as a missionary to Lorraine, where he founded a church and preached for half a century . . . Sedulius travelled through a large part of the world, finally settling down in Rome, where he composed the fair total of almost fifty theological tracts and many sacred hymns which are still used today in the Catholic ritual . . . The fiery Columbanus had the task of reforming the French Church and, after stirring up a civil war in Burgundy with his sermons, he left for Italy where he became the apostle of the Lombards and founded the monastery of Bobio.

(*OCPW*, 111)

Whatever Joyce's objections to modern-day Catholicism, and they were substantial, he takes great pride in the scholastic tradition. The list of achievements continues with references to Frigidianus, St Gallus, Finian 'the Learned', St Fiacre, Fursey, Arbogast [*sic*], St Virus, Disibod, Rumold, Albinus, Kilian, Sedulius the Younger, and to the heresiarchs John Scotus Erigena, Macarius and Virgilius Solivagus. The offhanded summary of the period as 'an interrupted record of apostles, missions, and martyrs' cannot cancel the obvious pleasure taken in the achievements of such figures as John Duns Scotus who 'according to legend . . . once listened to the arguments of all the professors of the University of Paris for three whole days and then, speaking from memory, confuted them one by one'; or of Petrus Hibernicus, 'the theologian who had the supreme task of educating the mind of. . . St Thomas Aquinas, perhaps the keenest and clearest mind known that human history has ever seen.' Moreover, it is precisely this account of the early Church which, like O'Connell in theearly days of the Catholic Association, Joyce uses to justify the assertion that 'the Irish nation's desire to create its own civilization is not so much the demand of a young nation wishing to link itself to Europe's concert, but the desire by an ancient nation to renew in a modern form the glories of a past civilization' (*OCPW*, 111–14).[5]

The controversial connection made between Catholic intellectual history and the national identity is accompanied by a refusal to see revivalism in its Anglo–Irish form as an authentic extension of Celticism. Indeed, Joyce mounts a full-bodied account of Anglo–Ireland's complicity in the subjugation of native Irish culture, which began to die with the English invasion. By the eighteenth century the process was all but complete, with 'Protestants, who had now become *Hibernis Hiberniores*, more Irish than the Irish themselves . . . inciting the Irish Catholics to oppose the Calvinist and Lutheran fanatics from across the water'(*OCPW*, 115). Joyce may be entirely willing to claim the likes of Berkeley, Goldsmith, Swift and Burke for Ireland, but he denies them any connection to what he calls 'the glories' of the 'ancient national spirit'. 'Just as ancient Egypt is dead', he writes, 'so is ancient Ireland' (*OCPW*, 125).

There is an interval of almost eight centuries from the date of the invasion of the English to the present day. I dwelt a little on the preceding period with the purpose of enabling you to discern the roots of the Irish temperament, but I do not intend to detain you with an account of the affairs of Ireland under foreign occupation. I do this mainly because Ireland then ceased to be an intellectual force in Europe. The decorative arts, at which the ancient Irish excelled, were abandoned and the sacred and profane culture fell into disuse.

(*OCPW*, 114)

Joyce fully recognizes that 'To deny the name of patriot to all those not of Irish stock would be to deny it to almost all the heroes of the modern movement' (*OCPW*, 115). He acknowledges the diversity of 'Our civilization' where no 'race or language can nowadays claim to be pure. No race has less right to make such a boast than the one presently inhabiting Ireland' (*OCPW*, 118). At the same time, he is not prepared to indulge in what he calls 'a convenient forgetfulness of the facts' (*OCPW*, 116). The essential fact of 'Ireland, Island of Saints of Sages' is the English invasion and the analysis of Anglo–Ireland as a 'hybrid' to a Celtic/Catholic root which produces a period of general cultural collapse. Colonized Ireland produces some exceptional writers, but these 'adopted the English language . . . and almost forgot their native country' (*OCPW*, 122). They have little or no connection with anything that could be termed an 'authentic' national culture.

This kind of material, which echoes throughout the critical and political writings, was particularly controversial because of what it implied not just about Ireland's cultural past but about the cultural present as represented by contemporary revivalism. It shapes Joyce's self-identification with Mangan, the one important Catholic writer produced by Ireland in the nineteenth century as far as Joyce was concerned. In 'James Clarence Mangan' (1907), he celebrates the 'gloomy and indolent child . . . preoccupied with religious questions', whose writings later 'attracted the attention of the enlightened' (*OCPW*, 128), elevating the dissipation and despair that Yeats found brutish and unmanly into an embodiment of racial consciousness, an echo of which may be found in *A Portrait* where Davin is repelled by Stephen's sexual revelations and Stephen replies that, 'This race and this country and this life produced me . . . I shall express myself as I am' (*P*, 170).[6] Mangan was working 'with no native literary tradition', but, for Joyce, he nonetheless takes on the role that Yeats had reserved for Samuel Ferguson (a Protestant Unionist and a Trinity man), as 'the most distinguished poet of the modern Celtic world'. Mangan 'subsumes into himself the spirit of an age and country'. One tonal characteristic of this national poetry is the expression of grief: 'This is the theme of much of Irish poetry, but no other Irish song is as full as those of Mangan of nobly suffered misfortunes and such irreparable devastations of the soul.' Another feature is 'the spirit of revenge' (*OCPW*, 130–5).

There is a strongly politicized consciousness at work in these pieces; one that finds it 'a bit naïve to heap insults on the Englishman for his misdeeds in Ireland. A conqueror cannot be amateurish' (*OCPW*, 119) and sees no good in fulminating 'against English tyranny while the tyranny of Rome still holds the dwelling place of the soul' (*OPCW*, 125). At the same time, Joyce is deeply sensitive to the workings of imperial tyranny, as a piece like 'Ireland at the Bar' (1907) shows with particular force.[7] Joyce is profoundly suspicious of English politics and doubtful about Ireland's capacity for extricating itself from dependency. He is highly sensitive to Protestant claims to speak for Ireland and to the kind of landlordist cultural history which commonly excluded Catholic Ireland. At the same time, his is a modern and modernizing perspective, one that sees the return to Celticism, a major Irish response to the collapse of the parliamentary nationalism, as a complete failure to face reality – an attempt to somehow resurrect a nineteenth-century Anglo–Irish cultural intervention (revivalism) as a culture of antiquity that remains somehow 'ours'.

These responses to modern Ireland converge in the insistence on the virtues of realism emphasized in so many of these pieces. In 'Realism and Idealism in English Literature' (1912) Daniel Defoe becomes the 'great precursor of the Realist movement' (167); in 'A Neglected Poet' (1903) George Crabbe is applauded as 'a champion of realism' (90); a minor melodrama, T. Baron Russell's *Borlase and Son* (1903), is praised because it has 'the merit, first of all, of "actuality"' (*OCPW*, 99). The sharpest criticism is reserved for the romanticists, especially the Irish romantics claiming to speak for or represent Ireland. William Rooney, who had worked with Arthur Griffith on the founding of the *United Irishman*, is lampooned as 'An Irish Poet' (1902) for writing 'issued from headquarters' and the production of poems that are in their enthusiastic patriotism the 'false and mean expression of a false and mean idea (*OCPW*, 61). In 'The Soul of Ireland' (1903), a review of Lady Gregory's *Poets and Dreamers: Studies and Translations from the Irish*, Joyce pokes fun at Lady Gregory's departure from 'legends and heroic youth' into a land 'almost fabulous in its sorrow and senility. Half of her book is an account of old men and old women in the West of Ireland'; the other is comprised of transcriptions of stories told by 'feeble and sleepy' mind (*OCPW*, 74).

The imperative on the Irish artist to face reality was crucial to early Joyce, and became the theme of the first paper, 'Drama and Life', which he delivered to the Literary and Historical Society of University College,

Dublin on 20 January 1900. Mason and Ellmann, considered it to be to be 'one of . . . [his] most important artistic pronouncements', which may be the case.[8] Its force derives from the superiority it allows to the 'New School' of drama over what Joyce saw as a conservative contemporary preference for the old theatre classics, the 'bland blatancy of Corneille, the starchglaze of Trapassi's godliness, the Pumblychookian woodenness of Calderon' (*OPCW*, 24).[9] Rejecting the theatregoer's taste for 'old food', Joyce goes on to advocate passionately for a modern drama, exemplified by Ibsen, which is 'at war with convention' and fearless in its squaring up to reality. For the best in drama is not primarily a matter of 'ethical claims' or 'Beauty . . . the swerga of the aesthete' (*OPCW*, 27), but ultimately a confrontation with 'truth'. 'It is the function of art', Joyce argues in this rhetorical flourish,

> to give us light rather than darkness . . . Art is marred by such mistaken insistence on its religious, its moral, its beautiful, its idealising tendencies. A single Rembrandt is worth a gallery full of Van Dycks. And it is this doctrine of idealism in art which has in notable instances disfigured manful endeavour, and has also fostered a babyish instinct to dive under blankets at the mention of the bogey of realism . . . people want the drama to befool them, Purveyor supplies plutocrat with a parody of life which the latter digests medicinally in a darkened theatre, the stage literally battening on the mental offal of its patrons.
>
> (*OCPW*, 27–8)

For the young Joyce, just predating the beginnings of *Dubliners*, there was a question about whether modern life could be compatible with a drama of this passionately engaged kind, a question which he answered himself in the affirmative. 'Out of the dreary sameness of existence, a measure of dramatic life may be drawn. Even the most commonplace, the deadest among the living, may take part in a great drama.' In a comment that would have resonated particularly with the revivalists and Celtic enthusiasts, and would not have been lost on the clerics in the audience, Joyce spoke of how 'It is a sinful foolishness to sigh back to the good old times, to feed the hunger of us with the cold stones they afford. Life we must accept as we see it before our eyes, men and women as we meet them in the real world, not as we apprehend them in the world of faery' (*OCPW*, 28). This kind of declaration was a long way from the dry discourse of nineteenth-century aesthetics with which Joyce experimented in the Paris and Pola notebooks and later redeployed in *Stephen Hero* and *A Portrait*. It may have had a notional position in relation to the philosophy of the beautiful or of taste, but the primary engagement was with *fin de siècle* cultural politics and, especially, the cultural politics of revivalist Ireland.

Dubliners (1914)

The *Dubliners* stories were written quite quickly. Most were completed in Trieste between 1905 and 1906 at the same time as Joyce was working on the *Stephen Hero* manuscript, in the first flush of his 'exile' and new life with Nora. It may not be possible to know with any real certainty what fully motivates a writer, but there is often contextual material which at least indicates where a writer believes his work to be centrally positioned and this was the case with *Dubliners*. Across 1905 and 1906, the subject of *Dubliners* was prominent in the extensive correspondence Joyce had, notably with his brother, Stanislaus, and Grant Richards the eventual first publisher of Joyce's stories. To his brother Joyce confessed concerns about the tone of the stories and the 'mischievous' spirit that seemed to direct his pen. However much he considered 'contemporary Irish writing . . . ill-written, morally obtuse formless caricature', he worried whether his own versions of Irish life had done Dublin justice. 'The Dublin papers will object to my stories as to a caricature of Dublin life,' he predicted. 'Do you think there is any truth in this?' (*Letters* II, 99). Over a year later he was still engaged with this point, asking his brother whether he had been 'unnecessarily harsh' in *Dubliners* (*Letters* II, 166). The overriding issue for Joyce was clear. Had he finally produced in his short stories what fellow Irish writers, in his view, had failed to achieve, a realistic version of the modern colonial city? The exchanges with the publisher Grant Richards from October 1905 through to late 1906 confirmed the crucial importance of this difficult and highly controversial agenda for Joyce. He explained how Dublin had yet to be given to the world in literature, pointing out that 'the odour of ashpits and old weeds and offal [that] hangs round my stories', far from being his invention, was a reflection of realities he felt compelled to observe and expose. 'I seriously believe', he wrote, 'that you will retard the course of civilisation in Ireland by preventing the Irish people from having one good look at themselves in my nicely polished looking glass' (*Letters* I, 64). He was under no illusions as to the impact his stories would have – 'I have come to the conclusion', he wrote, 'that I cannot write without offending people'. But that did not alter the essential truthfulness of the picture Joyce was portraying. Indeed, what Joyce saw as the 'denouncement' of his stories only confirmed their validity. 'I have written it for the most part in a style of scrupulous meanness,' he claimed, 'and with the conviction that he is a very bold man who dares to alter in the presentment, still more to deform, whatever he has seen and heard' (*Letters* II, 134).

The imperative to make it real is fundamental to *Dubliners*. It is apparent everywhere in the writing strategies deployed in these stories and central to maintaining the sense of objective critical analysis that was so important to Joyce at this time. The emphasis on direct speech, for example, and idiom, strong in most stories and predominant in some, implies the insider's perspective. Stories like 'Counterparts', 'Ivy Day in the Committee Room' written almost entirely in direct speech and 'Grace' are particularly compelling in this respect. At the same time, the idea of precise transcription, even of the seemingly trivial, is also suggestive of the outsiderly scientism of a sociologist or anthropologist. The convention of marking direct speech is engaged here, with Joyce preferring the dash to inverted commas because it mediated less harshly in his view:

> Seeing that all were ready to start she [Aunt Kate in 'The Dead'] shepherded them to the door where good-night was said:
> – Well, good night, Aunt Kate, and thanks for the pleasant evening.
> – Good-night, Gabriel. Good-night, Gretta!
> – Good-night, Aunt Kate, and thanks ever so much. Good-night, Aunt Julia.
> – O, good-night, Gretta, I didn't see you.
> – Good-night, Mr D'Arcy. Good-night, Miss O'Callaghan.
> – Good-night, Miss Morkan.
> – Good-night, again.
> – Good-night, all. Safe home.
> – Good-night. Good-night.
>
> (*D*, 243)

Similarly, the style of narration which often involves using the idiom and registers that characters might themselves use if they were narrating the story, although indisputably writerly, is part of the same ambition to capture Dublin realities. Littered with expressions that suggest the voice, or rather voices, of Mrs Mooney and her family, the narrative of 'The Boarding House' has often been used to illustrate this dimension of *Dubliners*. Bob Doran becomes a good prospect for marriage to Mrs Mooney's daughter, Polly, because, 'She knew he had a good screw for one thing and suspected he had a bit of stuff put by' (*D*, 70); Jack Mooney, the son, plays a potentially important part in completing the deal as the physical power behind the throne – he was 'handy with the mits' (*D*, 67). Again, the narrative of 'Clay' involves copious use of the word 'nice' to suggest both Maria's talking style and the characteristic mechanism by which she deals with the world. She sets a 'nice' fire, works for 'nice' Protestants and a 'nice' matron. In preparation for going out on a 'nice' evening she admires her 'nice tidy little body' and buys something really 'nice' for the All Hallow's party. The man on the bus is 'very nice with' Maria, as is Joe (*D*, 110–17).

The apparent inconclusiveness of these seemingly plotless stories responds to the same agenda of making it real, as does the attention paid to street names and buildings. In a story like 'Two Gallants' the insistent naming of place – Rutland Square, Dorset Street, Dame Street, Earl Street, Trinity College, Nassau Street, Kildare Street, Hume Street, Merrion Street, Shelbourne Hotel, the Duke's lawn, Grafton Street, George's Street, Westmoreland Street and Ely Place – grounds the story in the physical environment at the same time as evoking a history of colonial appropriation and domination which resonates alarmingly against the story of how Corley, urged on by Lenehan, manages to obtain money from 'the slavey'. The importation of texts from outside reality, notional or otherwise – a memorial card ('The Sisters'); a music-hall song ('The Boarding House'); an imagined review of a non-existent book of poems ('A Little Cloud'); legal documents ('Counterparts'); parlour songs and songs from light opera ('Clay' and 'The Dead'); a newspaper article ('A Painful Case'); a candidate election card ('Ivy Day in the Committee Room'); poems ('A Little Cloud' and 'Ivy Day in the Committee Room'); a sermon ('Grace'), a speech ('The Dead') and letters ('The Dead') – work, again, in a similar way, establishing for *Dubliners* an apparently seamless contiguity with the real world it anatomizes.

The lacunae and inconsistencies of these stories, so often the focus of recent criticism on *Dubliners*, work in support of the same reality principle.[10] Many of these stories invest in unresolved puzzles. That is not to say that critical readings have failed but, rather, that Joyce sets up puzzles incapable of resolution, often because their maintenance is central to the representational depth of the stories. Here in the silences, secrecies, gaps and unresolved questions, the social and cultural fabric of colonial Dublin in the early-twentieth century is often at its sharpest exposure. In 'An Encounter', for example, the narrator as a young boy has a 'confused notion' about sailors and green eyes (*D*, 23). As it turns out, the 'pervert', who does something in the sight of the two boys who encounter him, although what he does is not made explicit, has green eyes. The resultant zone of expectancy is crucial to the story, as is the beautifully maintained silence that circumnavigates any too explicit an encounter with masturbation, sadism and homosexuality. Ironically for these stories, especially the stories of childhood, which particularly implicate confessional traditions, there is much that is not, or cannot, be confessed and faced directly.

'The Sisters' with its pervasive sense of mystery is the standard illustration here and for good reason. Secrecy and mystery are key to this signature story. The words 'paralysis', 'gnomon' and 'simony', famously invoked at the beginning, are apparently highly significant, but what of? There are questions about the old priest's death. From what, exactly, did he die, for example? There are also suggestive suspicions and innuendos about his life. What was 'queer' and 'uncanny' about him? Why would Old Cotter not like children of his own 'to have too much to say to a man like that'? (D, 8). What, exactly, was 'bad' for children to see in relation to the old priest? The narrator dismisses Old Cotter as a 'Tiresome old red-nosed imbecile' but his own dream of the priest's 'grey face', desiring to 'confess' something, smiling 'continually . . . the lips . . . so moist with spittle' (D, 9), only develops the sense of the mysterious suggested by Old Cotter and extended later when Father Flynn's sister, Eliza, raises a further series of questions. In later life, she says, there 'was something queer coming over him . . . Whenever I'd bring in his soup to him I'd find him with his breviary fallen to the floor, lying back in the chair and his mouth open. She laid a finger against her nose and frowned.' Her brother was 'a disappointed man' but why? His life was 'you might say, crossed', but in what sense? The beginning of 'his troubles' is associated with 'that chalice he broke', even though 'they say it was all right, that it contained nothing, I mean.' But this event apparently has a profound effect on the old priest, and one night he is discovered 'in the dark in his confession-box, wide-awake and laughing-like softly to himself' (D, 15–17). Here both loyalty to '*the* religion, the old, original faith' (D, 188) and the Church's great cultural status become deeply problematized as they are conflated, and contaminated, with superstition, gossip, secrecy, snobbery and the confused ambitions of a young boy. They are also firmly embedded in a colonial context (Flynn and his sisters live tellingly in 'Little Britain Street'), where mystification is part of the everyday landscape.

Although these gaps and silences have a particular resonance in the stories of childhood, they continue through the stories of adolescence, maturity and public life and punctuate 'The Dead'.[11] Typically the associations are with the politics of religion and sexuality, with Eveline, the character in the story of that name, never fully confronting the sexual panic and fear of punishment from the father authority that is generated by her planned escape with Frank. The failure to articulate what is 'awkward' in 'The Boarding House', echoed by the story's inability to say what really took place between Bob Doran and Polly, engages a similar terrain, as do the questions which surround Mr Duffy's dramatic aversion to Mrs Sinico's touch and its scarcely conceivable relationship to one of Duffy's characteristically pompous 'sentences': 'Love between man and man is impossible because there must not be sexual intercourse and friendship between man and woman is impossible because there must be sexual intercourse' (*D*, 69, 125).[12] Elsewhere secrecy, silence and mystification operate in a more conventionally political context as in 'Ivy Day in the Committee Room' where there are questions around Father Keon's status and his mysterious relationship with Mr Fanning, the sub-sheriff of Dublin, and a careful refusal to name 'a certain little nobleman with a cock-eye', the 'patriot' who is 'in the pay of the Castle' (*D*, 140).

There are further ways by which Joyce underwrites the realism of these stories, the intimacy of knowledge about, for example, church ritual in stories like 'The Sisters' and 'Grace'; about the local cultural scene in 'A Mother' and 'The Dead' and local politics in 'Ivy Day' (for which Stanislaus took the credit. See *MBK*, 206). This precise mapping was often carefully verified in letters home, asking for checks on such details as to whether 'a priest can be buried in a habit . . . Aungier Street and Wicklow Streets [were] in the Royal Exchange Ward . . . The police at Sydney Parade [were] of the D. division' and so on (*JJ*, 210). All testified to the importance that Joyce placed on absolute accuracy. Even the allusive quality of the collection, so much utilized in readings which see the meaning of the stories outside the realistic 'surface', often work to support the illusion of the real. In 'Eveline' it is clear that behind the references to the estate owner, 'a man from Belfast'; 'little Keogh the cripple'; to dust; 'the broken harmonium'; the Blessed Margaret Mary Alacoque, the saint in whom self-mortification produced paralysis and the priest who moved to Melborne, there is a network of implied meaning crucial to the story but which remains undeveloped, even seemingly unattached, because that is how things would appear to Eveline (*D*, 37–8).[13] By this means Joyce, again, gets depth into his stories without disturbance to realism.

Joyce knew perfectly well that his version of Dublin was deeply controversial, and this remains, to a significant degree, the great excitement of *Dubliners*. After Richards's printer objected to 'Two Gallants' and 'Counterparts', Joyce warned with some degree of relish, and perhaps unwisely, that things would not stop there.

> A Dubliner would denounce *Ivy Day in the Committee Room*. The more subtle inquisitor will denounce *An Encounter*, the enormity of which the printer cannot see because he is, as I said, a plain blunt man. The Irish priest will denounce *The Sisters*. The Irish boarding-house keeper will denounce *The Boarding-House*. Do

not let the printer imagine, for goodness' sake, that he is going to
have all the barking to himself.

(Letters II, 134)

There was no doubt that these stories were specifically designed to be
challenging and at odds with conservative contemporaneity. The treatment of sexuality in stories like 'An Encounter', 'Araby', 'The Boarding
House', 'A Painful Case' and 'The Dead' engaged with *fin de siècle* sexual
politics and aligned Joyce broadly with the sexual radicals of his day.
Dubliners also took political position by countering the jingoism of
Edwardian England with a complex and highly-nuanced representation
of a developed colonial metropolis. Crude oppression of the kind associated with the late-nineteenth century 'scramble' for colonies in Africa
had already been powerfully, if ambiguously, addressed by early modernism, but Joyce, as he claimed, was the first fiction writer to focus on
the metropolitan centre of the oldest British colony of all. 'I do not think',
he wrote to Grant Richards, 'that any writer has yet presented Dublin
to the world. It has been a capital of Europe for thousands of years, it is
supposed to be the second city of the British Empire' *(Letters* II, 122).
Here imperialism was much more established, producing a sophisticated geopolitics of street naming, statuary and architecture, 'the feudal
arch of King's Inns' *(D,* 77). It was also subtle in its phenomenology, at
work in everyday exchanges and the apparently commonplace where,
for example, the inferiority of being Catholic and Irish produced a thoroughly Anglicized culture and one, in Joyce's account, obsessed with
demarcations. It is in this context that the narrator of 'An Encounter',
worried enough to plan for disguises but still wanting to impress the
strange man of seemingly high-class literary tastes whose 'accent was
good', suggests that, if asked, he should adopt the typical English name
of Smith, while his friend, the more robust Mahony, should become
'Murphy' *(D,* 25). The classic colonial double bind is implied here. In
emulating high-status cultures of England, or the 'Continent', in order to
escape native 'inferiorities', colonial identities only become more clearly
defined. Such dynamics are everywhere in *Dubliners* – in the education
that Jimmy Doyle, in 'After the Race', gets in England; in Bob Doran's
fear that his family would 'look down on' Polly *(D,* 72); in the general
disbelief that a Lord Mayor of Dublin should send *'out for a pound of
pork chops for his dinner' (D,* 143); in the sense that the Morkan's small
party, their 'annual dance' is a 'great affair' *(D,* 199). Some stories, like 'A
Painful Case' and 'The Dead' are centrally, even obsessively, concerned
with social demarcation. In the latter Gabriel Conroy distinguishes
himself as a man whose 'grade of culture' differs from that of his aunts
and their friends *(D,* 203). His mother, 'sensible of the dignity of family

life' names her children accordingly, Constantine and Gabriel (*D*, 212). When Molly Ivors remembers that Gabriel's wife, Gretta, comes 'from Connacht', he corrects her, 'shortly' with the observation that 'Her people are' (*D*, 215). Gabriel's first attempt at counter attack when Gretta reveals the story of Michael Furey, the young man who may have died of love for her, is a question which challenges Michael's status 'What was he?' (*D*, 251). That list is far from inclusive; it only illustrates the great many exchanges motivated by concerns over social status in the story that Joyce wrote as a 'coda' to *Dubliners*.

The psychological dimensions of colonial appropriation are apparent in many other ways. In 'After the Race' the notable silence around whether Jimmy Doyle is being welcomed to the international circle of youth and glamour that so attracts him or fleeced by it, responds to empire politics. Significantly, at the end of a raucous night of gambling it is the Englishman, Routh, who wins and Jimmy Doyle who is among the 'heaviest losers' (*D*, 51). In 'Counterparts', Farrington's frustration and subsequent brutality is framed by the subservience owed to and demanded by his superior, Mr Alleyne, a man with 'a piercing North of Ireland accent' (*D*, 95) and by Farrington's failure to 'uphold the national honour' in an arm wrestling match with Weathers, an Englishman (*D*, 106).

In representing the micropolitics of empire in such ways, *Dubliners* took a radical political position, one which inevitably interfered with the romanticizing traditions of much contemporary Irish culture, whether in the form of revivalist traditions, heroic and Celticizing and mocked in stories like 'A Little Cloud' and 'A Mother', or Church traditions which defined the national identity its terms of its piety, learning and loyalty. Indeed, it was here that the Joyce revolt was at its most potentially controversial and its underpinning justification was precisely the writing performance that Joyce defined so centrally in terms of the real. If Joyce could not reproduce the sober, spiritual, pure and Gaelic-speaking Ireland powerfully made manifest in revivalist and Church culture, that was because such an Ireland, in his view, was a romantic, and indeed, conservative fantasy.

Although, as we have seen, however careful Joyce was in correspondence with Grant Richards to justify his stories in terms of realism, with his brother he was less confident about exactly how accurate his representation was. Here there was always the concern that perhaps he had gone too far, not by making his stories somehow too realistic, but by failing to control the wicked energy that was always so evident in Joyce's work and which, like the writerly performance of the real, was intimately bound up with his radical sense of self. Indeed, in *Dubliners* it is the exercise of these particular muscles that produce the most 'ruthless realism' of all, as in the description of Sunday morning piety in 'The Boarding House' – 'The belfry of George's Church sent out constant peals and worshippers, singly or in groups, traversed the little circus before the church, revealing their purpose by their self-contained demeanour no less than by the little volumes in their gloved hands' (*D*, 68–9).[14] A similarly wicked satirical instinct is evident in the representation of Little Chandler's ambition to become a poet of 'the Celtic school' and recognized by 'the English critics'. He imagines his review *'Mr Chandler has the gift of easy and graceful verse . . . A wistful sadness pervades these poems . . . The Celtic note'* (*D*, 80). The comment that Mrs Kearney, in 'A Mother', 'respected her husband in the same way as she respected the General Post Office' is, again, particularly sugges-tive of an implied author persona, as is the observation that the young tenor in the same story 'marred the good impression by wiping his nose in his gloved hand' (*D*, 159–60). Indeed this kind of intervention is eve-rywhere in *Dubliners*, in the deeply ironic use of romance novelese at the beginning of 'Two Gallants' and the equally ironic layering of the Tristan and Isolde story over 'A Painful Case';[15] in the description of the Inchicore sightseers watching the car race as 'the gratefully oppressed' (*D*, 44) and in Lenehan's ambition to find 'some good simple-minded girl with a little of the ready' (*D*, 62). As fascinating as the appearance of realism is, these sharp and comic interventions are also fundamental to the marking out of *Dubliners* as a characteristically Joycean text and distinguish it from what Joyce typically referred to as the 'whinging' of his revivalist contemporaries. His brother, wrote Stanislaus, 'Surfeited with the tawdry melancholy of patriotic Irish poets . . . used to say that Ireland had contributed nothing but a whine to the literature of Europe' (*MBK*, 167), which is consistent with Joyce's caricature of Yeats in 'The Holy Office' being consoled 'when he whinges' by 'giddy dames'.[16] In January 1905 he wrote in similar vein to Stanislaus *'What* is wrong with all these Irish writers – what the blazes are they always snivelling about?' (*Letters* II, 78). Many critics have argued that in *Dubliners* there are signs of the experimentalism of *Ulysses* and *Finnegans Wake*, the later and much more dramatic interferences with novel culture. One of the more substantial senses in which this is so is in the fascinating play which enables comic satirical intervention to become somehow sub-sumed in what is a masterly performance of reality.

Portraits of the Artist (1904–1914)

In January 1904 Joyce wrote an autobiographical paper entitled 'A Portrait of the Artist'. When it was rejected by the editors of the Irish periodical *Dana*, he decided to develop the material into a novel, called, at Stanislaus Joyce's suggestion, *Stephen Hero*. By March 1906 Joyce was informing Grant Richards, the publisher, that he had written 'nearly a thousand pages' or 'twenty-five chapters about half of . . . [a] book', which was 'in some sense autobiographical' (*Letters* II, 131–2). All that remains of this draft is an unrevised fragment comprised of eleven chapters dealing with the University College period.

In 1907 he began rewriting *Stephen Hero* according to a new scheme of just five chapters, instead of sixty-three. Three chapters were completed between September 1907 and April 1908, at which point he stopped once more, starting again with the encouragement of his language student, Ettore Schmitz, who had published two novels in Italian under the pen name of Italo Svevo. In 1911 Joyce, maddened at the difficulties of finding a publisher for *Dubliners*, threw one of these manuscripts, either the *Stephen Hero* version or the revision, into the stove. The 'charred remains of the MS were rescued by a family fire brigade and tied up in an old sheet where they remained for some months. I then sorted them out and pieced them together as best I could and the present MS is the result' (*Letters* I, 136). *A Portrait of the Artist as a Young Man* was finally brought out in book form by W. B. Huebsch in America in 1916, with book versions appearing in England under the Egoist imprint in 1916 and 1917. The Jonathan Cape edition of 1924 was reset with corrections by Joyce himself, who thereafter did no further work on the text.[17]

For earlier reviewers of *A Portrait* it was again the book's realism and its apparent counterpart, the perceived 'filth' and 'bestial coarseness', that stood out. *The Irish Book Lover* saw it as fascinating and 'unsparing' in its 'realism', but Joyce's relatively frank treatment of schoolboy and adolescent sexuality and the language used by his undergraduates in chapter five meant that 'no clean minded person could possibly allow it to remain within reach of his wife, his sons or daughters' (*CH*, 1, 102). The reviewer for *Everyman* wrote that 'the description of life in a Jesuit school and later in a Dublin College, strikes one as being absolutely true to life – but what a life!' (*CH*, 85) and the *Southport Guardian* saw it similarly as a 'ruthless, relentless essay in realism', the word 'essay' here being suggestive (*CH*, 1, 102). For these early reviewers, though often astonished by the book's veracity, had strong doubts about its artistic value and great difficulties in recognizing it as a 'genuine' novel. In a reader's report he produced for Duckworths, Edward Garnett – an important figure in English letters and publishing – declared the book 'formless' and by its end 'falling to bits' (*Letters* II, 371–2). *Everyman* regarded it as 'impressionistic', again especially in its ending which somehow seemed symptomatic. *The Literary World and Reader: A Monthly Review of Current Literature* thought it more 'a study of a temperament' than a 'story' and confessed 'that it is very difficult to know quite what to say about this new book by Mr Joyce'. The *Rochester (New York) Post-Express* found it 'chaotic' and *The Irish Book Lover* saw it as a 'pseudo autobiography'. The reviewer here posed the question 'Is it Art?' and provided a more or less clear answer – 'We doubt it' (*CH*, 1, 102).

These criticisms and confusions responded in part to the complexities of a text that seemed both highly autobiographical, as it was, and yet related in highly ambiguous ways to some very familiar literary forms. In particular, Joyce's novel was a highly transgressive and modernizing treatment of the *bildungsroman*, or novel of youth, and its variants – the *erzihungsroman*, where the emphasis was on formal education and training, and the *künstleroman*, which focused on the development of the artist. Narratives of these kinds, often linked by literary historians to the development of European romanticism, derived their particular force from the symbolic and highly politicized resonance they constructed around youth and adolescence in the age of nationalism.[18] Most typically they constructed young aristocratic or otherwise advantaged males in metaphorical relationship to cultural development, the latter usually being imagined in racial or national terms and frequently conceptualized as potent antitheses – across conservatism and progressivism, for example, where most typically the promise of national growth and development was pitched against the threat of decadence and degeneration. *A Portrait* is a critical engagement with these forms and traditions, drawing emphatic attention to the most Anglicized product of *bildungsroman* culture – public school literature, where, in the standard nineteenth-century form, 'juvenile development gained new value as a metaphor for wider social progress and political reform'.[19] The connections that this literature made between nation building and adolescence, and its later deployment of the discourses of racial fitness and national efficiency, ensured that this nowadays humble literary culture was once centrally engaged and of obvious relevance for Joyce in *A Portrait*.

The opening chapters of *A Portrait* in particular are built around the clichés of the public school narrative. Bullying, initiated when Stephen is 'shouldered' in 'the square ditch' by Wells – 'It was a mean thing to do' (*P*, 11) – and extended into chapter 2 and Stephen's encounters with Heron, was a standard theme in this literary culture and invariably linked to the question of whether such treatment was both natural and a valuable part of toughening up young boys too much dependent on their mothers, or simply brutalizing. The narrative line that begins with Stephen being falsely accused and beaten by Father Dolan and ends with him being elevated to the schoolboy hero, declared by 'the people' to 'have been wrongly punished' (*P*, 44–5), was *the* standard narrative of this often reformist genre. Similarly with the general emphasis on discipline and punishment and the relationship between fear and adolescent socialisation, evoked from the opening chapter of *A Portrait* through to the sermon at the retreat and Stephen's terrified response to it – this was the essential domain of the public school novel. The sick schoolboy, his illness connected to moral correction – in chapter 1 of *A Portrait*, Stephen's fever becomes the context in which he is reminded of his father's advice to 'never to peach on a fellow' (*P*, 7) – were also characteristic narrative devices, as was the contrast between combative masculinity, represented in Joyce's novel by Rody Kickham, 'a decent fellow', and the more feminized sensitivity and outsiderliness imaged in the figure of a young Stephen feeling 'small and weak' and 'on the fringe of his line' (*P*, 6). The estrangement from the father and the imperative on the hero to formulate his engagement with society and culture on his own terms, a particular focus of chapter two of *A Portrait* and the trip Stephen takes to the old stomping grounds where his father was once well known as 'the handsomest man in Cork' (*P*, 77) – again, all this material, whatever its relation to autobiography, was also typical of public school literature and positions *A Portrait* firmly in relation to that genre.

A Portrait is framed, then, by the traditions that produced such popular classics as Thomas Hughes's *Tom Brown's Schooldays* (1857); F. W. Farrar's *Eric, Or, Little by Little* (1858) and a host of school histories and Victorian and Edwardian biographies and popular magazine writing. There was also an Anglo–Irish dimension contributed to by such figures as Maria Edgeworth and Percy Hetherington Fitzgerald who both wrote novels in the genre. In almost all other respects, however, Joyce's version is completely atypical. It draws on these traditions, but at the same time establishes a highly transgressive relationship to them and not simply through the frankness that so alarmed early reviewers, where schoolboy sexuality and gossip around such practices as 'smugging' are never far from the surface of things (see *P*, 33–8).

The characteristic narrative voicing of *A Portrait*, for example, is a fundamental breach in the authorizing traditions of the *bildungsroman* and the public school narrative. Partly in order to get closer to the stages of his central character's psychological development, Joyce compromises the 'objective' authority of third person narrative in favour of a series of narrative styles adapted to suggest babyhood, childhood and various emotional states usually associated with youth. Here the narrator is brought very much closer to the subject identity of the central character, one of the central aesthetic developments that distinguish *A Portrait* from the more conventional *Stephen Hero* fragment. Whereas

Stephen's family members and friends have a relatively independent life in *Stephen Hero*, now, in *A Portrait*, it is Stephen's viewpoint which dominates, even in the famous Christmas dinner scene where a terrified Stephen recedes as the political and religious passions of Mrs Riordan, Simon Dedalus and John Casey run riot. The world and its inhabitants are as they are perceived or conceptualized by Stephen. The beginning of the first chapter is particularly illustrative. As an infant, he sees his father as a man who 'looked at him through a glass: he had a hairy face'; his mother is represented in terms of her scent – she 'had a nicer smell than his father'. Figures appear without explanation or frame as does Dante who 'had two brushes in her press. The brush with the maroon velvet back was for Michael Davitt and the brush with the green velvet back was for Parnell' (*P*, 5). Later, with Stephen, aged 7, attending Clongowes Wood School, the language of the narrative shifts similarly with minimal explanatory context, as when schoolboy idiom slips easily into the first part of the narrative ('Rody Kickham was a decent fellow but Nasty Roche was a stink' – *P*, 6). Confusions about matters which would be trivial in the adult world – whether it is 'right to kiss [one's] . . . mother or wrong' (*P*, 11) – remain just as puzzling as the big issues, around religion, for example, ('there were different names for God in all the different languages of the world . . . still God remained always the same God and God's real name was God'); or politics ('It pained him that he did not know well what politics meant' – *P*, 13). All persist as confusions conceptualized in Stephen's own terms. At the same time, the chapter constructs a world strongly characterized in terms of sensual perceptions. Chapter 1 echoes with references to smell, taste, sound modulated as Stephen opens and closes 'the flaps of his ears' (*P*, 10), to the experience of heat and cold and to a visual world frequently signified by the colours red and white. Sometimes all the senses are evoked virtually simultaneously: 'And the air in the corridor chilled him too. It was queer and wettish. But soon the gas would be lit and in burning it made a light noise like a little song. Always the same: and when the fellows stopped talking in the playroom you could hear it.' (*P*, 9)

This virtuoso performance is repeated in different terms in later chapters as Stephen gets older. His moods, states of mind and intellectual capacities predominate over his sensual experience of the world as he grows and develops but, again, these become reproduced in narrative styles, rendering the narrative pious when Stephen fears for his soul, and suitably ecstatic when he finds a way of transferring his sexualized imagination into a framework shaped not by a Catholic conception of sin but by a late-nineteenth century aesthetic discourse. The following extract is from the end of chapter 4, the conclusion of the wading-girl scene and a hymn to the transforming power of beauty. It is also the beginning of Stephen's serious identification with outsiderly roles framed emphatically in *fin de siècle* cultural terms. These combine in Stephen in the last chapter of *A Portrait* to help place him as a modern egoist aligned with an avant-garde that was dominated in historical reality by the aesthetic philosophy of Walter Pater and such figures as Arthur Symons, Daniel Gabriel Rossetti and Yeats (see *AP*, 257–61).[20]

> He closed his eyes in the languor of sleep. His eyelids trembled as if they felt the vast cyclic movement of the earth and her watchers, trembled as if they felt the strange light of some new world. His soul was swooning into some new world, fantastic, dim, uncertain as under sea, traversed by cloudy shapes and beings. A world, a glimmer, or a flower? Glimmering and trembling, trembling and unfolding, a breaking light, an opening flower, it spread in endless succession to itself, breaking in full crimson and unfolding and fading to palest rose, leaf by leaf and wave of light by wave of light, flooding all the heavens with its soft flushes, every flush deeper than other.
>
> (*P*, 145)

The resulting *entrelacement* of narrator and character has usually been seen as problematizing the question of 'tone', the stance the novel takes towards Stephen Dedalus as the developing *fin de siècle* artist. Indeed, this question of how ironic Joyce's portrait was intended to be, formulated as 'the problem of distance', dominated criticism of the novel throughout the 1960s and 70s. From a different perspective, however, this narrative positioning has the effect of undermining the authoritative narrative which once turned the public school novel into a kind of guide for the development of the gentleman and the ruling elite. The narrative convention which traditionally mediated between the developing subject and the society he is destined to take his place in is here displaced, not only by a much more relative, contingent narrative identity, but one which crucially has no access to the progressive future imagined more typically in the *bildungsroman* generally and the public school novel in particular.

This undermining of progressivism is also implied in the novel's highly original treatment of the pursuit of the gentlemanly ideal. Stephen, confident that his father is 'a gentleman' but worried that he is not a 'magistrate' (*P*, 6), is urged from an early age to be himself a gentleman above all things and instilled with the importance of associating with 'bloody good honest Irishmen . . . fellows of the right kidney' (*P*, 77) – a lesson which he learns thoroughly but very much in his own way, identifying with aristocratic heroes of romantic literature, Edmund Dantes in *The Count of Monte Cristo*, for example, and later with the aristocratic rebel, Lord Byron.

But the gentlemanly ideal so attractive in these forms is also deeply problematic. It is both compromised and powerfully shaped by Stephen's battle against 'the squalor of his life', the developing fall from material grace crucially connected with Parnell's fall and the collapse of Irish parliamentary nationalism. He also struggles with 'the riot of his mind' (*P*, 76), the growing sexuality pathologized by his Church and the dysgenic enemy of 'progress, control and order'.[21] By chapter 5 of *A Portrait* the gentlemanly ideal as represented by Stephen has not degenerated, as some of the early critics appeared to believe, into the upper-class vulgarity and decadence that was its standard Victorian antithesis but, rather, has transmuted into something much more interesting and of contemporary currency – a modern Irish anti-self: the seemingly self-contained egoist, extremely sensitized to coarseness and poverty of mind and spirit, who fully knows himself to be a product of 'this race and this country and this life' (*P*, 170).[22]

Similarly, and again in an architectural way, the determinedly progressivist structure essential to the public school narrative where the young hero re-enters social culture as a young man, reformed, engaged and ready to take his place in society, is displaced in *A Portrait* by a determinedly circular structure. First identified by Hugh Kenner in *Dublin's Joyce* (1959), this involves an end of chapter or section triumph, followed immediately by failure, or a shift in perspective so radical that any sense of pride in achievement is destroyed.[23] Thus chapter one leaves Stephen bringing a brutalizing regime at Clongowes to a higher authority and having its injustice overturned, a deed brought crashing down to earth in chapter 2 where Father Conmee and Stephen's father conspire to patronize Stephen's 'heroism' as the work of both 'an impudent thief' and a '*Manly little chap!*' (*P*, 60). The effect of such sharp shifts in perspective is to relativize progressivism out of existence, a countering of the fundamental ideological drive of the public school novel towards establishing authentic leadership values and the dispensation of just social authority.

Joyce thoroughly undermines the literary form of the *bildungsroman*, not just as a disruptive aesthetic exercise but in order to challenge the ideological consistency that once supported so many of these stories of 'youth'. Both the training and development narrative and the fundamental insecurities that underpin obsessions with order and progressivism are wrecked as the idea of the unitary subject is challenged and the conditions of the 'miserable Godforsaken island' (*P*, 181) in which Stephen attempts to flourish work against him. The monologic narrative voice becomes a device put to the service of psychological realism and is itself often fragmented, even overwhelmed. Sometimes its disappearance is the product of a genuinely powerful cultural intervention. The long and largely unmediated religious sermon in chapter 3 where 'the priest's voice takes over', for example, is not only a 'scandalous breach of the rules of modern fictional construction', but also a compelling assertion of Church ideology operating on the mind of the young.[24] Elsewhere it is the growing confidence of Stephen Dedalus himself that displaces the narrative voice, as in the extended discussions on aesthetics and, most dramatically, in the removal of the narrative voice altogether as it gives way to Stephen's diary extracts at the end of the novel. In either case, the novel proceeds not by the management and eventual alignment of narrative subject, mediating narrative and ideology, but by a fluctuating conflict of power relations rooted in Irish and colonial conditions. The end result is a complete breakdown – the space that is filled exclusively by Stephen's own voice in the form of his diary extracts as he prepares to leave Ireland, with all the insecure excitement and ambiguity that implies.

Stephen's position outside a meaningful progressivist narrative is framed in part by the 'psychological idea' that Stanislaus Joyce first described in his account of the novel's apparent original scheme:

> In Dublin when he set to work on the first draft of the novel, the idea he had in mind was that a man's character, like his body, develops from an embryo with constant traits. The accentuation of those traits, their reactions to hereditary influences and environment, were the main psychological lines he intended to follow, and, in fact, the purpose of the novel as originally planned.
>
> (*MBK*, 39)

That sense of continuity is not just described in *A Portrait* but enacted in a network of repeated phrases and images, and by the recurrent characteristics that become identified with Stephen irrespective of his circumstances or age – the creative engagement with words, for example, which begins with Stephen's interest in the multiple meanings of the word 'belt' (see *P*, 7), and the word 'suck' (*P*, 9), continuing right through to chapter 5 and the politically loaded discussion of the English word 'tundish' (see *P*, 158), which the English dean of studies at University College wrongly assumes to be an Irish word. Detachment similarly remains specifically associated with Stephen, from his early position on the 'fringe of his line' to his eagerness to escape with Cranly from the handball players in chapter 5 and the development of the much quoted Flaubertian aesthetic that positions the detached artist 'like the God of the creation . . . [remaining] within or behind or beyond or above his handiwork, invisible, refined out of existence, indifferent, paring his finger nails' (*P*, 181).

Such elements form Stephen's individuated nature in the book, but they also mutate into culturally familiar identities that resonate against the stereotypes of the public school novel and are profoundly shaped by the historical circumstances in which Stephen finds himself. The 'lazy bitch' (*P*, 147) of chapter 5 who sings Elizabethan songs and writes love poetry, continues to embody elements of the sensitive, feminized character who traditionally either falls by the wayside, or, in a novel like *Tom Brown's Schooldays*, becomes the moderating counterpart to the necessarily forceful masculinity of the 'Coming Man'. Equally, Stephen, as the rebel who will not serve, contains elements of unreconstructed aristocracy, usually punished in popular fiction as the decadent succumbing to disease and sometimes early death. But Stephen also figures as the serious, dispossessed representative of a new generation of Irish gentlemen – thus his sensitivity to any suggestion that he is somehow not pedigree. When Davin wonders whether 'with your name and ideas and your ideas . . . Are you Irish at all?', Stephen replies firmly, 'Come with me now to the office of arms and I will show you the tree of my family' (*P*, 169–70). He cultivates in himself the manners of the gentleman aristocrat against all the material and ideological odds generated by living in an Ireland symbolized for him by 'the old sow that eats her farrow' (*P*, 171). Oppressed by 'The grey block of Trinity . . . set heavily in the city's ignorance like a great dull stone set in a cumbrous ring' (*P*, 151) – a powerful reminder of a long colonial history and the power relations Trinity was crucial in maintaining – Stephen identifies with 'The soul of the gallant venal city which his elders had told him of had shrunk with time'. This is the 'Ireland of Tone and Parnell' that seems 'to have receded in space' (*P*, 154–5)', glossed by Gifford in Enlightenment terms as 'the Ireland that aspires to realize itself as a nation and as a republic with religious and civil liberties for all' (*AP*, 234). However reduced in circumstances and squalid his surroundings, when he takes leave of his family by 'kissing the tips of his fingers adieu' (*P*, 147), he re-enacts the gentlemanly ideal, albeit in knowingly ironic forms. With rather less self-knowledge, Stephen formulates himself as is an art aristocrat searching 'for the essence of beauty amid the spectral words of Aristotle and Aquinas' (*P*, 148), for 'an esthetic philosophy, [which] was held no higher by the age he lived in than the subtle and curious jargons of heraldry and falconry' (*P*, 151). Surprised and sometimes pleased 'to find himself still in the midst of common lives' (*P*, 148), he sees his contemporary Davin, a country boy, adopting 'the attitude of a dullwitted loyal serf' (*P*, 152).

He also reserves for himself the hugely ambitious-sounding role of going forth to 'to encounter for the millionth time the reality of experience and to forge in the smithy of my soul the uncreated conscience of my own race' (*P*, 213).

What these poses and ambitions mean in the modern world, however, have become greatly problematized. Without any material base, they become egoistic and practically ridiculous. Stephen is not only, as many critics have pointed out, no poet in any substantial sense – he also has no land, no property, no status. They also contain inherent and compelling contradictions which derive from Stephen's particularly historicized position as an Irish intellectual at the turn of the century. His statement at the end of *A Portrait* appears to be nationalistic at some level and yet bears little or no relation to the formations of cultural nationalism evident in Stephen's immediate environment and which he generally despises and mocks – Davin's 'rebellion with hurleysticks' (*P*, 169). The declaration about forging the 'uncreated conscience' of his race also appears to be radical, yet remains outside of the familiar liberal tendencies espoused by a figure like McCann (see *P*, 164–7). It looks forward to a future and in that sense could be interpreted as progressivist, and yet there is no indication of what sort of future might be implied, and for whom. The point being that these contradictions do not suddenly appear at the end of *A Portrait*. Fundamentally, they develop from the kind of gaps, inconsistencies and contradictions that the absence of a unified narrative has been signifying with great subtlety, virtually from the beginning of this 'autobiography' of a disestablished young Irishman learning how to articulate the voice of dispossession, 'the voice of Esau' (*U* 9.981).[25]

Exiles (1918)

Exiles was started in late 1913, simultaneously with the early sketches for *Ulysses*, and completed by March 1915. It was eventually published in May 1918 in the UK and USA by Richards and Huebsch respectively, accompanied by the usual furore over decency. In rejecting the play for the Stage Society in 1916, one member wrote of the need to resist 'Filth and Disease' (*JJ*, 415). First produced in 1919 in Munich, the play was withdrawn immediately, 'a flop' as Joyce put it, leaving one critic wondering why 'All that noise for an Irish stew' (*JJ*, 462). Yeats refused it for the Abbey theatre on the grounds that 'it is a type of work we have never played well. It is too far from the folk drama' – 'peasant dramas' as Joyce typically referred to them. Yeats thought the play 'sincere and interesting' but not 'at all so good as "A Portrait of the Artist" which I read with great excitement'. This view was shared by Pound who found the play 'exciting' but 'not nearly so intense as Portrait' and thought it unlikely 'to do for the stage' (*JJ*, 401–2). Joyce, thinking 'An unperformed play . . . like a dead deportee' (*Letters* II, 456–7), continued to champion *Exiles* with theatre companies until the mid 1920s.

Early Joyce critics tended to confirm that with *Exiles* Joyce had fallen below par, producing a self-indulgent play that was somehow not play-able. Harry Levin in *James Joyce* (1954), found the play, like Joyce's early poetry in his view, 'incurious and conventional' by comparison to the 'later experiments'. More specifically *Exiles* suffered from the influence of Ibsen, displaying 'a literal-minded subservience to another conven-tion, to the school of Ibsen and the naturalists' – misleading not least because naturalism was only one phase of many in Ibsen's long play-writing career and Joyce knew them all.[26] William York Tyndall writing in 1959 in *A Reader's Guide to James Joyce* was the first of many to con-struct the play as an exorcism of personal pain 'not objective enough to be a play. Inclining to what Stephen would call "lyric" art, *Exiles* fails to play on a stage, remote from the author, where a play must play'.[27] Of the early critics, Hugh Kenner, also writing in the1950s, was one of the few to see *Exiles* as anything more than a diversion from the main trajectory of Joyce, and he did so by understanding it as he understood *A Portrait*, as a thoroughly ironic dispersal – a sophisticated joke on the themes of Irish exile and the modern. 'In *Exiles*', Kenner wrote, 'he brings [in the character of Richard Rowan] an Ibsen hero to nullity within the context of an Ibsen play'.[28] There was some limited consensus here to the extent that both Kenner and Tyndall thought *Exiles* not so much a play as an exercise of pathological individualism. But whereas Tyndall wrote of *Exiles* in terms of breaks, inconsistencies and a falling off in quality, Kenner saw a clear continuity. 'Joyce drew off the rebellious heroics and cast them as a running sub-plot to his later works: first Richard Rowan, then Stephen Dedalus, then Shem the Penman; a metamorphosis of sham personae containing and controlling all the errors implicit in the relation between Dublin and its "liberated" victim'.[29]

Exiles is Ibsenite in its intense claustrophobia. As the fascinating, sometimes strange, notes that Joyce wrote as a commentary on the play make clear, it was, like all Joyce's work, deeply rooted in his own life, albeit in a fantasist sort of way. The Richard Rowan apparently standing in for Joyce returning to Ireland to honours awarded by the Protestant intelligentsia with nothing short of awe was some considerable way short of reality in any period close to 1912. In particular *Exiles* is linked to an extraordinary series of events which took place during his 1909 trips to Dublin, when Joyce was temporarily persuaded by Vincent Cosgrove, and his own insecurities, that Nora had been unfaithful. The resultant despair and anger seem to have been resurrected during Nora's trip to

Galway in 1912, which led Joyce to follow Nora out to Ireland for what was to be his final visit home. Once this obsession with Nora's infidelity began to die down, as Ellmann points out, Joyce began to consider 'constancy', or 'betrayal', in what he thought of as 'jesuitical' terms (see *JJ*, 284). *Exiles* is first and foremost, then, a surgical investigation of sexuality in modernity, a transformation of the intense emotions that were to produce, among other sexual adventures, the infamous 'dirty' letters designed by Joyce and Nora 'as aids to self-stimulation' (*N*, 142) and which they sent to each other between September and December 1909 while Joyce was in Ireland (see *N*, 137–47).

This focus is largely what gives the play contemporary relevance for many late productions, Harold Pinter's 1970 version, for example, and especially James MacDonald's at the Cottlesloe (2006). Revivals such as these have helped change the perception of *Exiles*, with one influential theatre critic now hailing it as a 'missing link' between Ibsen and late modern drama.[30] Characterized by 'ideas about sexual freedom and experiment within a traditionally closed marital framework', *Exiles* is a powerful reminder that some Edwardians were 'free radicals'.[31]

Not only does the play's sexual energy take place outside marriage and relate sexuality to personal freedom, the familiar territory of *fin de siècle* sexual liberationists, it also explores other kinds of sexual activities that sexologists had been cataloguing and analyzing since the late nineteenth century – the voyeuristic imagination, for example. Richard's questioning of Bertha in Act 1, excites him, as he and Bertha know. Indeed part of the deeper motivation for his seeming encouragement of Bertha's sexual 'freedom' is the pleasure Richard receives at imagining her with another man. In this context Robert's question, 'You were watching us all the time?' (*E*, 75), is loaded, as Richard fully understands and freely admits 'Because in the very core of my ignoble heart I longed to be betrayed by you and by her – in the dark, in the night – secretly, meanly, craftily' (*E*, 88). There are elements of passivity in the other character in this foursome, Beatrice. She is attracted to what she sees as the cruelty of Richard's mind (see *E*, 17); Richard thinks her 'running away' and 'afraid' because she cannot give herself 'freely and wholly' (*E*, 22). For all his romantic posturings, there are also strong elements of sadism in Robert, as the play notes make explicit. These describe the play as 'a rough and tumble between the Marquis de Sade and Freiherr v. Sacher Masoch' (*E*, 157) and refer directly to 'The sadism in Robert's character – his wish to inflict cruelty as a necessary part of sensual pleasure' (*E*, 158). In the play Robert sees Bertha as 'little', although in reality she is imposing. He wants to dominate her and she, responding to this desire, invites him to 'take' a kiss (*E*, 40). Robert himself talks of those 'moments of sheer madness when we feel an intense passion for a woman. We see nothing. We think of nothing. Only to possess her. Call it brutal, bestial, what you will' (*E*, 79) and Richard fears that Robert might be prepared to use violence against Bertha (see *E*, 92). There is, then, a cruelty in Robert which he exercises with particular pleasure over his cousin, Beatrice, and to which she submits. Beatrice's relative quietism in the play, far from being suggestive of underdevelopment, a charge which Joyce appears to have predicted (see *E*, 149), is a specific part of a highly patterned sexualized landscape.

The play also involves an exploration of homosexuality in an essentially heterosexual environment .The 'motive deeper still' that encourages Richard to expose his 'wife' to Robert is the desire to get physically closer to Robert (see *E*, 87–9). Robert's feelings towards Richard are similarly shaped around the idea of Bertha as a physical mediator. 'You are so strong', he claims, 'that you attract me even through her' (*E*, 78). The notes confirm the reading, indicating how 'The bodily possession of Bertha by Robert, repeated often, would certainly bring into almost carnal contact the two men. Do they desire this?' (*E*, 156–7). Even the pleasure which Joyce found in 'everything connected with excretion' (*N*, 139), at least for a period, is suggested in the play, when Robert talks of his attraction to the 'commonest' qualities in women 'how her body develops heat when it is pressed, the movement of her blood, how quickly she changes by digestion what she eats into – what shall be nameless' (*E*, 49). Again the notes, which refer also to menstruation and lesbianism (see *E*, 148, 156), make it clear just how challenging Joyce's analysis of sexuality and sexual motive could be. Here in a curious mix of scientism, poeticism and the biblical, he probes the issue of what Bertha might assent to in the way of accommodating 'emission' and why:

> Bertha is reluctant to give the hospitality of her womb to Robert's seed. For this reason she would like more a child of his by another woman than a child of him by her. Is this true? . . . Is her reluctance to yield even when the possibility of a child is removed this same reluctance or a survival of it or a survival of the fears (purely physical) of a virgin? . . . As for the accomplishment of the act otherwise externally, by friction, or in the mouth, the question needs to be scrutinized still more. Would she allow her lust to carry her so far as to receive his emission of seed in any other opening of the body where it could not be acted upon, by the forces of her secret flesh?
>
> (*E*, 157–8)

Drawing no doubt on a highly sexually creative period of his life with Nora, Joyce engages with sexuality here in terms of psychology and in ways suggestive of both the religious text and late-nineteenth and early-twentieth-century sexology. At the same time *Exiles* invokes different kinds of ideological resonance which overlap with the sexual identities of Richard and Robert. The contrast and conflict between these protagonists echoes the *fin de siècle* struggles of nineteenth-century libertarianism to define itself against social Darwinism and its later incarnations as eugenics and philosophic egoism, a theme that engages Joyce over and over in his creative life. Richard's demands for freedom and equality are set against Robert as a Darwinist or Nietzschean, a figure, like Mulligan in *Ulysses* and Shaun in the *Wake*, who has 'come up from a lower world' (*E*, 52), and is engaged in 'the fight' and fights to 'win'. The ambition to overpower Richard is expressed in terms of ownership of the house they once shared but above all is imminent in the competition for Bertha. 'No man', argues Robert, 'ever yet lived on this earth who did not long to possess – I mean to possess in the flesh – the woman whom he loves. It is nature's law'. Richard's response, delivered '*Contemptuously*' is highly suggestive of a fundamentally opposed rationalist and egalitarian response to the world: 'What is that to me? Did I vote it?' (*E*, 79). This battle between the brute force of the biological and psychological condition and the painful dispensation of free will is fundamental to the play. 'Every step advanced by humanity through Richard is a step backwards by the type which Richard stands for' (*E*, 152), as the notes put it, indicating how the play interrogates the historiography articulated by Nietzsche where the French Revolution and the consequent surge of European egalitarianism became the catastrophic wrong turning of nineteenth-century history.[32]

Equally important to the play are its Irish dimensions. As well as being framed by the clash of ideas represented by Richard and Robert, betrayal is linked to Ireland and Irish political life, with Joyce in the notes returning to his old fascination with the notion of the Irish betraying themselves and the prototype 'adulterous wife of the King of Leister who brought the first Saxon to the Irish coast' (*E*, 160). Significantly, when Bertha arrives for the 'secret' assignation at Robert's house, she is met first by Richard, who greets her with a deeply ironic 'Welcome back to old Ireland!' (*E*, 91). The overlays of the Tristan and Isolde story – Isolde is Bertha's 'sister-in-love' (*E*, 157) – reinforces this dimension, as does the fact that Richard Hand is a Protestant. Here the love quadrangle in *Exiles* becomes linked to territoriality and dispossession quite explicitly, which is presumably why Protestant and Catholic identities, and antipathies, become so much engaged. Richard's mother is reported as having referred to Beatrice as '*the black protestant*, the pervert's daughter' (*E*, 24); and Bertha, jealous of what she sees as Richard's flirtation with Protestant intellect, makes angry reference to Beatrice and 'her clan' (*E*, 69) who are, she says incapable of real generosity. Robert, allegedly a modernizer and above such social and religious divisions, and also exercising his instinct for cruelty, criticizes the protestant culture which produced him, but of which Beatrice, he claims, is a truer representative. He refers to the harmonium in Beatrice's father's parlour as 'The asthmatic voice of protestantism' (*E*, 32) and to the protestant strain in Beatrice herself – the 'gloom, seriousness and righteousness' which when it 'prevails' (*E*, 33), sends her off on retreat to Youghal. This is a town that has particular significance in Anglo–Irish history as a Norman walled seaport that declared for parliament in 1649 and became the headquarters of Cromwell. Pre-empting his own creation of Molly Bloom and ALP, Joyce also raises the 'vain question' about Bertha's status in the play as a new Celticized model for Western notions of female beauty. 'Europe is weary even of the Scandinavian women (Hedda Gabler, Rebecca Rosmer, Asta Allmers)', he writes, 'whom the poetic genius of Ibsen created . . . On what woman will the light of the poet's mind now shine? Perhaps at last on the Celt' (*E*, 158).

There are further Irish dimensions to *Exiles*, in Robert's glib association of Richard's visit with the 1912 Home Rule Bill, constructed by Robert in his article on the writer's return as Ireland's 'longawaited victory' (*E*, 129) – and by Joyce in his essay 'The Home Rule Comet' as a cynical piece of *realpolitik* (see *OCPW*, 155–9). Above all there are the contrasts between political and art exiles, developed, again in Roberts's article, by the further distinction made between 'spiritual' and 'economic' exiles. This element positions Richard and Bertha alongside, and yet suggestively separate from, the waves of Irish migrants that characterized nineteenth-century Irish history.

It may be that *Exiles* is overburdened, as well as enriched, by the sheer weight of these overlays as they combine with the play's substantial engagement with sexual politics and *fin de siècle* philosophy. It could be argued that form here is not sufficiently developed to support what Joyce appears to demand, with the result that many of these allusions are lost in performance. Whatever, it clearly is the case that the play is much more accomplished than was at one time thought. Far from being a diversion from the main directions of Joyce's work, *Exiles* confirms and develops the now established territory typical of Joyce and, in some ways, points to its new disposition in the text that was to become the classic work of high modernism – *Ulysses*.

CHAPTER 3

Going Forth By Day – *Ulysses*

Preliminaries

Ulysses has been the subject of forensic analysis for some 90 years. There is now clarity about what happens in a narrative sense – the old uncertainties about whether Leopold Bloom actually takes or merely imagines himself taking a bath at the end of 'Lotus-eaters', for example, were cleared up long ago. Likewise with the issue of exactly how many lovers Molly Bloom has had. We also have the benefit of annotations – not complete and probably never definitive, but nevertheless full. Latin, Greek, Hebraic, French and Italian expressions used in *Ulysses* have been translated; allusions to apostles, heretics and aestheticians have been identified and the many local references to Dublin's everyday life fixed and contextualized. We also have a large body of criticism and exegesis at our disposal. Our knowledge about the composition of the *Ulysses* text, while it still has some gaps, has been considerably refined and we can now characterize the narrative styles deployed in *Ulysses* and discuss their effects in highly sophisticated ways. Indeed we know enough about *Ulysses* to be able to assert with confidence that everything in it has purpose. We are also at a position where the status of *Ulysses* is so high that most would accept the idea that those who make the considerable effort required to read it have achieved something. That level of confidence may not be found in respect of *Finnegans Wake*, which demands even more of our time and energy.

At the same time *Ulysses* remains hugely complex and challenging. For all the critical efforts, fundamental questions remain. Take Bloom's status, for example. How central is Bloom to this book? Is the equanimity with which he meets the challenges that face him; the general kindness with which he approaches his fellow citizens; the penetration of his outsiderly comments on Dublin society really sufficient to carry *Ulysses* off, as was once widely held? For many readers, now as in the earliest days of *Ulysses*, there is something attractive, even compelling, about this unorthodox Dublin Jew and his anthropologically engaged perspectives on Dublin life, but is that enough to support the high cultural status *Ulysses* now has? Or is this book with its shifting perspectives and spectacular techniques simply too big for Bloom, as most contemporary traditions of criticism currently maintain? And what about that bigger book? The problem of why *Ulysses* is constructed on such a large, overarching scale and yet at the same time engaged so much in minutiae remains. Why does it take such great pains to establish itself as the highpoint of realism – there is perhaps no book so devoted to reproducing life as we think we live it – and yet at the same time draw so much attention to itself as a fabricated product, a book? This is a novel which seems made to undermine itself, at the same time as it designs the epic dimensions that take it beyond undermining.

Just to emphasize the point, it is not that critics have failed to address such issues – on the contrary, these are among the most fundamental questions asked about *Ulysses* – but, rather, that the book itself seems specifically set up to problematize engagement with the expectations we bring to it. This chapter shows how *Ulysses* positions itself in this way. The primary aim is to illustrate the extraordinary textuality that characterizes *Ulysses* by focusing on some of the most basic questions generally asked of fiction – how was it made, what story does it tell, what does it mean – and being prepared to reframe such questions where necessary. If, for example, this large scale novel has no correspondingly large scale story to tell what, then, does it set out to do?

Before addressing such issues, a few brief practical ideas on how to approach *Ulysses*. One of the most obvious difficulties of this book is that it takes allusiveness to new extremes. As well as thousands of cross references to itself, it also contains thousands of references to the world outside itself. The opening three chapters of *Ulysses*, the Telemachia, are particularly problematic in this respect because they focus on Stephen Dedalus and Stephen's range of reference is wide, intellectual and obscure. Because of who he is, then, the chapters are allusive in very particular and quite challenging ways. The first word positioned in Stephen's mind – 'Chrysostomos' (*U* 1.26) is symptomatic in this respect. Presumably the word refers to a man, but who was Chrysostomos and why is he being referred to? By the time we reach 'Proteus', more consistently interior than 'Telemachus' and 'Nestor',[1] the density of allusiveness has accelerated. The first twenty lines of this episode, for example, are formulated substantially out of books II and III of Aristotle's *De Anima*; the ideas of the theologian Jacob Boehme; Gotthold Ephraim Lessing's 1776 work on aesthetics *Laokoon*; *Hamlet*; Dante's 'Inferno' and lines of poetry associated with Los, the figure created by William Blake to represent divine aspects of the imagination. Something like Weldon Thornton's

Allusions in 'Ulysses' (1973) or Don Gifford's *'Ulysses' Annotated* (1989) will help locate such references, although search engines on the Internet are also helpful in this respect, often leading to fuller explanations than those available in either Thornton or Gifford. There are also hypertext versions of *Ulysses* now available online, one of which utilizes Gifford's annotations. The availability gives everyone connected to the web the tools to work with this aspect of Joyce's fiction very easily, providing one has the time and inclination.

The further option, however, is to worry less about the detail and aim for an understanding of the more general – the point being that the substantial issues usually, and certainly in the early stages of *Ulysses* reading, are much more important than chasing down the allusions. There is a more 'everyday' level to the book where straightforward questions often ignored by contemporary criticism are actually quite pressing. Why is there such tension between Stephen and Mulligan in 'Telemachus', for example? Clearly Stephen feels dispossessed in some way, but what of and who by? Many of the scenes imagined and remembered in Stephen's mind in 'Proteus' are constructed in stylized and often very beautiful ways, but to what end? Here, for example, he imagines a medieval Dublin, initially under assault from the Vikings:

> Galleys of the Lochlanns ran here to beach, in quest of prey. Their bloodbeaked prows riding low on a molten pewter surf. Dane Vikings, torcs of tomahawks, aglitter on their breasts when Malachi wore the collar of gold. A school of turlehide whales stranded in hot noon, spouting, hobbling in the shallows. Then from the starving cagework city a horde of jerkined dwarfs, my people, with flayers' knives, running, scaling, hacking in green blubbery whalemeat. Famine, plague and slaughters. Their blood is in me, their lusts my waves. I moved among them on the frozen Liffey, that I, a changeling, among the spluttering resin fires. I spoke to no-one: none to me.
>
> (*U* 3.300–9)

Knowing that the Lochlanns were among the earliest Danish invaders of Ireland; that 'when Malachi wore the collar of gold' is a direct quote from a Thomas Moore song about a tenth-century king of Meath who became Ireland's High King; that the Liffey did freeze over in December 1338 – all this may help in a number of possible ways. The more important issue, however, is the question of how to read the self-conscious poeticizing of this passage and the uncharacteristically intimate connection made between Stephen and his 'people', here and elsewhere in the Telemachia. Such questions will have an impact not just on our understanding of the character but of the wider book in which Stephen Dedalus now figures.

If all else fails with the 'Telemachia', my cavalier advice is to skip it and go to the first three Bloom chapters (episodes four to six). These are more reader friendly. Most will find them more accessible once the movement between 'outside' narration and inside 'monologue' becomes familiar. As with the Telemachia, the prose can be very allusive, but here it will be easier to get from the specific references to the more general point. We might not know precisely who Kate Bateman is in the sentence 'How he used to talk of Kate Bateman in that' (*U* 5.197–8) for example, but we will realize from the context that she was an actress, admired by Bloom's father. The density of allusions to Dublin theatre life is consistent with Bloom's wider relationships, both as the son of a theatre-going father and as the husband of a semi-professional singer. The reference also helps position him in the realm of 'popular' culture, which, for him, as for most of us, is just culture and entertainment. This, then, is notionally a more familiar world and reading it with confidence may help a return to the different demands of the 'Telemachia'.

Thereafter *Ulysses* develops as something like a game structured around levels of difficulty. There are periodic returns to the narrative styles most associated with Bloom and Stephen throughout, but from 'Aeolus' onwards 'style' begins to make more and more demands on the reader and it becomes increasingly obvious that our notions of what a novel is are being challenged. The critical point here is to accept the game and respond to the challenge. Even if the later episodes have seemed excessively indulgent to some commentators, there is always purpose and design to the dramatic stylistic shifts of *Ulysses*. The first question to ask of chapters like 'Sirens', 'Oxen of the Sun' and 'Ithaca' is identificatory. The radical styles of 'Ulysses' are usually imitative and parodic. What do they imitate? The second question is analytical in a different way. *Ulysses* is challenging and often playful but it is also purposeful; it has ambitions, takes position and is often appropriative. What is being engaged with through these textual or stylistic 'experiments'?

These kinds of questions should take you a long way with *Ulysses*. Remember above all, however, that *Ulysses* is a hugely comic text. Although scholars have repeatedly reminded us of this fact, they (and I include myself here) have also been responsible for the institutionalised culture of gravitas that can have the effect of separating out the 'significance' of *Ulysses* from its comic vision. Under such conditions, it is always worth emphasizing that there is no 'level' to *Ulysses* that is somehow immune from the comic. This suggests another question that should become second nature to *Ulysses* readers, a book that has become increasingly funnier as it grows older – what's the joke?

The Making of the Text

The history of the composition of *Ulysses* is long, complex and problematic. Joyce's extraordinary methods of composition, characterized by seemingly endless revision and expansion of text, combined with the fact that there are serious gaps in the manuscript evidence, especially for the earlier episodes, make it extremely unlikely that there will ever be a definitive reconstruction of the development of the *Ulysses* text from initial notes through to the final publication of the whole book. Indeed for many specialists working in the field of text development, the very idea of a complete *Ulysses* text is little more than a fantasy. Putting such positions aside, at least temporarily, it is possible, however, to reconstruct an outline story that will satisfy most general curiosities on this issue.

In September 1906 Joyce wrote to Stanislaus about a new story intended for inclusion in *Dubliners*, given the provisional title 'Ulysses' and focusing on a 'Mr Hunter', a real life Dubliner rumoured to be a Jew (*Letters* II, 168). The story never got written. In later life Joyce frequently claimed that *Ulysses* had its origins in this Rome period, but the real development of *Ulysses* began more seriously, and measurably, rather later.

Joyce began making notes for *Ulysses* between 1912 and 1914. Towards the end of this period, while still working on the proofs of *A Portrait* and *Exiles*, he was planning both early and late chapters, indicating that he had a sense of a complete structure at this relatively early time. After a redesigning of the initial chapters involving a 'foreshortening' of the Telemachia (chapters 1 to 3) and moving 'Scylla and Charybdis' to a more central place, Joyce wrote to Harriet Shaw Weaver in October 1916 explaining that the 'first part' of *Ulysses*, the 'Telemachia', was 'almost finished' and that he had 'written out part of the middle and end' (*Letters* II, 387).[2]

There were, however, substantial structural revisions to come. A major reworking took place between 1919 and 1921 when the earlier parts of the book, more conventionally realistic, were rewritten to make them more consistent with the complexities and innovations of the later chapters – although, as Michael Groden pointed out in the 1970s, as keen as he was to make such changes Joyce did not visualize a complete conversion. According to Groden, Joyce 'never entirely abandoned a set of aesthetic principles, even when new ones dominated his writing', which meant that *Ulysses* retained its status as a palimpsest, a work of development rather than a seamless whole, even in the final version.[3] It would seem that Joyce wanted a degree of revision consistent with the radical aesthetic of chapters like 'Circe' and 'Ithaca', but he also wanted the growth of his text to be on show, like the rock sediments in a cliff face. This made the development of the text a central part of the design of *Ulysses*.

The reworking of *Ulysses* was more or less coincident with its early publishing history. With Pound as its European editor, *The Little Review* undertook to serialize *Ulysses* in late 1917, the subsequent deadlines now dictating the pace of the book's progress with episodes being worked on in regular succession up to 'Oxen of the Sun' and December 1920. It was at this point that a New York court intervened, ordering *The Little Review* to cease publishing after a complaint by the New York Society for the Suppression of Vice which followed publication of the 'Nausicaa' episode. This is the chapter where Leopold Bloom, often seen as the Everyman centre of *Ulysses*, walks to the beach at Sandymount shore and finds himself worshipping 'at the shrine' of a young stranger, Gerty McDowell (*U* 13.564). Stimulated by the sight of Gerty leaning back, ostensibly to view a firework display but also putting her underwear on show, Bloom commits an act of public or, at least, open-air indecency. It was this episode, incidentally, that lead an early reviewer to describe Joyce, 'in his more delicate moments' as imitating George Moore and 'writing sentimentally about pale young girls and their underclothing' (*CH*, 193). In fact, although the first half of 'Nausicaa' is written in a mock-sentimental style – 'namby-pamby jammy marmalady drawersy (alto lá)' (*Letters* I, 135) – this chapter, which has Bloom detaching a stuck foreskin (under what circumstances does a Jew possess one?) and constructing a disabled Gerty McDowell as 'that little limping devil', is as earthbound, and as subversive, as anything in *Ulysses* (*U* 12.851–2). The offending 'tableau' also produces the most exciting sequence of Bloom's day ('Will she? Watch! Watch! See! Looked round . . . Darling, I saw, your. I saw all. Lord! – *U* 13.936–7), a highpoint famously celebrated by the coincidence of Bloom's ejaculatory climax with the spectacular finale of the firework display.

The legal decision to ban the title forced Joyce's American publisher, Huebsch, to withdraw his offer to publish *Ulysses* without alterations. After prompting from Joyce, Sylvia Beach agreed to produce the book, originally with a release date of October 1921 which was eventually delayed until 2 February 1922 – Joyce's fortieth birthday. The process of imminent production saw the book through to completion and resulted in extensive revision to the proofs pulled by the French printer Maurice Darentiere, many sections requiring 'five or six sets of proofs; some needed up to nine'.[4] These revisions involved not just corrections, but an astonishing degree of textual expansion, the accretive growth characteristic of Joyce's method of working in both *Ulysses* and the *Wake*. A 2009 account of this history points out that 'In all, *Ulysses* grew

Joyce's schema for Ulysses

Title	Scene	Hour	Organ	Art	Colour	Symbol	Technic	Correspondences
I. TELEMACHIA								
1. Telemachus	Tower	8 am		Theology	White, gold	Heir	Narrative (young)	Stephen: Telemachus, Hamlet; Buck Mulligan: Antinous; Milkwoman: Mentor
2. Nestor	School	10 am		History	Brown	Horse	Catechism, (personal)	Deasy: Mentor; Sargent: Pisistratus; Mrs O'Shea: Helen
3. Proteus	Strand	11 am		Philology	Green	Tide	Monologue (male)	Proteus: Primal Matter; Kevin Egan: Menelaus; Cocklepicker: Megapenthus
II. ODYSSEY								
4. Calypso	House	8 am	Kidney	Economics	Orange	Nymph	Narrative (mature)	Calypso: Nymph; Dlugacz: The recall; Zion: Ithaca
5. Lotuseaters	Bath	10 am	Genitals	Botany, Chemistry	White, black	Eucharist	Narcissism	Lotuseaters: the cabhorses, communicants, soldiers, eunuchs, bather, watchers of cricket
6. Hades	Graveyard	11 am	Heart	Religion		Caretaker	Incubism	Dodder, Grand and Royal Canals, Liffey: The 4 rivers; Cunningham: Sisyphus; Father Coffey: Cerebus; Caretaker: Hades; Daniel O'Connell: Hercules; Dignam: Elpenor; Parnell: Agamemnon; Menton: Ajax
7. Aeolus	Newspaper	Noon	Lungs	Rhetoric	Red	Editor	Enthymemic	Crawford: Aeolus; Incest: journalism; Floating island; press
8. Lestrygonians	Lunch	1 pm	Esophagus	Architecture		Constables	Peristaltic	Antiphates: Hunger; The Decoy: Food; Lestrygonians: Teeth

Episode	Scene	Hour	Organ	Art	Colour	Symbol	Technic	Correspondences
9. Scylla and Charybdis	Library	2 pm	Brain	Literature		Stratford, London	Dialectic	Rocks: Aristotle, dogma, Stratford Whirlpool: Plato, mysticism, London Ulysses: Socrates, Jesus, Shakespeare
10. Wandering Rocks	Streets	3 pm	Blood	Mechanics		Citizens	Labyrinth	Bosphorus: Liffey; European bank: Viceroy Asiatic bank: Conmee Symplegades: groups of citizens
11. Sirens	Concert Room	4 pm	Ear	Music		Barmaids	Fuga per Canonem	Sirens: barmaids Isle: bar
12. Cyclops	Tavern	5 pm	Muscle	Politics		Fenian	Gigantism	Noman: I Stake: cigar Challenge: apotheosis
13. Nausicaa	Rocks	8 pm	Eye, Nose	Painting	Grey, blue	Virgin	Tumescence. detumescence	Phaeacia: star of the sea Gerty: Nausicaa
14. Oxen of the Sun	Hospital	10 pm	Womb	Medicine	White	Mothers	Embryonic development	Hospital: Trinacria; Nurses: Lampetie, Phaethusa; Horne: Helios; Oxen: fertility; Crime: fraud.
15. Circe	Brothel	Midnight	Locomotor Apparatus	Magic		Whore	Hallucination	Circe: Bella
III. NOSTOS								
16. Eumaeus	Shelter	1 am	Nerves	Navigation		Sailors	Narrative (old)	Skin the Goat: Eumaeus Sailor: Ulysses Pseudangelos Corley: Melathius
17. Ithaca	House	2 am	Skeleton	Science		Comets	Catechism (impersonal)	Eurymachus: Boylan Suitors: scruples Bow: reason
18. Penelope	Bed		Flesh			Earth	Monologue (female)	Penelope: earth Web: movement

approximately one third longer from additions Joyce made on the type-scripts and proofs'.[5]

Consistent with the ambition of the book, its composition was nothing less than epic in scale. Larbaud described the notesheets and drafts as 'a genuine example of the art of mosaic . . . They are entirely composed of abbreviated phrases underlined in various-coloured pencils'.[6] The letters where Joyce wrote about the number of drafts for 'Circe' for example (given variously as six and nine), or the one thousand hours he estimated working on 'Oxen of the Sun' (see *Letters* I, 146, 156, 141), provided further testimony to the sheer labour identified with the production of *Ulysses*.

Moreover, *Ulysses* apparently had evolved according to a detailed plan, the most immediate and accessible registration of the creative energy that had gone into realising its huge ambition. In 1921, word began to circulate about the plan's existence. Joyce had showed it to the Italian critic Carlo Linati in the previous year and now lent it to Larbaud who was preparing a lecture to coincide with the publication of *Ulysses*. Jacques Benoît-Méchin, commissioned to write a French translation of 'Penelope' for the publication celebrations, also asked to see the elaborate scheme but at this stage Joyce became uneasy about giving 'it all up immediately, I'd lose my immortality' (quoted in *JJ*, 521). Eventually, however, the scheme was printed, in Gilbert's 1954 account, *James Joyce's 'Ulysses'* and since then a number of versions have appeared. (see page 50-1)[7]

It shows how *Ulysses*, designed as 'an epic of two races (Israelite–Irish)' also corresponded to 'the cycle of the human body' (*Letters* I, 146) with each chapter beyond the Telemachia corresponding to a human organ, chapters 1 to 3 being excluded from this part of the scheme because Stephen was predominantly 'mind'.[8] Each episode of Joyce's book was also identified by a place (the tower, the school, the strand, the house and so on) and the hour at which it occurred. Each was associated with a colour, a symbol, a 'technic' or style (narrative, catechism, monologue, for example) and by its 'correspondences'. *Ulysses*, the scheme insists, evolved according to an intricately designed blueprint and here the full extent of Homeric correspondence became transparent.

The Politics of Homeric Correspondence

Very quickly after publication critics began to discuss what turned out to be one of central selling points of *Ulysses* – one of the key qualities that initially made *Ulysses* indispensable to art literature. If the new Joyce book, even more than the preceding ones, was a decadent assault on human values, Richard Aldington's 'tremendous libel on humanity'

(*CH*, 188), it also deployed a parallel with one of the great classics of European culture, Homer's *Odyssey*. Writing for the *Quarterly Review*, Shane Leslie connected the filth with the intertextuality to produce an immoral 'Odyssey of the sewer' (*CH*, 207). Others were not so sure. As early as 1923, Ernest Boyd in the second edition of his *Ireland's Literary Renaissance* (1923) could write with justification that 'Much has been written about the symbolic intention of this work, of its relation to the *Odyssey*' (*CH*, 305), the vague use of the word 'symbolic' here implying Boyd's sense of the seriousness of the matter, because symbolism would have been suggestive of depth to Boyd. In an article entitled 'Mr Joyce and the Catholic Tradition', Cecil Maitland wrote without elaboration of *Ulysses* as 'the *Odyssey* retold' (*CH*, 273). Gilbert Seddes put more flesh on things when he explained that *Ulysses* was 'built on the framework of the *Odyssey*' but 'burlesques the structure of the original' (*CH*, 236), a view shared by Aleister Crowley who, in an interesting article written for *New Pearson's Magazine* in 1923, enthused about how 'Mr Joyce has taken Homer's *Odyssey* and made an analogy, episode by episode, translating the great supernatural epic into terms of slang and betting slips, into the filth, meanness and wit and passion of Dublin today' (*CH*, 288).

That *Ulysses* is somehow 'based on' Homer's *Odyssey* is of much less interest now, but, from publication through to the 1960s, criticism was once dominated by the issue – not least because Joyce himself, intensely engaged in the process of transposing 'the myth *sub specie temporis nostri*', had been so insistent on establishing correspondence as a central condition of *Ulysses* (*Letters* I, 147).[9] Frank Budgen's early account *The Making of Ulysses* (1934), reproduced in some detail Joyce's version of this relationship, emphasising the significance of Odysseus, the most 'complete man in literature' and the reasons why he stood as a prototype for Bloom, a modern 'hero' (*MU*, 16).

But, as Budgen also indicated, the importance of the *Odyssey* went far beyond any idea of character modelling. Primarily, Joyce saw his book as 'a modern *Odyssey*' (*MU*, 20) in architectural terms with the prototype providing a 'ground plan' for his novel (*MU*, 15). In the schematics Joyce produced, the basic tripartite division of the book into Telemachia, Odyssey and Nostos (Return) was Homeric in design. Each episode was not only referred to by its Homeric name – in the scheme and also in correspondence and *The Little Review* versions – but also positioned in relation to a narrative event taken from the *Odyssey*.[10] Indeed, all the columns in the schema were related in some way to the prototype text, with the single exception of an anti-epic column denoting the time of day at which each episode took place. In the 'symbol' designations, for example, the symbol for 'Telemachus' was heir; for 'Nestor' horse; for 'Proteus' tides' and for 'Calypso' nymph – all

Homeric, although the way they actually appeared in *Ulysses* was comically deflationary, mock heroic.

Some of the 'art' designations were, again, Homeric – magic was designated the art of 'Circe', for instance. Likewise the bodily organ listings, which had lungs representing 'Aeolus' and the ear representing 'Sirens'. The 'correspondence' column itself, unsurprisingly, was particularly rich in Homeric parallels. This column identified both the reasonably transparent – Stephen's correspondence to Telemachus and Mulligan's to Antinous – and the ingenious, not to say absurdly strained. In the correspondences for 'Hades', Martin Cunningham figures as Sisyphus; Father Coffey as Cerberus; the Prospect cemetery caretaker as Hades; Daniel O'Connell as Hercules; Paddy Digham as Elpenor; Parnell as Agamemnon and John Henry Menton as Ajax.

All in all, then, the columnar scheme insisted on a central intertextuality, apparently driving *Ulysses* at a very wide range of levels, but often virtually impossible to spot without the benefit of the plan. It seems hardly surprising that when the book was finished, Joyce advised his favourite aunt, Josephine Murray, if she wanted to read it, to 'better first get or borrow from a library a translation in prose of the *Odyssey* of Homer' (*Letters* I, 174). At the same time, the patterning was also determinedly skewed, typically ironic with the epic geography of the *Odyssey* being reproduced as a walk through Dublin; epic heroism as kindness to birds; epic revenge becoming Bloom's capacity for accepting Molly's infidelity and so on.

This overdone interaction with the *Odyssey*, described as simple 'scaffolding' by Ezra Pound, clearly raised more fundamental issues. What was Joyce getting at by bringing antiquity into proximity with modernity in such extremely determined but also wildly convoluted ways? In response, T. S. Eliot set the tone which enabled reconciliation of Joyce with the 'great tradition' version of literature, a case of 'the introduction of the new (the really new)' being introduced to 'the existing monuments [i.e. the canonical texts that] . . . form an ideal order among themselves.'[11] In the influential essay, '*Ulysses* order and myth', Eliot, like other early commentators, focused on the importance of 'the mythical method' and its originality, arguing that with the deployment of this device literature could bring to aesthetic heel what he saw as the anarchy of the modern world. 'In using myth' he wrote, 'in manipulating a continuous parallel between contemporaneity and antiquity, Mr Joyce [has discovered] . . . a way of controlling, of ordering, of giving shape and significance to the immense panorama of futility and anarchy which is contemporary history. Instead of narrative method, we may now use the mythical method.'[12] Interestingly, this has become one of the most well-known critical descriptions of *Ulysses* of all time.

But 'the mythical method', however much pursued by Joyce, is never used with the kind of piety that Eliot's analysis seems to require. How, for example, does the identification of Gerty McDowell's mouth as being 'Greekly perfect' (*U* 13.89), or the transmutation of Lestrygonians into 'teeth', restore order to chaos? When it came to revisions, Homeric correspondence also helped shape textual expansion, again often in seemingly comic and excessive ways. In 'Aeolus', for instance, the Homeric prototype, notably the Aeolian 'bag of winds', developed into a barrage of rhetorical devices and a whole wind lexicon. There are phrases like 'what's in the wind' and 'raise the wind'. The vocabulary includes breath, puff, draught, zephyrs, breeze, squalls, gale, whirlwind, hurricane, cyclone and a range of allusive words and phrases, like bladderbags, afflatus, breath, flatulence and so on. Similar lexicons feature in 'Ithaca', where the root is the idea of return; in 'Sirens' where musical terminology corresponds to the sirens' song and in 'Proteus' where the idea of change and mutation is linked to wordplay. How does this indulgence, again, 'control the futility and anarchy' of 'contemporary history'?

There are further questions to be asked of Eliot's commentary, especially of the assertion that Joyce invented the 'mythic method'. He might have been the first to extend myth structure to the novel so determinedly, but other writers had used the broad idea of correspondence, at all historical periods, in a wide range of literary forms – not least Eliot himself in his iconoclastic anti-modern poem, *The Waste Land* published in the same year as *Ulysses*. More than that, the broad strategy of positioning modernity in relation to a prestige culture of antiquity was entirely familiar outside the field of literature and aesthetics. It was already being used to give shape to history in the politics of nationalist identity formation, where European states, both established and aspirational, went to great lengths to identify themselves in relation to cultures that embodied 'the progress of the human race'[13] – not only Greek and Roman, but also Anglo–Saxon, Teutonic, Judaic, Gothic and Celtic cultures. In this respect the elaborate ghosting of *Ulysses* intersected with a wide set of cultural and political practices that pre-existed Joyce's book by centuries but which had particular shape and definition in late-nineteenth and early-twentieth century Europe. Connected to the conversion of Darwinism into progressivist evolutionary scales applied across a wide range of fields of knowledge, the elaboration of 'correspondences' between contemporary and classical cultures became a trademark practice of late modernity, the means by which both new and older nations attempted to define their pedigree, their 'evolution'. Potent in terms of legitimizing the modern state, as in the Napoleonic empire and the development of the German and Italian states in the later nineteenth century, such parallel thinking also figured prominently both in more aspirational cultural theory, like Yeats's romantic mythologizing of the Celt and in darker *fin de siècle* degeneration literature – Otto Spengler's *The Decline of the West* (1918), for instance. Joyce's handling of the *Odyssey* positioned his work in terms of these wider cultural strategies that were defining modernity and its modernisms in crucial ways.

At the very beginning of *Ulysses*, Haines, an Englishman whose 'old fellow made his tin by selling jalap to Zulus' (*U* 1.156), seeks to make a contribution towards the Celticizing of modern Ireland, and Buck Mulligan proposes joining forces with Stephen Dedalus in order to 'Hellenise it' (*U* 1.158) – a proposal which Stephen inwardly ridicules as an infantile misappropriation of English Victorian cultural theory.[14] In the same way, the *Odyssey* throws *Ulysses* generally into a dialogue with antiquity, and, more specifically, with the very process of 'correspondence' in its modern forms, except that here in a spectacular example of mock one-upmanship the strained and wilful practices necessary to conduct the exchange are hilariously on show and anatomized. This is the central reason why Joyce's version of 'correspondence', often more misfitting than fitting, could function so powerfully as the starting point for the development of a Greek/Irish mock epic into a classic reference point of modernity and part of the reason why contemporaries especially understood *Ulysses* so much in terms of the 'ferociously satirical' (*CH*, 186).

'Not an implicit believer in the lurid story' – What Happens?

Joyce's output up to *Ulysses* had already demonstrated that he saw 'goahead plot' (*Letters* III, 146) perhaps partly as a guilty pleasure associated with lightweight entertainment value, but more substantially as inconsistent with a realist agenda constructed in fundamentally politicized terms. Typically the 'paralysed' *Dubliners* story, highly resistant to linear and progressivist movement, was made manifest as an epiphanic moment framed in the context of inescapable colonial conditioning. In *A Portrait* narrative was decentralized in the chaos of an unfolding life framed, again, more by the maturing of a consciousness rooted in the conditions of colonialism than a sequence of gripping events.

Plot in *Ulysses* is similarly closed down, tightly framed by its attention to precise movements that take place over the 24 hours of a single day. Here *Ulysses* becomes potentially much smaller in scale than Joyce's grandiose plan allowed, 'a little story of a day (life)' (*Letters* I, 146), which not only makes this book the precursor of all the literary, filmic and, indeed, musical texts later to be formulated around 'a day in the life', but also throws it into sharp cultural conflict with narrative forms

that insist on romanticism, adventure and completion. Here the expectancies raised by the massive structuring framework deployed in *Ulysses*
are wickedly deflated by the fact that against conventional standards
of narrative not much happens. The little that does is surrounded by
so much immediate detail and technical display that there is a point to
retrieving the outlines of the narrative sequence in a simplified form.

The novel opens famously with the tensions between 'Stately, plump
Buck Mulligan' (*U* 1.1) and a contrastingly down-at-heel Stephen
Dedalus. Triumphantly expecting to be on the move at the end of *A
Portrait*, Stephen, after his visit to Paris, is now back in Ireland. He is
temporarily accommodated in a round tower at some considerable
remove from the traditional symbol of Irish culture because this is a
Martello tower, built by 'Billy Pitt' – the present inhabitants pay rent
to 'the secretary state for war' (*U* 1.540). Far from being the '*omphalos*'
(*U* 1.544) imagined by Mulligan, the tower as conceived by Stephen is
the physical signature of Empire in Ireland. His mother has died a painful death and he earns a living teaching the sons of 'Welloff people' who
are 'aware of [his] . . . lack of rule and of the fees their papas pay' (*U* 2.24,
29). After his Thursday morning stint teaching at Mr Deasy's school,
Stephen takes a walk along Sandymount Strand (see the 'Proteus' episode). He thinks about the changing selves of his past and the possible
futures he may inhabit in a universe that is, likewise, perceived as ever
changing. As Joyce told Budgen, 'It's the struggle with Proteus. Change
is the theme. Everything changes – sea, sky, man, animals. The words
change too' (*MU*, 49), although, as he also told Budgen in a different
context, Stephen now 'has a shape that can't be changed' (*MU*, 107).

At the risk of unbalancing this summarizing of the *Ulysses* narrative, it is important to register just how deeply saturated this opening
of *Ulysses* is in colonial history. Here the precarious state of Homer's
Telemachus, 'mocked and taunted' by the suitors who would marry his
mother and usurp his succession to the throne of Ithaca, is brought into
parallel with a morose Stephen Dedalus whose '*mother is beastly dead*'
(*U* 1.198–9).[15] In this frame of correspondence the 'suitors' have established themselves over the estate and hold power in the land. As several
accounts of *Ulysses* have demonstrated, 'Telemachus' is saturated as a
colonial landscape.[16] The exchanges which circulate around Haines in
the episode are freighted with the histories of empire culture – as when
Stephen pointedly asks 'How long is Haines going to stay in this tower?'
(*U* 1.49) and Mulligan, who thinks Haines 'dreadful . . . A ponderous
Saxon . . . Bursting with money and indigestion' (*U* 1.51–3), nevertheless knows how important his patronage might be and so panders to his
needs – 'Kinch . . . come on down. The Sassenach wants his morning
rashers.' (*U* 1.232)

Notions of landlordism and servitude form a powerful undertow to 'Telemachus'. They reside in Mulligan's proprietorial blessing of the land and produce tense moments, as when Haines refers patronizingly to a visit to 'your national library' (*U* 1.469–70). They condition Stephen's sense of Ireland, Irish art and himself as servants and reach a culmination in the angry and bitter exchange that leaves Haines 'calmly' offering an apology on England's behalf. In response to Haines's confident assertion that Stephen is his 'own master', Stephen asserts that he is, in fact, the 'servant of two masters' and a third 'who wants me for odd jobs' (*U* 1.636–41). Haines asks for explanation, and gets a partial one:

> – The imperial British state, Stephen answered, his colour rising, and the holy Roman catholic and apostolic church.
> Haines detached from his underlip some fibres of tobacco before he spoke.
> – I can quite understand that, he said calmly. An Irishman must think like that, I daresay. We feel in England that we have treated you rather unfairly. It seems history is to blame.
>
> (*U* 1.643–9)

Haines's innocent-sounding remark about Irish identity – how 'an Irishman must think' – suggests, again, a patronizingly English perspective, but some such determinism as he imagines is nonetheless implied in this chapter and the rest of the Telemachia. These opening episodes decisively shape the world in colonial terms. The round tower, the figures in it and the powerful dynamics that take place between them cannot be disentangled from historical relationships. Haines, for all his interest in Celticism, and, indeed, partly because of it, inevitably figures as an English invader. Stephen is firmly located as a dispossessed Catholic and Mulligan as an Anglicized subaltern determined to make his way at all costs. In this guise the latter is a cultural stereotype. Modernized by Wildean elegance, he is, for Stephen, the familiar gay betrayer of Irish historiography – the servant artist, a 'jester at the court of his master' (*U* 2.44) performing in hope of praise and elevation. He is also the figure firmly designated by Stephen as his 'Usurper' – the word which closes 'Telemachus' so strongly (*U* 1.744).

This formulation, however much it derives from real history, is stylized in very literary ways in the 'Telemachia'. Everyday objects – a mirror, a finished-with shaving bowl, the key to the round tower – all become invested with particular meanings that resonate from the colonial framing. Similarly marginal figures from the everyday become charged, just as are the central protagonists. The obvious example is Stephen's famous elevation of the old woman who delivers the milk into a figure emblematic of Ireland itself, although Deasy, Sargent and even very minor figures – the cocklepickers and their dog on Sandymount Strand for example – are configured in similar ways:

> He watched her pour into the measure and thence into the jug rich white milk, not hers. Old shrunken paps . . . Old and secret she had entered from a morning world, maybe a messenger . . . Crouching by a patient cow at daybreak in a lush field, a witch on her toadstool, her wrinkled fingers quick at the squirting dugs. They lowed about her whom they knew, dewsilky cattle. Silk of the kine and poor old woman, names given her in old times. A wandering crone, lowly form of an immortal serving her conqueror and her gay betrayer, their common cuckquean, a messenger from the secret morning.
>
> (*U* 1.397–406)

This owes something only half ironic to the revivalism Stephen typically claims to despise. It also denotes a substantial shift from the Stephen of *A Portrait*. The Stephen who once declared his intention to fly by the nets of family, religion and nation now seems much more knowingly implicated – preoccupied with intimate memories of his mother ('Her secrets: old featherfans, tasselled dancecards, powdered with musk, a gaud of amber beads in her locked drawer' – *U* 1.255–6); identifying more strongly with Church schoolmen, both 'militants' and heretics (see *U* 1.650–60) and, above all, much more consciously saturated in the conditions that make him a colonial subject. He remains privileged in terms of intellect, but nevertheless appears humbled in Deasy's study before the 'princely presence' of a portrait of Edward the Seventh (*U* 2.299) and outwardly submits to the headmaster's naive assumption that he must be a Fenian. He determines that he can easily break the 'nooses' that tie him to working for a Unionist headmaster in a private school for the well-off (*U* 2.234), but for all such expressions of independence, he *is* in service. When Deasy doles out the sovereigns that are Stephen's payment, Stephen's response shows a servant sensibility. He gathers 'the money together with sly haste' and puts 'it all in a pocket of his trousers' (*U* 2.223–4). Similarly, for all the assertion that he 'will not be master of others or their slave' (*U* 3.295–6), he *does* run Deasy's errand and wear Mulligan's castoff clothes. Everyday details, in 'Nestor' and 'Proteus' as in 'Telemachus', again collude to enforce the point. In the protean world of *Ulysses* 3, the dog on the beach becomes a cur brought 'skulking back to his master' (*U* 3.354). The cocklepicker on the beach is seen in feudal terms, as a follower of 'her lord, his helpmate, bing awast to Romeville' (*U* 3.374–5). Secrets become 'tyrants,

willing to be dethroned' (*U* 2.171–2). At the very point when he makes
the decision not to return to the tower, Stephen imagines the effect of
his departure in master/servant terms: 'In the darkness of the dome
they wait, their pushedback chairs, my obelisk valise, around a board of
abandoned platters. Who to clear it?' (*U* 3.274–5). These are just a few
examples of how words and images connected with power, servitude
and dispossession carry such currency across the 'Telemachia'. The idea
of history being 'a nightmare' from which Stephen is 'trying to awake'
(*U* 2.377) is not abstract or theoretical, but refers to something real and
tangible which so shapes Stephen that even his expression of 'proud
intellect' is, as he well knows, the product of a historical dialectic.

To return to the broader outline of narrative, at *U* 4, 'Calypso', the
book effectively begins again with Leopold Bloom whose entrance
constitutes one of a number of important space-clearing moments in
Ulysses. Here the novel enters a new phase, characterized not least by
the introduction of a range and depth of comedy that, up to this point,
had not existed in Joyce's fiction. Bloom is a Dublin Jew who in most
respects is an ordinary citizen, employed as an advertising canvasser. In
his opening chapter he buys and prepares breakfast for himself and his
wife Molly. Apparently, for the first time in her life, Molly is about to
commit adultery, on this very day, with Blazes Boylan. Bloom, while he
cannot know with certainty, strongly suspects as much. In this respect,
16 June 1904 is not quite the ordinary day that many Joyceans have
imagined, for Molly and Leopold at least. Bloom makes valiant attempts
to avoid thinking about his wife's imminent rendezvous with Blazes
Boylan and tries, usually successfully, to maintain a level of balance,
even a kind of cheerfulness. Events, however, conspire against him. As
well as everything else, this is the day he intends to go to the funeral of
an acquaintance – Paddy Dignam. The occasion raises memories of a
deceased father, who committed suicide and Bloom's only son who died
as a baby – although even here Bloom's characteristic curiosity helps
to re-establish equilibrium. Personal memories are eventually ousted
by more objective consideration of the generic conditions of death and
decay. 'I daresay', Bloom thinks to himself, 'the soil would be quite fat
with corpsemanure [in a cemetery], bones, flesh, nails. Charnelhouses.
Dreadful. Turning green and pink decomposing. Rot quick in damp
earth. The lean old ones tougher' (*U* 6.776–8).

Stephen and Bloom are antithetical in many respects – one a uni-
versity-educated Catholic with serious intentions of becoming an artist, the other a Dublin Jew and canvasser for advertising space. In an
attempt to forge an aesthetic, Stephen grapples with ideas culled from a
fragmentary knowledge of such figures as Aristotle, Thomas Aquinas,
Blake and Lessing. Bloom, on the other hand, gropes his way towards

an understanding of such phenomena as light and heat refraction, floatation and gravity, litmus paper, anaesthetics, public health, heart physiology and the science of decomposition. Parallax, rainbows, perspective, astronomy, the law, politics and a whole range of other issues and subjects are all treated similarly. Stephen is an intellectual; Bloom by contrast is the ideal consumer of general knowledge imagined by the editors of the *Encyclopaedia Britannica* (which Joyce owned a copy of) – someone who really appreciates 'the general diffusion of knowledge and culture' that would eventually 'bring all extant knowledge within the reach of every class of readers'.[17]

Unsurprisingly, the two characters seemingly at the centre of this book are not much more than casually aware of each other's existence. While Bloom makes his way towards Dignam's funeral, Stephen is being asked by his employer, Mr Deasy, to place a letter written about the politics of foot and mouth disease in cattle. With this aim in mind, Stephen visits the offices of Myles Crawford, editor of the *Freeman's Journal* (at 12 noon). Later (at 2 p.m.) he visits the National Library and enters into an extended debate with his largely Anglo–Irish contemporaries. This is conducted through Stephen's articulation of a 'Shakespeare theory', a show-stopping performance built around the little accurate information known about Shakespeare's life.

Stephen and Bloom's paths cross at various points, although they do not yet meet. During the late afternoon/early evening the novel's focus remains on Bloom as he stays out of Molly's way, the circumnavigatory motive for many of his actions on this day. Typically he wants to avoid confrontation, although he is unknowingly moving towards an embarrassing exhibition that will bring into the open the anti-Semitism usually expressed by Dubliners in more subtle ways. He visits first the Ormond Hotel (at 4 p.m.) and then Barney Kiernan's bar (at 5), where he faces the famously patriotic 'citizen'. Excoriating, amongst many others, the English monarch Edward 'the peacemaker' – 'There's a bloody sight more pox than pax about that boyo' (*U* 12.1399–401), the citizen eventually turns to the subject of Jews 'coming over' to Ireland 'filling the country with bugs' (*U* 12.1141–2). The subsequent intensification of things, directed precisely at Bloom, culminates with the latter declaring in an uncharacteristically public display for the cultural importance of Jewry – 'Mendelssohn was a jew and Karl Marx and Mercadante and Spinoza. And the Saviour was a jew and his father was a jew. Your God.' (*U* 12. 1804–5). The citizen responds by threatening to 'brain that bloody jewman for using the holy name. By Jesus, I'll crucify him so I will. Give us that biscuitbox here' (*U* 12.1811–2). It is following this comically framed rumpus that Bloom takes himself off to 'the rocks' to calm down and enjoy the entirely different surprise afforded by the generous exhibitionism of Gerty McDowell. It is now 8 p.m. For all the final melancholy of 'Nausicaa' where Bloom, now deserted by Gerty, ponders the life of the cuckold, there is some suggestion, as there always is throughout the book, that the tide may be turning in Bloom's favour.

Night time, beginning with 'Oxen of the Sun', brings the episodes most technically extreme and most removed from conventional narrative, although even here a basic narrative structure is retained. Bloom (at 10 p.m.) turns up at the Holles Street maternity hospital to enquire after the progress of his friend Mina Purefoy, who is in childbirth. Stephen is already at the hospital, carousing with some of his medical student friends. Later they are joined by Mulligan and Alec Bannon, 'late come to town' (*U* 14.654) – presumably the young student to whom Milly makes a glancing reference in her letter, read by Bloom some 270 pages earlier. Stephen and Bloom finally meet in the flesh and exchange words. In an off-page event, Bloom, accompanying the well-oiled young men, observes that Stephen is deserted by his friends at Westland Row railway station and decides to keep an eye on a figure he sees as vulnerable. The drinking continues in Bella Cohen's brothel and ends up with a drunken brawl where Stephen is knocked to the ground by a soldier of the English Army, Private Carr. Able to use his considerable social nous to prevent the intervention of the police, Bloom takes Stephen off to a local cabman's shelter in an attempt to sober him up. Eventually they arrive at Bloom's home, 9 Eccles Street, where Bloom will offer his young guest a bed for the night, and possibly longer. It is sometime after 2 p.m. and Bloom's offer is politely refused. After a convivial cup of Epps cocoa, Stephen and Bloom urinate in the garden, under the night stars. Stephen takes his leave and Bloom turns in for the night. The final episode of *Ulysses*, 'Penelope', is comprised of Molly Bloom's soliloquy, an episode which, as much as any, displaces story in favour of voicing. We are now firmly inside Molly's head and time is indeterminate.

Such are the central 'events' of *Ulysses*. They are by any standards limited – even the weight of history so evident in the Telemachia operates at the level of the everyday. They are also inconclusive, especially so in the context of the overarching structures of *Ulysses*. Against such limited narrative possibilities, ideas of reconciliation and return, where Irishman meets Jew; father meets son; citizen meets artist and art meets science, can only reverberate. The overblown resonances of *Ulysses* where the wanderers and dispossessed of the world return home to regain their lost territories is wrecked against a narrative framework which by comparison is diminutive, and there is not much that Bloom can do to shift that fact. The laughs and humanist acceptance of things are always appealing, but neither goes far towards meeting the full potentialities activated in a book that, besides everything else, holds out such prospects as the dawn of a new era, the 'Nova Hibernia of the future' (*U* 15.1544–5) – the 'reform of municipal morals and the plain ten commandments. New worlds for old. Union of all, jew, moslem and gentile. Three cows and an acre for all children of nature' (*U* 15.1685–7). This is one respect in which there are echoes of *Dubliners* in *Ulysses*. As in that earlier text, paralysis seems to creep in – except that here the responses provoked are on a very different scale.

'By lorries along Sir John Rogerson's Quay' – *Ulysses* and the Spectacle of the Real World

If *Ulysses* seems constrained by the comic distance between inflated structure and a dead end narrative, in other respects it is unashamedly open and expansive. Indeed, almost everything about it *except* its determinedly minimalist plot could be described as large and extrovert. From its physical size to the overblown epic proportions of its scheme, *Ulysses* is a big and often loud book. Much concerned with the conditions of its own making, 'the usylessly unreadable Blue Book of Eccles' (*FW* 179,26–7) is not shy about drawing attention to itself. It is even given to extravagant mockery of its most overarching themes, especially in the later episodes. A ventriloquised cap in 'Circe', for example, announces 'Jewgreek is greekjew. Extremes meet. Death is the highest form of life. Ba!' (*U* 15.2097–8). At the other extreme where *Ulysses* focuses on minutiae, it does so with obsessive attention to detail, to the extent that it is often seen as 'encyclopaedic'.

Some critical responses understand this latter dimension of *Ulysses* in terms of the Aristotelian impulse to catalogue and record the objective world and its materialist mechanics – systems do sometimes come to life in particularly objectified ways in this book. The 'Wandering Rocks' episode, for example, was designed like a time and motion study, with a map of Dublin in one hand and a clock in the other and 'Aeolus' opens with the terminal at Nelson's pillar where the tram system takes on a life on its own and newspaper presses clank into action articulated as rhythm ('threefour time') and sound ('Thump, thump, thump' – *U* 7.101).[18] It is also true that *Ulysses* does register the names of thousands of streets, public buildings, public figures and historical events. Shops and businesses – butchers (Buckley's and Dlugacz's); undertakers (Nicholl's); chemists (Sweeny's); the Belfast and Oriental Tea Company; Meade's timberyard; Leask's the linseed crusher and so on – are never very far away. Pubs, often referred to by the names of their licensees – O'Rourke, Adam Findlater, Dan Tallon, McAuley – are especially ubiquitous. Among the huge number of products made, displayed, sold and consumed in *Ulysses* are Denny's sausages; Plumrose potted meat; Guinness's porter; Cantrell and Cochrane's Ginger Ale (aromatic) and Wheatley's Dublin hop bitters. Advertisement is part of the cultural world it registers, with the jingle for Plumrose's potted meat appearing as a poem would centralized on the page, italicized and returned to again and again:

> *What is home without*
> *Plumrose's Potted Meat?*
> *Incomplete.*
> *With it an abode of bliss.*

(U 5.144–7)

Ephemera such as this – religious sermons, newspaper articles, public speeches, pantomime acts, fashion – the full range of city life often constructed as 'popular culture', is everywhere in *Ulysses*. A census of contemporary magazines referred to in its pages, for example, would include *Titbits, Photo Bits, Answers, The Lady's Pictorial, Pearson's Weekly, The Princesses Novelette, Modern Society, The Gentlewoman* and *Lloyd's Weekly News*. Popular theatre is treated in a similarly comprehensive-looking way. The main Dublin theatres – such as the Queen's, the Gaiety, the Empire Theatre of Varieties (usually known in *Ulysses* by its earlier name, Dan Lowry's) – all figure in the text, not once but many times, as do the popular shows performed there and the performers. Mrs Bandmann Palmer, an actress; Eugen Sandow, the American strong man associated for some years with the influential producer Florenz Ziegfeld; the Irish comedian Pat Kinsella who Bloom remembers 'Showing long red pantaloons under his skirts' and playing 'the Shah of Persia liked that best' (*U* 8.603/*U* 11.1050–1) – these are just a few of the celebrities, once real people, who contribute to the fabric of *Ulysses*.

There is something here of the catalogue and, indeed, *Ulysses* is far from being immune to the pleasures of the list. It contains many – lists of 'Irish heroes and heroines of antiquity' for example, and the 'twelve tribes of Iar' in 'Cyclops' (*U* 12. 176,1125); of its own Homeric chapter titles and the contents of Bloom's library in 'Ithaca' – the latter including *Thom's Dublin Post Office Directory*; *The Useful Ready Reckoner* '(brown cloth)'; *Thoughts from Spinoza* and *The Beauties of Killarney* '(wrappers)' and so on (see *U* 18.1362–98). But for all this apparent inclusiveness, this book is not, of course, a list. However much its detail might suggest the audit account (and it contains one of those too, which shows that Bloom's balance for 16 June 1904 is £2–19s-3d – see *U* 18.1455–78) or encyclopaedia, it is, of course, very different from either.[19] Far more than a simple register, Joyce's book mounts a compelling reproduction of the ways in which people and their actions constitute the world and in turn are formed by it. Shopping, fantasizing, joking, disputing, welcoming, excluding, agreeing and dissenting are all parts of this everyday world, just as much as the more specifically physical and biological – eating, drinking, defecating and so on. Such activities and processes are essential to the domain of *Ulysses*, especially in the early chapters where the presentation of the everyday is shaped by what has become widely understood as the book's 'initial' style.

From the *Ulysses* scheme discussed in a previous section it might be imagined that 'style' changes from chapter to chapter in *Ulysses*, because each episode is given a distinct technic designation. In fact, the first six episodes are essentially made up of a single style, a stitching together of third person narrative and interior monologue – the latter being the style most commonly associated which *Ulysses* although it is not until the final episode, 'Penelope', that we see a fully unmediated interior monologue. This is the style, of course, which Joyce, in an untypical underplaying of his own originality, always insisted was modelled on *Les Lauriers sont coupés*, a relatively obscure novel by Édouard Dujardin which he had first read in 1903.[20]

The relative weight of third person and stream of consciousness varies both within chapters and across them. 'Proteus', for example, is far more heavily weighted towards interiority than 'Telemachus'. At the same time, Bloom's chapters are easily distinguishable from Stephen's because these characters experience the world in very different ways. In more general respects, however, the essential narrative style is reasonably stable in these early chapters, formulated as a switching between outer and inner worlds or, more accurately, often a collaboration where third person narrative shares space with a stylized representation of the inner voice. Running uninterruptedly from 'Telemachus' to 'Hades', this is the 'technic' returned to again and again throughout *Ulysses*, sometimes, as in 'Lestrygonians' and the second half of 'Nausicaa' in extended forms. It provides the signature sound where an ostensibly objective narrative voice cooperates with inner voices as they articulate against the outside world. The following illustration comes from Bloom's second chapter, chapter 5 ('Lotuseaters').

By lorries along sir John Rogerson Quay Mr Bloom walked soberly, past Windmill lane, Leask's the linseed crusher, the postal telegraph office. Could have given that address too. And past the sailors' home. He turned from the morning noises of the quayside and walked through Lime street. By Brady's cottages a boy for the skins lolled, his bucket of offal linked, smoking a chewed fagbutt. A smaller girl with scars of eczema on her forehead eyed him, listlessly holding her battered caskhoop. Tell him if he smokes he won't grow. O let him! His life isn't such a bed of roses! Waiting outside pubs to bring da home. Come home to ma, da. Slack hour: won't be many there. He crossed Townsend street, passed the frowning face of Bethel. El, yes: house of: Aleph, Beth. And past Nichols' the undertaker. At eleven it is. Time enough. Daresay Corny Kelleher bagged the job for O'Neill's. Singing with his eyes shut. Corny. Met her once in the park. In the dark. What a lark. Police tout. Her name and address she then told with my tooraloom tooraloom tay. O, surely he bagged it. Bury him cheap in a whatyoumaycall. With my tooraloom, tooraloom, tooraloom, tooraloom.

In Westland row he halted before the window of the Belfast andOriental Tea Company and read the legends of leadpapered packets: choice blend, finest quality, family tea. Rather warm. Tea. Must get some from Tom Kernan. Couldn't ask him at a funeral, though. While his eyes still read blandly he took off his hat quietly inhaling his hairoil and sent his right hand with slow grace over his brow and hair. Very warm morning.

(U 5.1–22)

The third person narrative is pervasive, but not exactly intrusive. Indeed both Bloom and the narrator are in curiously close alignment, working together in very intimate ways. The externalized detail about the slum kids, for instance, leads smoothly into Bloom's shifting thoughts on a young boy smoking – they move from superior disapproval, through pragmatism to characteristic sympathy. When the narrative registers 'Nichols' the undertaker', Bloom, without missing a beat, checks how much time he has at his disposal before Digham's funeral. The narrator's observation on a particular piece of religious adornment on a local building, the 'frowning face of Bethel',[21] segues easily into Bloom asserting his more or less everyday knowledge of Hebrew. 'Beth', the second letter of the Hebrew alphabet, means 'house'; 'El' is God's name. It is almost as if narrator and character are communicating with each other. Again, the narrative comment about the postal telegraph office in the first sentence leads seamlessly to Bloom's thought 'Could have given that address too', establishing a particularly close, indeed, contingent relationship between narrator and character from which, in this case, the reader is excluded – at least temporarily. Here the meaning of Bloom's fleeting interiorized comment is deferred for only a page or so, when Bloom reveals the post office address he *has* chosen (Westland Row Post Office) and the use he puts it to as a mailing address for an erotically charged correspondence between 'Martha Clifford' and his other self, 'Henry Flower'. Elsewhere meaning is deferred for many pages, even across chapters, or is dependent on the remembering of a very distant detail. The explanation for the lost 't' on Bloom's 'high grade ha' at *U* 11.876, for example, occurs no less that one hundred and eighty-three pages earlier at *U* 4.69–70.

This proximity of narrator to character, the intimacy established across narrative voice and interior thought, is the context for much of what is often seen as the dense complexity of *Ulysses* – the deferred meanings, cross referencing dimensions, the reader traps and so on – all potentially elements of the *auteur* novel and the writerly text. But this combination of external narration and interior monologue also captures the immediacy of everyday living. It is largely through such techniques that *Ulysses* becomes, in Clifford Geertz's terms, a work of massively 'thick description' – remarkable in its capacity for reproducing a sense of what it is like to experience living in the world.[22]

The 'initial style' also mirrors Bloom's closeness to the modern world and its workings, just as in the Telemachia it combines and colludes with Stephen's artistic ambitions. As 'Daresay Corny Kelleher bagged the job for O'Neill's' indicates with considerable economy, Bloom, for all the anti-Semitism that positions him as an outsider, is fundamentally at home in modernity. He knows exactly how things get done in contemporary Dublin and seems indicative of the modern on a larger scale. It is not coincidental that the first sentence of the above extract from 'Lotuseaters' positions Bloom precisely among transport systems (lorries and docks); communications (the post office) and manufacturers (linseed oil makers and tanners). Similarly the body and its workings become important in new ways in the Bloom chapters, as science but more fundamentally as conservative social performance where conformity and hygiene are at a premium. The detail about well-groomed hair is suggestive of the many associations made between Bloom, sober style and cleanliness. Appearance and self image is also very much linked to Bloom the engaged and canny modern consumer, an identity reinforced in this extract and elsewhere in these early chapters by his window shopping. The activity suggests not any particular acquisitiveness on Bloom's part, indeed he is typically restrained in appetite, but, rather, his professional appreciation of retail displays – one of many signifiers of his status as a representative of urban life at the *fin de siècle* and commodified modern culture, as well as reflecting, of course, his work as a advertising canvasser.

An 'inherited tenacity of heterodox resistance' – 'Filth', Molly Bloom and *Ulysses*

One suspects that for many readers, especially readers new to *Ulysses*, the attraction of the book is caught up with this spectacle of the real taken to such lengths. It has also shaped critical perceptions of *Ulysses* from virtually all schools. Indeed, it is hard to imagine any reading, however structuralist, or disengaged from historical and culturalist realities, that could avoid its impact. Whether the focus has been simply explicatory, to do with glossing allusions, or more broadly interpretative, the representational powers of *Ulysses* have been invoked everywhere.

No reading of *Ulysses*, however, can be sustained solely on the basis of the book's 'reality' or phenomenological persuasiveness, not least because representation in *Ulysses*, while comically evoking the list and catalogue and their associative claims of objectivity and inclusiveness, is far from being somehow just neutral. Just as Homeric correspondence, the absence of traditional plot and the 'encyclopaedic' principle are culturally engaged, so with the phenomenological *Ulysses*. This, too, is subject to the pervasive critical realism that throws the book into such radical articulation against its contemporary world.

Bloom's internal observations could be rendered as part of this dynamic. Observing Catholics at worship he thinks 'Makes them feel more important to be prayed over in Latin' (*U* 6.602). Later, in a darker part of the day, he is more deeply critical in his confused internal thoughts about a wealthy Catholic Church that keeps the poor in poverty by prohibiting contraception. 'That's in their theology or the priest won't give the poor woman the confession, the absolution. Increase and multiply. Did you ever hear such an idea? Eat you out of house and home. No families themselves to feed. Living on the fat of the land' (*U* 8.31–5).

But it was not the commonplace thoughts of the everyday social critic that produced the early uproar about the anarchic, destructive *Ulysses* or sustained its place in cultural history. These could easily be contained by modern liberal culture; indeed, they represented modern liberal culture in many ways. The more pervasive radicalism, as it was then perceived, derived not from Bloom the character but primarily two sources – from what was understood as the book's insult to literary tradition and, above all, from Joyce's unrelenting exposure of the 'shameful' private, the alarming discordance often evident between outward behaviour and inner thoughts. The Freudian conflict across social behaviour and secret desire might be drawn with relative innocence in a chapter like 'Lotuseaters', where Bloom is secretly trying to catch a glimpse of an aristocratic pair of female legs at the same time as engaging in polite chit chat with McCoy, a fellow Dubliner (see *U* 5.115–34). By the later chapters, however, the exposure of human sexuality has become a Rabelaisian anatomizing, deeply challenging to many modern sensibilities. Here framed by the 'technique' of 'hallucination', Bloom's mild inclinations towards the masochistic – inclinations which, in everyday life, are entirely under control – become dramatically unleashed.

Bloom now figures as 'Miss Bloom', under the authority of an extrava-gantly savage 'Bello':

BELLO

(*savagely*) The nosering, the pliers, the bastinado, the hang-ing hook, the knout I'll make you kiss while the flutes play like the Nubian slave of old. You're in for it this time! I'll make you remember me for the balance of your natural life. (*his forehead face swollen, his face congested*) I shall sit on your ottoman sad-dleback every morning after my thumping good breakfast of Matterson's fat hamrashers and a bottle of Guinness's porter. (*he belches*) And suck my thumping good Stock Exchange cigar while I read the *Licensed Victuallers's Gazette*. Very possibly I shall have you slaughtered and skewered in my stables and enjoy a slice of you with crisp crackling from the baking tin basted and baked like sucking pig with rice and lemon or currant sauce. It will hurt you. (*He twists her arm. Bloom squeals, turning turtle.*)

BLOOM

Don't be cruel, nurse! Don't.

(*U* 15.2890–914)

That material of this kind puzzled, alarmed and undoubtedly attracted the earliest readers of *Ulysses*, many of whom saw its satire as 'cruel and unflinching' or 'harsh and sneering' (*CH*, 188, 194), is of more than historical interest. It reminds us of a cultural impact that Joyce fully understood and worked toward and its impact was not limited to the 'fantasies' of 'Circe'. Indeed by far the most challenging example of it was to be found in the final chapter, 'Penelope' – a place where *Ulysses* famously reaffirms its commitment to the real.

For all the technical innovation interrupting the flow of the phe-nomenological, *Ulysses* never loses it grip on realistic representation. Indeed, its last chapter makes a final and especially pointed gesture in this respect, one which breaks the intimate and often complex relation-ship between the third and first person narrative of earlier chapters by removing mediation altogether. The punctuation marks so much deno-tative of the presence of words written on the page are almost entirely erased – only a space indicates that a 'sentence' has become complete. Apart from that, we are entirely in Molly's mind and here Joyce inflicts serious damage not just to the taboos that once surrounded the sub-ject of women's sexuality – although 'Penelope' *is* a devastating riposte to a idealizing and patriarchal cultures which denatured women – but also to a much wider politics governing family, marriage and, indeed, masculinities.

This exclusive positioning, far from marking a retreat from the real world, only makes the sense of its presence stronger. For all the schematizing of this 'gynomorphic' episode, where Molly apparently figures as 'mother-earth',[23] there is probably no episode of *Ulysses* that insists so strongly on the illusions of realism, precisely because it is so completely enclosed, so notionally out of bounds to any world outside – however much it might be defined by the outside. Here thought can be revealing to new degrees, which is why the portrait of a 'perfectly sane full amoral fertilisable untrustworthy engaging shrewd limited prudent indifferent *Weib*' is also 'more obscene than any preceding episode' (*Letters* I, 170).

In a comprehensive coverage of sexuality, 'Penelope' squarely faces the realities of the sexual imagination. Rarely do five lines pass without some reference to sex. There are, for instance, references to a range of fetishes, real and fantasized. Boylan seems to be a foot fetishist (see *U* 18.246–50); Bloom nurses a rather more complex desire to have Molly walk through horse manure (see *U* 18.267). The fetish most associated with Bloom, however, is his underwear obsession. As distinguished from Boylan – who, Molly suspects, prefers women with 'no drawers at all' – Bloom is 'mad on the subject of drawers' (*U* 18.289). He asked Molly for a piece of her underwear when they were courting and was given the drawers off Molly's doll. There is also a great deal of exhibitionism in the episode, with Molly lifting her 'orange petticoat' in public (*U* 18.308) and being asked by Bloom 'to pose for a picture naked' (*U* 18.560–61). At line 921, Molly thinks she was observed whilst washing, an experience she clearly enjoyed. She fantasizes about having sex in a train at line 367. At line 85 she expresses a desire for sex with a young man; at line 483 she'd like to try 'a black man's'. Molly remembers being touched in the Gaiety Theatre at line 1041 and thinks about dirty books at line 969. There is considerable sexual activity around breasts, at lines 535, 577 and 800, and Molly fantasizes about being a whore at line 1418. Sadomasochism is alluded to at 494 and fantasized about at line 963. Masturbation, perhaps the sexual practice most frequently referred to in 'Penelope', involves Molly masturbating a pre-Bloom lover, Mulvey, (see *U* 18.810), and herself fairly regularly – in fact '4 or 5 times a day sometimes' (*U* 18.1179). She masturbates Bloom with her feet at line 263 and would have tried a banana on herself at line 803, but was concerned that 'it might break'. She thinks about shaving off her pubic hair at 1134, and approves of having sex during the day, on the floor because of the noise from squeaky bed, at line 1133. Lesbianism is referred to at 1147 and oral sex, which Bloom does 'all wrong', at both lines 1250 and 1353 where Molly wants to kiss the statue of a boy 'all over also his lovely young cock'. Molly wonders about the sexual practices of her friends – 'Mrs Mastiansky told me her husband made her like the dogs do it and stick out her tongue as far as ever she could (*U* 18.417–9). Some of the most vivid material is saved for Boylan and his 'tremendous big red brute of a thing' (*U* 18.144). He 'must have come 3 or 4 times' and Molly feels 'fucked yes and damn well fucked too up to my neck nearly not by him 5 or 6 times handrunning theres the mark of his spunk on the clean sheet' (*U* 18.1511–12). Although Molly asserting her sexual power over a debased Bloom can also be quite pretty immediate – 'if he wants to kiss my bottom Ill drag open my drawers and bulge it right out in his face as large as life he can stick his tongue 7 miles up my hole as hes there my brown part then Ill tell him I want £1' (*U* 18.1520–3).

The resultant shock value of 'Penelope' is greatly increased by that fact that Molly is so rooted in the specifics of a particular milieu and, again, sheer detail is crucial here. Molly sings the popular songs of the period and reads the popular literature, like Mrs Henry Wood's *The Shadow of Ashlydat* (1863), which sold 150,000 copies in 1899, and Mrs Mary Elizabeth Braddon's *Henry Dunbar* (1864). She takes popular magazines like *Lloyds Weekly News* and *The Gentlewoman*, turning to them for ideas in fashion and to some degree assimilating their idiom: the face lotion she uses, for instance, 'made my skin like new' (*U* 18.459). She has a dressy taste in clothes and thinks about 'high buttoned boots'; 'violet garters'; 'orange petticoats'; 'kidfitting corsets'; 'silkette stockings' and 'cream muslin dresses' (see *U* 18.440–90). There are also suggestions of the unfashionable, like 'a pair of old brogues itself' (*U* 18.469). Molly's monologue is also full of references to contemporary figures, places and events. She calls to mind meeting Arthur Griffith of Sein Fein and Val Dillon; a visit to the City Arms Hotel and remembers the performance of Mr and Mrs William Hunter Kendal in *The Wife of Scarli* at the Gaiety Theatre and of Beerbohm Tree in *Trilby*.

'Penelope', then, is in many ways the culmination of a compelling reproduction of the phenomenological world, but also demonstrates how much, and in what ways, 'realism' is connected to critical engagement in *Ulysses*. But there are further reasons why a response to *Ulysses* in simple phenomenological terms cannot be sustained on its own. For at the same time as it reproduces the world in great detail, it also announces it own presence in that formulation with great inventiveness and gusto. The book that so completely, and courageously, embraces the mimetic function of literature is also responsible for the most thorough compromising of itself in this respect. And there is an accelerating dynamic here. The more *Ulysses* approaches its final chapter, the more it seems to subvert the critical realism to which it devotes so much creative and political energy.

'SOPHIST WALLOPS HAUGHTY HELEN SQUARE ON PROBOSCIS. SPARTANS GNASH MOLARS. ITHACANS VOW PEN IS CHAMP' – Narrative Disruption in *Ulysses*

Interior monologue was new and shocking to many readers of the novel in the 1920s, but it was not incompatible with expectations concerning the realist tradition. From 'Aeolus' onwards, however, albeit with many diversions and some circular routes, realist conventions begin to be displaced in ever more radical ways in *Ulysses*. The imperative to capture subject identity in the most complete and detailed fashion possible appears to diminish as in 'Aeolus', 'Scylla and Charybdis' and 'Wandering Rocks' Stephen and Bloom become dispersed more widely among the Dublin citizenry. In the latter episode, for example, they have no more or less notional importance than any figure in the enlarged Dublin scene. Corny Kelleher, a one-legged sailor, Katey and Boody Dedalaus, Blazes Boylan, Almidano Artifoni, Miss Dunne, Ned Lambert and so on – all figure in terms of '*symplegades*', the 'clashing rocks' that correspond to 'groups of citizens' viewed from above by a newly detached author with increased access to wide-angled vision. Here interior monologue remains but sporadically so and circumscribed by a narrative sometimes adopting the guise of the abstract system.

The opening out of *Ulysses* in this way is combined with even more serious disturbances. The captions in 'Aeolus', for instance, are disruptive of realist conventions simply through the typographical impact they make, but they also provide ironic commentary on the essentially conventional narratives they headline. 'IN THE HEART OF THE HIBERNIAN METROPOLIS' (*U* 7.1–2), for example, forms the prelude to a passage that does no more than describe the tram terminal at Nelson's pillar and the 'bawling' company timekeeper (*U* 7.7). 'THE WEARER OF THE CROWN' (*U* 7.14) refers to nothing more regal than the emblem displayed on an imperial mail van that contains 'sacks of letters, postcards, lettercards, parcels, insured and paid, for local, provincial, British and overseas delivery' (*U* 7.17–19). Elsewhere the headlines are simply reiterative – '" YOU CAN DO IT!"' (*U* 7.614) merely repeats the encouragement that Myles Crawford offers to Stephen at *U* 7.617; or they are otherwise redundant as in the case of 'IMPROMPTU' (*U* 7.812). Here 'style' is no longer smooth and seamless but, rather, comprised of contradictory elements that jar against each other with increasingly alienating results as the episode proceeds.

'Wandering Rocks' and 'Aeolus' are fractured by literal graphical interruption, but this is only the beginning of much more thorough going alienation. The interrogation of 'reliable' narration, in newspaper culture as in fiction, is extended much further in 'Sirens', an episode often seen as a gateway to the even more radical dislocations that follow. Here the narrator is freakishly on show. He makes up names, 'Kennygiggles' for Miss Kennedy (*U* 11.165) and 'Bloowho' (*U* 11.86) for Bloom, and mocks earlier narrative styles, especially Bloom's interior monologue, laughed at here for its comic fits and starts – 'Religion pays. Must see him for that par. Eat first. I want. Not yet. At four, she said . . . On. For Raoul' (*U* 11.187–9). This is a narrator who raises questions about narrative order, as if the tale he is telling unfolds in a spontaneous way outside his control and beyond his initial comprehension. In the following he is decidedly uncertain about identities in the real world, until part of the problem is resolved as a piano somehow reveals itself: 'Upholding the lid he (who?) gazed in the coffin (coffin?) at the oblique triple (piano!) wires' (*U* 11.291–2).

Yet there is, in fact, great narrative control and authority here, as well as personality. The narrator jokes and puns and is wildly inventive and energetic. He refers us back to much earlier parts of the novel which have only marginal relevance to events in the Ormond Bar, so that Simon Dedalus's indelicate remark 'Mrs Marion Bloom has left off clothes of all descriptions' (*U* 11.496–7) produces a narrative recapitulation of Molly in 'Calypso', where Molly smelled the burnt kidney Bloom cooked for his breakfast; asked her husband about the meaning of the word 'metempsychosis' and extolled the virtues of one of her favourite writers ('Mrs Marion. Met him pike hoses. Smell of burn. Of Paul de Kock. Nice name he has' – *U* 11.500–1). The narrator conjugates verbs at line 522; litters his own narrative with the direct speech of characters in and outside the bar (see, for example, line 527) and conflates soaring musical notes being sung in the moment with Blazes Boylan's rising sexual excitement as he rushes to meet Molly in another part of the city – 'Tenderness it welled, slow, swelling, full it throbbed. That's the chat. Ha, give! Take! Throb, a throb, a pulsing proud erect' (*U* 11.701–2). What Budgen calls 'the more banal tiddleypom aspects of music' (*MU*, 141) are reproduced in outlandish passages like the following:

> Bald Pat who is bothered mitred the napkins. Pat is a waiter hard of his hearing. Pat is a waiter who waits while you wait. Hee hee hee hee. He waits while you wait. Hee hee. A waiter is he. Hee hee hee hee. He waits while you wait. While you wait if you wait he will wait while you wait. Hee hee hee hee, Hoh. Wait while you wait.
>
> (*U* 11.915–9)

Here, then, narrative conventions and proprieties simply do not apply in any uniform way, which is why 'Sirens' has led some Joyceans to conceive of a narrative *character* at work in *Ulysses*, an 'Arranger', who greatly extends the territory normally occupied by the third-person narrator and, at the same time, thoroughly undermines the trickery behind the very idea of 'objective' narration.[24] This assumed narrative identity has sometimes been considered as being inimical not only to the novel tradition but also to the central characters of *Ulysses* apparently required to 'survive' these narrative offences.[25]

A realistic level of representation is sustained, here as in all the chapters of *Ulysses* – even in the icy detachment and scientism of 'Ithaca', but there can be no doubt that 'Sirens' raises the prospect of narrative ungovernability in a particularly acute form. The dynamics of a more traditional novel are being kept in play. Stephen and Bloom never actually disappear, indeed it could be argued that they are seriously tested – Bloom by his wife's infidelity and the one-eyed bigotry of the citizen in 'Cyclops', for example, and Stephen by what he sees as the betrayal of his friends and the guilt that produces a horrific vision of his mother in 'Circe'. To the extent that they survive these and other assaults, they could be said to 'develop'. Certainly the novel maintains the promise that somehow the Stephen/Bloom axis contains potential. Thus the two characters remain actively present throughout, until the end of the 'Penelope' episode which circulates around the pair, re-imagining their pasts and futures and confirming their status in the present.

At the same time, there is from 'Cyclops' onwards an increasing weight of 'textuality', where the emphasis shifts away from representation towards a different kind of enterprise and ambition. It is not so much that technical innovation in *Ulysses* overwhelms the characterizations set up in chapters 1 to 6, indeed it seems to build from the central dynamics which Stephen and Bloom both represent and engage with. But there can be little doubt that in chapters like 'Cyclops', 'Oxen of the Sun' and 'Circe', 'technic' moves to the centre. The sheer textuality and virtuosity of such episodes may remain at the disposal of the wider novel, but more substantially they push *Ulysses* towards the revolution where, to many critics, probably most nowadays and across a range of approaches, 'style' appears to become entirely caught up with substance.

The following chapter takes this position, arguing that from 'Sirens' onwards the dynamics of *Ulysses* shifts away from mimetic representation. Here the historical themes announced so emphatically at the opening of Joyce's book and returned to in episodes like 'Aeolus' and Scylla and Charybdis' make a dramatic return to *Ulysses* where they shape and determine the cultural strategics that operate precisely across the more radical innovations that Joyce termed 'technic'.

CHAPTER 4

Ulysses, Ireland, Empire

Joyce and History – Critical Traditions

Joyce studies has many diverse strands, but it is also the case that over relatively recent years the focus on historicizing the Joyce text has moved to the centre and now informs readings of *Ulysses* almost as matter of course. This chapter is primarily an introduction to reading the Irish contexts of the *Ulysses* text, especially its later chapters, in historical ways. As such it draws on transformations in literary criticism that since the 1970s have had a major impact on the Joyce world. Clearly to go into that history in any sustained way would be a major diversion from the central concerns here. At the same time, to avoid the theoretical shifts of the last 50 years altogether would produce a serious gap in our understanding of how and why Ireland and empire have become so important to Joyce studies, certainly since the mid 1990s. What follows, then, a return to some of the issues raised briefly in the introduction to this study, is a simplified overview of these developments.

There has always been considerable critical interest in the idea of the history and politics of the Joyce text but not necessarily in relation to Irish culture. In the early days of Joyce criticism, Ireland figured largely but as part of the more general terrain in which biography, annotation and critical exegesis took place. In order to understand Joyce's fiction it was thought necessary to know about Irish history, literature and music and mythology at some level, just as it was apparently important to know about many other things. His writing may have made demands on our knowledge of, say, Irish political life at the *fin de siècle*, but it also required us to have read Shakespeare and be familiar with early twentieth-century fashion and popular science. It was self-evident, even at this early stage, that Ireland was one of the more important contexts to reading Joyce, but it had no fundamental place in terms of critical reading. Indeed for academics working in Joyce studies in the 1950s and 60s it was apparent that 'deep' meaning in Joyce was not contingent on Ireland at all. The 'surface' *Ulysses* might be packed with the stuff of Irish life and culture, but its real significance was positioned elsewhere, alongside the universals of a celebrated and innovative Western individualism.

This positioning was the product of an influential version of modernism associated especially with the American academy in the post-1945 period and such figures as Maurice Beebe, Richard Ellmann, Hugh Kenner and Harry Levin.[1] The modernist reader *The Modern Tradition* (1965) stood for some of the central elements in this critical culture. Edited by two eminent American critics – Charles Feidelson, formerly Bodman Professor of English literature at Yale and Ellmann, arguably the most influential Joycean of the post-war period – it insisted on modernism's essential concern with 'the theme of human freedom' and 'subjective life at its most intense . . . personal and private, wholly individual':

the value of subjective reality in this sense is a modern article of faith. The individual person has turned round upon himself, seeking to know all that he is and to unify all that he knows himself to be. The totality of the self has become the object of an inner quest. The cultivation of self-consciousness – uneasy, ardent, introspection – often amounts to an almost religious enterprise.[2]

At the same time and for all their apparent individualism, the canonical moderns, 'one of the most remarkable constellations of genius in the history of the West',[3] were typically seen in terms of continuity as cultural defenders, conservatives in the broadest sense, as well as iconoclasts – 'classicists, custodians of language, communicators, traditionalists in their fashion'.[4] Hugh Kenner, for instance, understood modernism as a 'rectification of twentieth-century letters' coming out of the 'best of nineteenth-century culture'.[5] In this way just as Joyce in a heroic act of individualism had escaped in 'exile', so his texts, however steeped in Ireland they may have been, were liberated from what was perceived as the parochialism of everydayness to represent the apogee of high status Western literary culture – the supreme expression of Western freedom and individualism. Joyce's writing also became part of a rearguard action, an elitist defence of 'real' culture against a modern world designed for the amusement of Pound's 'half educated simpering general . . . with brains like those of rabbits'[6] – an alarmingly extreme formulation that needed refashioning in the 1950s and 1960s when modernists were associated more typically with disgust at 'urban trivialities' and contempt of '*l'homme moyen sensual*'.[7]

In almost all senses the turn to post-structuralist theory in the 1970s, an assault on universalism of all kinds – progressivist history, the unified subject and so on – worked against the confident practices of exegesis and interpretation that produced some of the classics of Joyce criticism in the American modern tradition. It did little or nothing, however, to reposition the Joyce text in direct relation to Ireland, at least initially. Figures like Cixous, Derrida, Deleuze, Kristeva and Lacan appeared uninterested in the local 'detail' reproduced in the Joyce text, except in terms of the theoretical meaning of the reproduction of detail. *Ulysses* and *Finnegans Wake* in particular were now understood not as repositories of cultural value to be somehow unlocked by Joyce 'experts', but rather as exemplary practices or performances that both encompassed and exposed the ambiguities, gaps and inconsistencies in the Enlightenment project, performing their own acts of radical deconstruction in what Derrida called the 'onto-logico-encyclopedic field'. [8]

This was a revolution against Western metanarratives of history and being, but an essentially playful one, understood by Lacanians in terms of endlessly open potential – *jouissance*. In a curious echo of the modernism it effectively overturned, deconstruction repeated the idea of literature performing a 'revolution' beyond any specific historical determinacy and, again, the American academy was central to the articulation of these positions, certainly in relation to Joyce. In the 1990s it produced a number of readings – James Fairhall's *James Joyce and the Question of History* (1993), for example, and Robert Spoo's *James Joyce and the Language of History* (1994) – that focused not on historicizing Joyce, but rather on the idea of the Joyce text as an escape from history and its discourses. This was a 'freedom' quite reconcilable with the discourse of American individualism, where the structuralist 'prisonhouse of language' became displaced by 'infinite semiotic openness; instead of entrapment, we might see freedom – at least a freedom from absolutist concepts and ideologies. It is this idea of freedom and liberation which links Joyce's attitudes to language and history.'[9]

Joyce's mature texts were particularly well suited to survival outside of precise historical dimensions. Colin MacCabe's *James Joyce and the Revolution of the Word* (1979) and Derek Attridge and Daniel Ferrer's *Post-Structuralist Joyce* (1984), marked the beginnings of the theoretical shift in Joyce studies where the late Joyce texts 'characterized by a foregrounded poetics or linguistic self-absorption . . . became turned in upon themselves . . . with the result that their "political" potential [took] chiefly a metaphysical rather than historicized form' – not too far away at all from the spiritual, ahistorical revolt of the American modern.[10] Modernist studies more generally, however, were not positioned so fortunately in the 1980s. A handful of texts might have remained in

the cultural present, but modernism more broadly was seriously displaced as a contemporaneous condition in the 1980s. No longer the
culture of an end of history in the *now*, it had become the culture of
an ideologically-informed *then*, a predominantly male and Eurocentric
monoculture inscribed with conservative ideology. At the very moment
that the standard historiographies were being thus crucially undermined by deconstruction, modernism found itself as a culture which
could only be approached historically – a culture of a past that had to
be in some way reproduced by literary critics living in the new age of
the postmodern.

Partly as a result of being so firmly fixed by such paradoxes, a contrary modernist studies was able to adapt and hybridize quite quickly,
combining what on the face of it could not easily be reconciled – deconstructive strategies with defiantly historicized reconstruction and cultural studies. For all the theoretical difficulties, a new approach to a
pluralist *modernism*, now sometimes identifying as *fin de siècle* studies,
emerged in the 1990s with such publications as Elaine Showalter's *Sexual
Anarchy: Gender and Culture at the Fin de Siècle* (1992); Lyn Pykett's
Engendering Fictions: the English Novel in the Early-TwentiethCcentury
(1995); the influential collection of essays edited by Sally Ledger and
Scott McCracken, *Cultural Politics at the Fin de Siècle* (1995) and Kelly
Hurley's *The Gothic Body: Sexuality, Materialism, and Degeneration at
the Fin de Siècle* (1998). These texts and others used a combination of
deconstruction, gender performance and postcolonial theory to challenge the 'clean break' tradition, understanding modernism not as
being somehow 'above' history or in terms of an abstract 'metaphysical'
revolution but, rather in precise historical terms, as 'a late-nineteenth
century discourse of rupture'. Here 'the projected transcendence of history found in the works of what has come to be regarded as canonical
high modernism' could be deconstructed, initially from the structural
perspective of a new feminist historiography, 'as an attempt to build a
new order from the ruins of masculine history – a degenerate (for some
a feminized) state which prefigures its own end'.[11]

Joyce and Ireland and its now familiar corollaries, 'history' and
'politics', began to be reconvened in entirely new ways as a product
of these complicated intellectual histories. From intersections across
quite disparate but interrelated fields, the Irish margin that once operated as the mere fabric of the Joyce text now moved to the analytical
centre – colonialism and race becoming crucial to the formation of a
newly constituted politics of modernist literature more generally. Enda
Duffy's *The Subaltern 'Ulysses'* (1994) had little difficulty in separating
Joyce out from the conservative modern now so much associated with
Eliot, Pound and Wyndham Lewis. He also fixed the implications of

contemporary rereadings starkly, and with some drama, by opening his account with a series of questions that must have seemed challenging at the time (one suspects that they remain challenging, but not in ways originally intended by Duffy) – 'Might an IRA bomb', he asked, 'and Joyce's *Ulysses* have anything in common? How might an IRA terrorist read *Ulysses*?' Without troubling too much over the substantial issues raised by an American cultural critic wanting 'to reclaim *Ulysses* . . . for Irish readers as the text of Ireland's independence', he developed a reading of *Ulysses* in 1921 republican terms – where Joyce's book became 'a covert, cautious, "guerrilla" text'.[12]

Vincent Cheng's study *Joyce, Race and Empire* (1995) appeared the very next year. This much more considered account drew on Seamus Deane's *Celtic Revivals* (1985) and his insistence that assumptions about Joyce's indifference to politics and Ireland were badly unsafe. *Joyce, Race and Empire* also acknowledged its debt to deconstruction and postcolonial theory and such figures as Derrida, Franz Fanon, Edward Said, Homi Bhabha and Gayatri Spivak.[13] On the basis of such materials, Cheng, like Duffy, became one of the first critics 'to produce a comprehensive account of Joyce as a dissident colonial subject specifically engaged in a revolt against the dominant power'.[14] A much more politically committed writer than we had previously seen, Cheng's Joyce was also angry, his works less militaristically disposed than in Duffy's account but nevertheless bristling 'with resentment against the imperiums of State, Church and Academy' and fundamentally engaged with ideas around the construction of race and racisms.[15] If the focus on 'Orientalism' in Cheng's study missed the mark in some ways – because the construction of exoticized otherness, as important as it was to Cheng, is actually quite marginal in Joyce's formulation – others working with different historical materials were able to build on this landmark text to demonstrate in different ways how far a politically radical instinct penetrated both the detail and substance of the Joyce text.

My own 1998 account, *Joyce and the Anglo–Irish*, for example, engaged with the complexities of Irish nationalism and its fundamentally fractured nature, showing the extent to which issues of cultural identity shaped Joyce's politics. Andrew Gibson's *Joyce's Revenge* (2002) was also concerned with Anglo–Irish culture, but operated more consistently as a highly-specified historical account of Joyce's engagement with imperial culture and politics. Katherine Mullins's *James Joyce, Sexuality and Social Policy* (2003), following on from Richard Brown's early study *James Joyce and Sexuality* (1985), constructed the representation of sexualities in Joyce's fiction in terms of apparatuses of the colonial state.

That brief overview of readings devoted to historicizing the Joyce text in various ways could go on – writers such as Mary Lowe Evans,

Anne Fogarty, Colin Graham, David Lloyd, Joseph Valente, John Nash and many others, have all made contributions to the literature. The above is probably sufficient, however, to indicate how the 'Joyce and Ireland' framework developed to form a new, if now waning, ortho-doxy. As should be clear, such historical approaches to Joyce, while they may have produced communities of interest, did not represent anything like a critical consensus. The business of inserting the Joyce text into late-nineteenth and early-twentieth-century Irish culture, an inherently complex critical procedure both practically and theoreti-cally was never going to be neutral. Historicizing Joyce engaged with a number of quite distinct critical traditions, each with their own agen-das. More than that it raised the question of to whom or what the his-torical Joyce belonged. For such reasons, Joyce and Ireland, as much as anything in Joyce studies, became a highly contested site.

Not surprisingly, it has been the Irish academy that has been most open to the idea of what is at stake in returning the Joyce text to critical frameworks where history, culture and national identity become fully engaged. Writing in the 1980s and early 1990s Luke Gibbons, a central figure here, articulated what he saw as an Irish need for 'a body of critical work'. Making a perhaps arbitrary but important strategic distinction, Gibbons described an Irish culture that 'as if bearing out the anti-intellectualism of the Celt', had been rich in 'creative energies' but, in his view, 'less successful in generating its own criticism, or intellectual terms of reference'.[16] Powerfully shaped by the deconstructive insight that posi-tioned 'logocentrism' as 'a uniquely European phenomenon',[17] scholars like Gibbons began to articulate what the terms of reference might be for a critical Irish intellectual culture where 'tradition' and 'modernity'; 'centre' and 'periphery' became highly problematized terms – not just as absolutes but also as forces that could be counted upon to be in opposi-tion. As Gibbons made clear, in the colonial context the standard polari-ties became not just reversed but unplugged. 'Tradition', for instance, looked entirely different from the perspective of a 'country with a frac-tured, colonial past'. Its typical associations with 'order, stability and the inherited wisdom of the ages' were thoroughly undermined because here tradition operated at the cultural margins, not at some originary centre. Its position as the antithesis of 'the modern against which both "progress" and "enlightenment" must define themselves' was similarly wrecked because in the Irish context, according to Gibbons, tradition was so often at the vanguard of change. Again, Irish society did not 'have to await the twentieth century to undergo the shock of modernity', Gibbons argued, because 'disintegration and fragmentation were already part of its history, so that in a crucial but not always welcome sense, Ireland experienced modernity before its time.' All this called, for a reversal of the standard view which presents the modernist movement – particularly as represented by Joyce and Beckett – as turning its back on the torpor of tradition in Ireland in order to embrace the exhilaration of the metropolitan avant garde: if anything these writers' vital contacts with mainland culture proved productive precisely because they were carrying with them the nightmare of Irish history the 'ruin of all space, shattered glass and toppling masonry' of the Irish political landscape.[18]

In a series of essays written in the 1980s and 1990s, collected as *Transformations in Irish Culture* (1996), Gibbons was to articulate how these profound shifts operated across twentieth-century culture, literary and otherwise. The effects on Joyce studies were significant. Drawing on the work of Gibbons, Deane and others, Emer Nolan's *James Joyce and Nationalism* (1995), for example, attempted to reinvent Joyce's fictions in postcolonial terms at central levels, arguing, for example, that the 'realism' of *Dubliners*, usually taken as 'the healthy opposite to [romanticising] national myth' contained strong elements of the 'pre-realist (folktale)'.[19] She was also one of the first to suggest that the absence of linear plot in *Ulysses*, or rather its displacement by 'a knot of superimposed complimentary narratives', was neither a version of historical escapism (as the liberal tradition had it), nor (as in the standard deconstructive accounts) 'a vision of apparent endless possibility at the level of language', but rather the product of colonial decentring – these were tales awaiting completion, a view that has influenced this present account.[20] More controversially still, Nolan took the idea that from the reversed position of 'an anticolonial frame', nationalism was 'radically different from the imperious, aggrandizing forms it assumes in the great colonial or world powers' and applied it to 'Cyclops'.[21] Switching the terms of a chapter which had become central to most if not all politicized readings of *Ulysses* and Ireland, Nolan argued against the widely held view that Bloom in 'Cyclops' articulated a reasonable and 'multivocal' internationalism against the verbal violence and bigotry of the citizen. She saw the episode as being in complicity with 'the community's language'.[22] Far from being a satirical attack on one-eyed nationalism, the episode here became a celebration of the citizen's virulent energy, which in turn echoed the textuality of *Ulysses* more generally – a text which bears everywhere the marks of 'colonial experience'. For all the presentism involved in removing nationalism from its often contradictory and wider early-twentieth-century dimensions, Nolan's reading was to constitute an important challenge to some of the most basic views once commonly held about *Ulysses*.

The situation in Joyce studies now on this front, then, is complex. There is hardly a consensus about precisely how the Joyce text functions across the Ireland/Britain dynamic. Some critics see Joyce as ambiguous and conflicted in relation to both Irish and British culture – Nolan herself constructed a Joyce 'deadlocked' and 'uncertain' who 'may not be able to provide a coherent critique of either colonised or colonialist'; his fictions thus represent 'the divided consciousness of the colonial subject'.[23] Others have argued for a stronger sense of commitment in Joyce's writing, a more powerful sense of grievance and a greater degree of control. The one-time orthodox view of Joyce's relation to a modernism set in antithesis to a 'backward' Ireland has been rightly challenged but there is no general agreement about how the Joyce text steers across the Ireland/modern nexus, or indeed, as to whether the issue needs to be thought through in those terms at all. The one certainty, however, is that the Irish context is fundamental to Joyce's fictions. Most would accept that they do address the postcolonial world at some level of centrality, and most would see *Ulysses*, of all Joyce's fiction, as the most developed version of that articulation, although some work has been published on the *Wake* in this respect.[24]

Such a perspective has enabled what many readers now understand to be the most compelling characteristic of Joyce's writing, its technical innovation, to be related to Ireland and politics, establishing the Joyce text in terms of political strategies. These become texts that formulate a complicated interrogation of ideologies of race and nationalism, not just by their representation of the colonial subject but through the appropriation of colonial and Irish nationalist discourses. *Ulysses* in particular is seen in terms of these kind of cultural strategies. Episodes of *Ulysses*, like 'Scylla and Charybdis' and 'Oxen of the Sun', became the most obvious examples of what is now seen as a pervasive engagement with English and Anglo–Irish cultural models, and 'Cyclops' the highpoint of a complex interaction with forms of cultural nationalism now seen to be central to the *Ulysses* project as a whole. What follows below is not a synthesis of such views – just to be clear, it is far from easy to visualize such a thing given what appears to be at stake in terms of the great cultural value placed on the Joyce text. It should be possible, however, to indicate, now in a more focused way, something of the textual foundation which has enabled contemporary Joyce studies to devote so much critical energy to the question of Joyce, Ireland and empire.

Voices of Esau

In the analysis of the relative absence of 'plot' and of the comically subversive Homeric correspondence, but most obviously in the account of the 'Telemachia' which so emphasises the importance of dispossession and betrayal at the opening of *Ulysses*, the potential importance of

Irish colonial history to the *Ulysses* project has already been strongly indicated. That framing continues in the episodes that follow 'Proteus', especially in those most associated with Stephen Dedalus. The 'Aeolus' episode, for example, can be read in terms of its complex and highly nuanced social setting. By contrast to the earlier 'Telemachia', and for all his continuing wariness, Stephen here seems emphatically drawn to a group of men with whom he appears to empathize – and there is some evidence to suggest that they reciprocate. Suggestively, both Professor McHugh and Myles Crawford are keen both to encourage Stephen and to protect him from the bitter cynicism of J. J. O'Molloy – a cynicism which seems to be presented as a common fate for members of the Irish Catholic intelligentsia. The origin of this empathy is in a shared social status and historical consciousness, thus the clannishness about the men in the *Telegraph* office which is not just a matter of acquaintance or friendship. They are a gathering, a gathering of failure and unful-fillment. In the 'OMINIUM GATHERUM' section, Stephen, McHugh, Crawford, O'Molloy and Lenehan are elevated to the status of a quin-tet of high performance talent. They represent literature, the classics, the press, the law and 'the turf' (*U* 7.604–7), although the ironies of these designations are obvious. In reality, these are the underachievers and the wasted potential is not simply a matter of personal dissipation. On the contrary, the relevant historical context is the collapse of a once dynamic middle-class Catholic nationalism, a wider context of cultural and political failure and displacement alluded to everywhere in the episode – in the perceived degeneration of journalism and oratory, for example, the two key cultural forms which fashioned and reflected Irish public opinion in the late-nineteenth and early-twentieth centuries.

In 'Scylla and Charybdis' the debate between intellectuals is more hostile, a product of a quite distinct social environment where the sense of Catholic community is fractured and displaced by something more conflicted and bifurcated. The participants make a show of conducting the debate courteously but, as the super-polite responses suggest, this is a contrived courtesy and there are occasions when the pretence slips. Stephen's Anglo–Irish contemporaries become openly irritated by what he has to say. His preference for Aristotle over Plato makes Eglinton's 'blood boil' (9.80). His critical method is seen as crude sensationalism. With appropriate Anglo–Irish disdain, AE regards Stephen's biographi-cal approach to reading Shakespeare as the work of an intellectual menial, 'Interesting only to the parish clerk' (*U* 9.184). The Shakespeare debate, moreover, is not itself the only source of antagonism in 'Scylla and Charybdis'. It is but one episode in a history of conflict, a history that finds its strongest expression in the hostility and resentment of Stephen's asides but which also includes Stephen's review which slates

Lady Gregory's literary efforts; the accusation that he pissed on Synge's hall door and the rumour that Synge is out to 'murder' him. There is clearly more at stake here than the relative merits of Aristotle or Plato, more behind the 'dialectic' enacted than an academic examination into the truth of an opinion. Indeed, the fundamental issue in this episode, one which underlies the antagonism between protagonists and will determine the direction of the debates on aesthetics and Shakespeare, is the legitimacy of Anglo–Ireland's claim to be forging from nothing more than an appropriation of Irish myth and folk-tale, nothing less than the consciousness of a nation. This is an issue which, for all its contemporary edge, raises old antipathies across a former Protestant hegemony and a rising Catholic middle class.

These relatively early chapters, then, are steeped in the conditions of colonial Ireland – a context of historical conflict that has no chance of being resolved, closed or otherwise smoothed out by a heroic narrative. As we have seen, the question of where the text goes is now responded to at the level of 'technic'. Just how loudly, however, does the stylistic innovation of *Ulysses* reverberate against colonial history in the modern world?

'Cyclops' to 'Circe' – Novel/Discourse

In all the episodes from 'Cyclops' to 'Circe' imported discourses exemplify modern culture, even where they least appear to. Ancient Celtic culture, plantation history and Irish resistance – all are key reference points in 'Cyclops'. The gigantic 'interpolations' point to the past and appear to be located there – indeed they rewrite the present world of the I-narrator as if it were an ancient and heroic past. The following extract illustrates how the components of the bi-narratives of 'Cyclops' work against each other in this way:

> – Come around to Barney Kiernan's, says Joe. I want to see the citizen.
> – Barney mavourneen's be it, says I. Anything strange or wonderful, Joe?
> – Not a word, says Joe. I was up at that meeting in the City Arms.
> – What was that Joe? Says I.
> – Cattle traders, says Joe, about the foot and mouth disease. I want to give the citizen the hard word about it.

So we went around by the Linenhall barracks and the back of the courthouse talking of one thing or another. Decent fellow Joe when he has it but sure like that he never has it . . .

In Inisfail the fair there lies a land, the land of holy Michan. There
rises a watchtower beheld of men afar. There sleep the mighty dead
as in life they slept, warrior and princes of high renown. A pleasant
land it is sooth of murmuring waters, fishful streams where sport
the gurnard, the plaice, the roach, the halibut, the gibbed haddock,
the grilse, the dab, the brill, the flounder, the pollock, the mixed
coarse fish generally and other denizens of the aqueous kingdom
too numerous to be enumerated.

(*U* 12.58–74)

Such interventions (here italicized), however, are not authentically
ancient at all. They derive from modern Celticism and the Irish literary revival, the cultural version of nationalism that rose to prominence
in Ireland following the fall of Parnell and the effective collapse of the
Irish parliamentary party. Of the thirty-one interpolations in 'Cyclops',
thirteen, mostly positioned towards the beginning of the episode as
if to establish a keynote, reproduce and engage with the style features
of revivalist culture. The later interpolations, if not entirely derived
from this romance literature, are invariably implicated in the wider
discourses of revivalism which in historical reality did indeed spread
outwards from literature and language. Sports reportage in 'Cyclops',
for instance, is concerned with the 'resuscitation of the ancient Gaelic
sports and pastimes, practised morning and evening by Finn MacCool'
(*U* 12.909–10). One of two interpolations which parody legal discourse
involves 'sir Frederick the Falconer' administering the ancient law of
Ireland, 'the law of the brehons' (*U* 12.1121–3).

In its over-exposure of Anglicization – in anti-heroic Englishisms
like 'denizens of the aqueous kingdom', 'too numerous to be mentioned'
and in the poeticism 'in sooth' – the above 'fish-run' interpolation
mocks a revivalism that in reality took Victorian forms, a highly sani-
tized 'translation' of a Celtic culture thought too crude and grotesque
in its original version. Some commentators have suggested that the
'Cyclops' interpolations restore some of the characteristics of Celtic literature which Anglo–Irish nineteenth-century 'translators' edited out.
But the exaggerations of size, the double epithets and the lists or 'runs'
in this episode are hardly legitimately antiquarian. Colliding with the
contemporaneity of the I-narrative, these imported texts are subjected
to hilarious interference – the long list of 'Irish' heroes in the fourth
interpolation, commemorated by shells on the citizen's belt, includes
Napoleon Bonaparte, a Celticized Patrick W. Shakespeare and Brian
Confucius, as well as the Last of the Mohicans, Dick Turpin, Ludwig
Beethoven, the Queen of Sheba, Lady Godiva, Jack the Giant Killer and
Gautama Buddh (see *U* 12.168–205).

Just as revivalist texts were faked Celtic, so the 'Cyclops' interpolations are faked revivalism. These are comic versions of the modern prototype. Far from supporting the I-narrative, the alternate perspective in 'Cyclops' which is modern in quite a different way – streetwise, cynical, demotic, everyday – the interpolations run alongside at hopeless variance. Indeed the satire of 'Cyclops' strikes most incisively at the angle where 'gigantic' interpolation meets the realist I-narrative. The transformation of 'Little Alf Bergan . . . squeezed up with the laughing' into the grandiose O'Bergan *'godlike messenger . . . radiant as the eye of heaven'* (*U* 12. 249–50/244–5) is patently absurd, as is the gigantic transformation of 'that bloody old pantaloon Denis Breen' into *'an elder of noble gait and countenance, bearing the sacred scrolls of law'* (*U* 12.253/246–7); or the transformation of Paddy Dignam, the Dublin burgher who in death becomes a national myth – '*O'Dignam, sun of our morning. Fleet was his foot on the bracken: Patrick of the beamy brow. Wail, Banba, with your wind: and wail O ocean, with your whirlwind'* (*U* 12.374–6, my italics throughout) – and so on through the entire episode. Here the discourse of a specific kind of cultural nationalism, though of the modern world, is rendered entirely unstable and practically unusable. Its only status is as a source of hilarity in a mechanics of bizarre juxtaposition.

In 'Cyclops', 'parody' operates as sharp interruption of an I-narration – the I-narrator having no access to the interpolations, although his lively, exaggerated rhetoric does invokes a kind of gigantism of its own.[25] Elsewhere, in the first part of 'Nausicaa' for example, discourses normally kept outside novels, or, at least, implicated in less disruptive ways, are mixed up with, rather than interpolated against, more conventional narrative forms – in this case a third person narrative. The effects are different, but, again, operate in a highly politicized domain. Kiernan's bar is suggestively positioned in Little Britain Street. In 'Nausciaa' the Martello Tower reappears as a sandcastle built by 'Master Tommy and Master Jacky'. True to 'the maxim that every little Irishman's house is his castle', Tommy and Jacky fight over the sandcastle's design (*U* 13.46–7), while Gerty McDowell, 'as fair a specimen of winsome Irish girlhood as one could wish to see' (*U* 13.80–1), looks on with just the right amount of styled detachment:

> A sterling good daughter was Gerty just like a second mother in the house, a ministering angel too with a little heart worth its weight in gold. And when her mother had those raging splitting headaches who was it rubbed the menthol cone on her forehead but Gerty though she didn't like her mother's taking pinches of snuff and that was the only single thing they ever had words about, taking snuff. Everyone thought the world of her for her

gentle ways. It was Gerty who turned off the gas at the main every night and it was Gerty who tacked up on the wall of that place where she never forgot the chlorate of lime Mr Tunney the grocer's christmas almanac, the picture of halcyon days where a young gentleman . . . was offering a bunch of flowers to his lady-love with oldtime chivalry through her lattice window. You could see there was a story behind it.

(*U* 13.325–37)

In this instance, narrative again becomes an anomalous composite. It features a self-consciously refined voice substantially derived from popular ladies magazines once produced in England and distributed across the Empire – magazines like *The Princess's Novelette* and *the Lady's Pictorial*, both referred to in the episode. These publications form a staple of Gerty's cultural diet and combine with a saccharine version of Catholicism which runs through the episode as a religious service heard in the background, 'the voice of prayer to her who is in her pure radiance a beacon ever to the stormtossed heart of man, Mary, star of the sea' (*U* 13.6–8). It is through these prettifying perspectives that Gerty views the world. The result is a jangling narrative punctuated by lapses of decorum as the narrator attempts to reconcile fantasy with the realities of Gerty's ordinary life, where in one of her roles she keeps the lavatory clean and bright, carefully cloaking what goes on in 'that place'. In this way the 'Nausicaa' narrative reproduces popular modern culture as a romanticizing discourse that both distorts Gerty's world and helps her to live in it. Here, as throughout the Joyce canon, the representation of colonial identity is deep and intimate, tied in this instance to cheap metropolitan magazines that paraded Anglicized notions of beauty and behaviour. It is highly politicized in a characteristically Joycean way – both seriously engaged and comically disposed.

In a reverse colonization that writes back to church, state and the conservative Celtic nation, the parodic dimensions of these mid-to-late chapters of *Ulysses* allow Joyce to return Dublin/Ireland as a political, psychological and cultural contemporaneity. 'Oxen of the Sun' is particularly suggestive in this respect. At the realistic level, a discussion among drunken medical students about childbirth, embryology, population control, national efficiency, sexology and so on, 'Oxen' is also a reproduction of English literary history as it was once configured in the anthology tradition represented by such texts as James Davies's, *English Literature from the Accession of George III to the Battle of Waterloo (1760–1815)* (1882); William Peacock's anthology *English Prose from Mandeville to Ruskin* (1903); A. F. Murison's *Selections from the Best English Authors (Beowulf to the Present Time)* (1907) and George Sainsbury's *A History of English*

Prose Rhythm (1912). As Andrew Gibson points out, in an age 'that sees a rapid expansion of education franchise and a rapidly expanding mass readership, the [literary] anthology became a crucial point of transmission of the national literary tradition' both in England itself and across the Empire where such anthologies stood for universal standards of taste and quality.[26] It is this tradition that is assimilated in 'Oxen'.

The following extract sees Mulligan's appearance at the drinking party and broadly illustrates how the parodies work. In this case they evoke eighteenth-century styles suggestive of Addison, Steele and Sterne – although it is often representative stages in the development of English prose that are interfered with here rather than individual writers:

> Our worthy acquaintance Mr Malachi Mulligan now appeared in the doorway as the students were finishing their apologue accompanied with a friend whom he had just rencountered, a young gentleman, his name Alec Bannon, who had late come to town, it being his intention to buy a colour or a cornetcy in the fencibles and list for the wars. Mr Mulligan was civil enough to express some relish of it all the more as it jumped with a project of his own for the cure of the very evil that had been touched on. Whereat he handed round to the company a set of pasteboard cards which he had had printed that day at Mr Quinnell's bearing a legend printed in fair italics: *Mr Malachi Mulligan. Fertiliser and Incubator. Lambay Island.* His project, as he went on to expound, was to withdraw from the round of idle pleasures such as form the chief business of sir Fopling Popinjay and sir Milksop Quidnunc in town and to devote himself to the noblest task for which our bodily organism has been framed. Well, let us hear of it, good my friend, said Mr Dixon. I make no doubt it smacks of wenching.
>
> (*U* 14.651–65)

In mimicking the historical span of 'English literature' with such apparent ease, at the same time as subjecting that history to the structural ambitions of the episode, 'Oxen' asserts its will and authority, bringing a disruptive level of comic liberation to the apparently serious business of collecting 'the noble aspirations, hopes and illusions of which the centuries have left their record in prose' (*CH*, 237).[27] Here *Ulysses*, not for the first or last time, establishes control in a precisely located cultural engagement.

The last episode in the 'adventures' section of *Ulysses* is 'Circe', a play – strongly linked again to revivalism and the Irish theatre – and one firmly located in psychoanalytic theory. Whereas earlier chapters mimic in their 'technic' the style features of various discourses, 'Circe' situates psychoanalytic culture at a more structural level. Here the switches from realistic levels of representation to the 'hallucinations' of unconscious fears and desires – transformations that echo Circe's magical transformation of Odysseus's men into pigs – form a kind of syntax underpinning the episode.

Of all these mid-to-late chapters, 'Circe' is by far the longest and, in many ways, the most challenging. Like 'Nausicaa', 'Cyclops' and 'Oxen', it invokes modernity at the level of 'technic'. Freud is at the heart of the episode, a usage that no more indicates a commitment on the part of Joyce to Freud, than the usage of romance literature in 'Cyclops' implies commitment to revivalism.[28] On the contrary, it is clear that Joyce's exposure of the workings of the unconscious is a mock, cartoon-like version. In the following extract, Bloom slips from modest conscious concern at being observed in Nighttown, the red-light district –'down . . . in the haunts of sin' (*U* 15.395) – to an existential condition of guilt and shame, formulated as 'hallucination'. Thus the appearance of Bloom's father, prompted in part by Bloom having bought 'a lukewarm pig's crubeen' (*U* 15.158). Rudolph, dead in the real world, appears here as a still-admonishing Jewish stereotype drawn, appropriately enough, from stage representations:

RUDOLPH

Second half crown waste money today. I told you not go with the drunken goy ever. So you catch no money.

BLOOM

(*hides the crubeen and trotter behind his back and, crestfallen, feels warm and cold feetmeat*) Ja, ich weiss, papachi.

RUDOLPH

What you making in this place? Have you no soul? (*with feeble vulture talons feels the silent face of Bloom*) Are you not my son Leopold, the grandson of Leopold? Are you not my dear son Leopold who left the house of his father and left the god of his fathers Abraham and Jacob?

(*U* 15.252–62)

With its elaborate representations of self loathing and narcissism and its wild inflations of Bloom's interests in voyeurism and masochism, 'Circe' represents a intellectual culture that by the1920s had come to terms with Freud. To the extent that the psychoanalytic paradigm could be culturally exploited and laughed at, Freud had become assimilated. As strange as 'Circe' seems, it is familiarizing in this respect. It reduces the power of the Freudian to shock – part of the effect of its carnivalesque atmosphere is to normalize guilt and, most tellingly, the desires that Freud considered to be indicative of sexual pathology. At the same time, however, 'Circe' *does* shock, as a powerful challenge to conservative forces, but also in the dramatic reconfiguration where church, state and nation appear in familial terms to reshape Freud's conception of the crucial psychic drama. In the extended climax that forms the end of 'Circe', Stephen's mother, far from being an object of sexual desire, becomes an objectification of the Church ghoulishly demanding her son's repentance. The authoritative father figure is represented both by a bumbling Edward the Seventh – *'robed as a grand elect perfect and sublime mason with trowel and apron, marked* made in Germany' (*U* 15.4454–5) – and the henchman apparently responsible for discipline and order, Private Carr ('I'll wring the neck of any fucking bastard says a word against my bleeding fucking king – *U* 15.4644–5). And, as Stephen says in the very beginning of things, 'a third there is' (*U* 1.641). Ill-defined in 'Telemachus', this third master appears precisely in 'Circe' as 'Old Gummy Granny', the crone who is both Ireland and 'Ireland's sweetheart . . . Strangers in my house . . . Silk of the kine!' (*U* 15.4584–6). This figure urges Stephen to die for his country – 'you will be in heaven and Ireland will be free *(she prays)* O good God, take him!' (*U* 15.4738–9) – and is crucial to Stephen's realization that his rebellion must first take place in his head. 'Break my spirit, all of you', he declares, 'if you can! I'll bring you all to heel!' (*U* 15.4235–6), before tapping 'his brow' and facing the psychodynamic fact that, whatever else, 'in here it is I must kill the priest and the king' (*U* 15.4436–7). This redrawing of the psychological landscape, part assimilation, part appropriation, is as characteristic a Joycean turn as anything in *Ulysses*, one which confronts conservative Ireland with a scientific perspective both European and modern, but which at the same time confronts Europe with the modern world as represented by the colonized state.

Clearly, the narrative innovation of late *Ulysses* is not nihilistic but functional. This functionality extends beyond engagement with aesthetics and playful interference with the novel form, although *Ulysses* does operate at such levels. Joyce's 'technic' serves the imperative of 'correspondence' with Homeric prototypes, but it is equally apparent that the implications of technic in these chapters go far beyond the solution of a series of purely technical problems generated from the building of a modern mock epic out of the *Odyssey*. In moving away from the securities of narrative convention through its styles and techniques, *Ulysses* begins to reinscribe Dublin as the backwater of empire with which Stephen struggles, one that yet stands as the site of modernity initially embodied by Bloom. Again and again contemporaneity is fashioned in terms of Irish history and culture and conditioned by the realities of colonial life, not only through the representation of individual characters but now through a direct engagement with the discursive material that makes up the colonized world. The expansion of this broad contingency into 'technic' extends the range of *Ulysses* yet again, engaging its satirical capacities and political interventions in new ways. It also shifts the periphery, configuring Dublin/Ireland as the centre of discourses linked to modern nationalism, psychology and literary cultures in both popular and 'high' forms – a repositioning which helps to explain why *Ulysses* has been of such great interest to deconstructive, postmodern and postcolonial theorists in recent years and why the idea of cultural strategics has played such an important part in Joyce criticism since the 1980s.

Ricorso – the Idea of Return in *Ulysses*

The last section of this chapter demonstrates the developing textuality of *Ulysses* in relation to 'Eumaeus' and 'Ithaca'. It is these chapters that must somehow adapt most precisely to the central narrative dynamic of Homer's *Odyssey* – the idea of return, the restoration of lands and legitimate authority. How this is done in a twenty-four hour book not only takes us further into the stylistic adventures of *Ulysses*; it also illustrates how innovation in Joyce always looks outward, registering against the real world.

The idea of return is fundamental to *Ulysses*, a novel that is both obsessively self-referential and so subject to expansion and travel that it becomes necessary at times to return to the base camps established in the earlier chapters. 'Scylla and Charybdis', with its emphasis on usurpation and engagement with the Anglo–Irish revival is a re-articulation of 'the voice of Esau' (*U* 9.981) first heard in the Telemachia, just as 'Lestrygonians' and the second half of 'Nausicaa' return us to Bloom – insiderly yet outsiderly, orthodox yet heterodox and, above all, defined by modernity in its most familiar manifestations – business, commerce, bourgeoisification. The *Nostos* section, however, is the return most central to the overall structure of *Ulysses*. If we persevere with the idea that what happens between Stephen/Bloom is driving this novel, expectancies about the capacity for resolution will be high. The styles of both episodes wickedly exploit such expectations. At a time of impending closure, 'Eumaeus' seems peculiarly devoted to storytelling and for this reason seems to promise movement towards closure. It relates stories about the Westland Row railway station incident and Corny Kelleher's intervention in Nighttown; gossips about

John Corley's true aristocratic parentage and in turn relates Corley's story about Bags Comisky. The mysterious D. B. Murphy figure is a habitual storyteller. Through the filter of the 'Eumaeus' narrative we hear his tall tales about a Simon Dedalus who was a sharpshooter; magical Chinese pills; the man killed in Trieste and the demise of Antonio who was 'Ate by sharks' (*U* 16.691). The episode is stuffed with tales of shipwrecks and mistaken identity, but for all these narrative possibilities the story which the reader has most investment in, the Stephen/Bloom story, remains not just unresolved, but virtually untouched. Despite Bloom's attempts at engagement, and partly because of them, Stephen is incapable of achieving vague interest, let alone the atonement that the structuring of *Ulysses* promises – 'Over his untastable apology for a cup of coffee, listening to this synopsis of things in general, Stephen stared at nothing in particular' (*U* 16.1141–2).

'Ithaca' works in a similar way, except that here it is a high status discourse of rationality, fact and scientific procedure that offers the prospect not just of a closed ending but of supremely confident understanding. The problem in 'Ithaca', however, is that this narrative style, far from resolving anything, has such a flattening effect that meaning is in danger of completely disappearing. There are facts in abundance but no value-system in which to place them:

What relation existed between their ages?

16 years before in 1888 when Bloom was of Stephen's present age Stephen was 6. 16 years after in 1920 when Stephen would be of Bloom's present age Bloom would be 54. In 1936 when Bloom would be 70 and Stephen 54 their ages initially in the ratio of 16 to 0 would be as 17½ to 13½, the proportion increasing and the disparity diminishing according as arbitrary future years were added, for if the proportion existing in 1883 had continued immutable, conceiving that to be possible, till then 1904 when Stephen was 22 Bloom would be 374 and in 1920 when Stephen would be 38, as Bloom then was, Bloom would be 646 while in 1952 when Stephen would have attained the maximum postdiluvian age of 70 Bloom, being 1190 years alive having been born in the year 714, would have surpassed by 221 years the maximum antediluvian age, that of Methusalah, 969 years, while if Stephen would continue to live until he would attain that age in the year 3072 A.D., Bloom would have been obliged to have been alive 83,300 years, having been obliged to have been born in the year 81,396 B.C.

(*U* 17.446–61)

If the *ricorso* implies a return to a familiar world of the novel where end-ing means resolution and closure, 'Eumaeus' and 'Ithaca' fail to deliver. Indeed the shifting, expanding and appropriative dynamic of the chap-ters from 'Cyclops' to 'Circe' continues. Both chapters are developing an engagement with discourse and both are profoundly contracted to modernity. 'Eumaeus' adopts a pretentious, pedantic idiom linked remorselessly to bourgeois values. It displaces the chaos of 'Circe' with orderly prioritizing, and the sound of middle-class, Edwardian England – 'Preparatory to anything else Mr Bloom brushed off the greater bulk of the shavings' (*U* 16.1–2) – proceeding by 'bringing common sense to bear' (*U* 16.31). There is the confident anticipation that, by putting 'a good face on the matter' (*U* 16.32), trusting providence and observing the proprieties, useful outcomes will accrue, undoubtedly to Stephen and Bloom's mutual benefit. The question and answer format of 'Ithaca' is decisively linked to the world of science where mathematics, physics, mechanics and engineering rule, as here in the response to a question about whether water flowed from the tap in Bloom's kitchen:

> Yes. From Roundwood reservoir in county Wicklow of a cubic capacity of 2400 million gallons, percolating through a subter-ranean aqueduct of filter mains of single and double pipeage con-structed at an initial plant cost of £5 per linear yard by way of the Dargle, Rathdown, Glen of the Downs and Callowhill to the 26 acre reservoir at Stillorgan, a distance of 22 statute miles . . .
>
> (*U* 17.164–9)

The textuality of these episodes, then, establishes a context where moder-nity seems firmly in control. The homeland in the *ricorso* is not just domestic territory – 7 Eccles Street with Molly Bloom as 'Penelope' – but a world under contemporary authority, where the idea of heroic return so central in Irish cultural history, and to Homer's *Odyssey*, is reduced to an irreverent handling in Anglicized popular culture – Bloom's com-mission to write 'a topical song . . . on the events of the past . . . entitled *If Brian Boru could but come back and see old Ireland now* (*U* 17.417–19).

This authority, however, is also subject to the kind of comic interfer-ence evident in the earlier chapters, as the extract from 'Ithaca' con-cerning Bloom and Stephen's relative age shows. It summons up all the certitude of the scientific age for calculation of a proportional relation that does not even exist. In this sense the exercise is purely that, a rou-tine and of no significant value. The passage aims for certitude, but ends up in a cycle that could go on forever without getting anywhere. If there is a potentially interesting idea here, that Stephen and Bloom get closer, as it were, as they get older, that idea is swamped by a process of calculation that is highly vulnerable to error. Indeed the proportion 16-0 cannot operate in the calculations set up because Stephen would always be at zero, an 'error' entirely characteristic of Ithaca, the chapter in which Bloom is credited with a very small chest (28 inches) and a very large neck (more than 17 inches).

Critics once found such apparently cold, pointless passages revealing of 'the bleak and terrifying universe in which man seems minute, insignificant and at the mercy of powers beyond his imagination',[29] just as some found the narrator of 'Eumaeus' a dark 'posturer' who speaks a 'deadly' 'concealing' language.[30] But such views surely miss the point. The effects of the manipulation of these discourses are hardly dark. They subject obsessive, petty, pretentious identities to the same kind of comic interventions apparent elsewhere in *Ulysses* and produce a similar kind of unravelling. Order, clarity and certainty are ambitions, but prove more than problematic to sustain. Both episodes are always on the verge of exhaustion, even defeat, as in the following extract from 'Eumaeus' which implodes as pronouns lose referents and subjects become utterly obscure.

> Briefly, putting two and two together, six sixteen which he pointedly turned a deaf ear to, Antonio and so forth, jockeys and esthetes and the tattoo which was all the go in the seventies or thereabouts even in the house of lords because early in life the occupant of the throne, then heir apparent, the other members of the upper ten and other high personages simply following in the footsteps of the head of the state, he reflected about the errors of notorieties and crowned heads running counter to morality such as the Cornwall case a number of years before under their veneer in a way scarcely intended by nature, a thing good Mrs Grundy, as the law stands, was terribly down on though not for the reason they thought they were probably whatever it was except women chiefly who were always fiddling more or less at one another it being largely a matter of dress and all the rest of it.
>
> (*U* 16.1195–207)

In terms of more familiar kinds of novelistic endings, these chapters prove decisively disappointing. There is a certain amount of confused 'getting-on' between Stephen and Bloom in both 'Eumaeus' and 'Ithaca', and some resolution in the equanimity with which Bloom faces Molly's infidelities, although little shift in Stephen. The portentously signalled symbiosis, however, simply never materializes. As 'technic', however, these episodes register loudly. They set to work from the inside on authorities of the modern world, establishing a kind of satirical convergence with despair at the modern empire. The resultant hilarity hardly makes Joyce's *ricorso* an advocate of contemporaneity, but there is an easy comic manipulation here that is highly distinctive and has a powerful resonance. In the staking out of new territory for the Irish artist, there is the mature expression of dispossession and repossession. Joyce, in these chapters as elsewhere in *Ulysses*, appropriates conditions of the modern world. Far from being a victim of colonization specifically or modern culture generally, the text itself controls and masters these contingencies. The essential significance of 'Eumaeus' and 'Ithaca', then, is that here, not for the first time, Joyce takes his trade to the materiality many thought inimical to the 'real' Ireland to produce a demarcation of urban modernity as the Irish novel's true domain.

Ulysses was and remains an epically large-scale novel, remarkable for its mastery of realism but also for its extension of our sense of what novels can do and how they operate in the world. It not only deployed a radical understanding of how reality was constructed by discourse but also created new spaces for literature to reproduce, interrogate and engage with. To the extent that it established Irish literature, an Irish Odyssey, at the very centre of modern European modernism, it was the postcolonial novel *par excellence* and made a defiant cultural statement. The fact that it did so at the same time as mounting a hilarious analysis of conservative cultural nationalism was not a contradiction. Rather this position defined Joyce not only in relation to Irish politics, but also in terms of a world politics decisively shaping up around ideological extremities. For many it was a liberating artistic achievement, but so wide-ranging and disruptive that it was perceived as leaving nowhere for the novel to go. Malcolm Lowry was not the only major novelist to consider giving up after *Ulysses*. Scott Fitzgerald made the theatrical gesture of threatening to jump out of Sylvia Beach's window 'in honour of Joyce's genius' (*CH*, 2, 420) and there were many others who thought that Joyce had bought the novel certainly to a crossroads and perhaps to the end of the road.

That issue of where to take the novel now, applied to Joyce as much as anyone. Having brought the novel to *Ulysses*, where could it go? The response to that issue was to engage Joyce for some seventeen years and finally produce a text as different from *Ulysses* as the latter was from *A Portrait*. As it began to emerge in the late 1920s, it began to be clear from *Work in Progress* that readers trying to keep up were now being asked to engage with a text that had moved even further away from representation and from the 'parodies' of *Ulysses* so central to that novel. Indeed Joyce's new work, although it seemed to refer to just about everything in world history and culture, appeared, at the same time, to owe nothing to any literature that went before. At best it seemed as if Joyce was trying to produce an openness that somehow embraced all and every meaning; at worse *Work in Progress* was, for many, a horrible jumble of image and sound, the 'witless wandering of literature before its final extinction' (*Letters* III, 102–6) as Stanislaus put it. In creating what appeared to be writing in a new language, Joyce was accused of 'aesthetic dishonesty' (*CH*, 2, 393), because no purpose could be seen behind his ingenuity. There were however, even at this early stage, more supportive opinions, some of which showed real insight. I'm thinking here especially of William Carlos Williams who thought of Joyce's new work as being 'truth through the break up of the beautiful'. It was composed, Williams continued in a 'style' that began 'not without malice' (*CH*, 2, 377).

CHAPTER 5

Reading *Finnegans Wake*

Preamble

The pre-*Wake* fictions are rich and challenging, but they have become more substantially fixed in critical terms than they once were. They continue to be read as contemporary culture, but over the last two decades they are often approached by the academy through genealogical frameworks as historical literature.

There are signs that *Finnegans Wake* may be going the same way. The transcriptions and commentaries on the *Wake* notebooks published by Brepols and the lost manuscript evidence that has resurfaced in recent years have helped to reinforce fundamental shifts in conceptual readings of the *Wake*. Deconstruction has again been crucial here. It has displaced the once familiar view that the *Wake* is a lyrical celebration of 'guilt-stained, evolving humanity' and 'a mighty allegory of the fall and resurrection of mankind'[1] with an entirely contrary view. Here the book is seen as a 'machine' that sets out to subvert 'the most cherished preconceptions of Western culture'.[2] Reformulated as a decentred text, the *Wake* becomes not a confirmation of fantasies about the human condition but, rather, an 'unraveling' of universals – as a 2007 account puts it.[3]

It is this radical overarching perspective that has enabled some critics to assert with more confidence how the *Wake* might operate in terms of twentieth-century modernism. New ways of understanding the *Wake* as historical culture are being formulated. This does not alter the fact that the *Wake* appears to establish itself outside of any historical specificity, but it does mean that we can now read that positioning itself as a cultural strategy which registers in fascinating ways.

Before considering such ideas, the current chapter seeks to introduce the *Wake* text. To do so it uses strategies adopted from an earlier chapter on *Ulysses* (Chapter 3). Here too the decentred nature of the *Wake* is demonstrated in relation to some of the basic questions that might be asked about this text or indeed any 'novel' – how was it written? What is its story? What does it mean? The chapter shows how the radical *Wake* was a product of design and not just an invention of critical fashion; how its obsession with narration undermines narrative and likewise how multiple frameworks of meaning render singularity of meaning impossible.

Illustrated by a section which examines the relation between the *Wake* and one its many source books, the *Encyclopaedia Britannica*, the chapter that follows reads these characteristics of the *Wake* text against epistemological crises of the early-twentieth century. Subsequently these ideas are developed in relation to race discourse and European politics in the early decades of the twentieth century, in particular to the 1920s and 1930s – which is not to say that there is only one way to historicize the *Wake* text; there are many. This one, however, is particularly illustrative of how the politics of the *Wake* work.

By way of further preamble, a few brief and general comments about *Wake* reading. Although density of 'allusions' are only part of the *Wake*'s difficulty, they are often seen as a primary hurdle to understanding and for good reason. There is a great acceleration of things here from *Ulysses*. The word 'Chrysostomos' on the first page of *Ulysses* (*U* 1.26 and see page 89 above) disrupts an otherwise quite familiar language world to invoke something quite particular – the idea of a golden-mouthed orator; perhaps, according to Thornton, Dion Chrysostomos, the first-century Greek rhetorician or St John Chrysostomos, a fourth-century father of the Greek Church.[4] Whatever, from here the point of the reference, made in relation to Buck Mulligan, becomes clear. Although the word remains unspoken, it is part of a more general jibing that takes place between Mulligan and Stephen in the 'Telemachia,' where Stephen is a 'dreadful bard' (*U* 1.134) and 'the unclean bard' (*U* 1.475) and Mulligan a 'gay betrayer' (*U* 1.405). 'Chrysostomos' is an insult.

In the *Wake*, however, language is much more disrupted and multiple meanings become standard. The very 'first' line of the *Wake* – 'riverrun, past Eve and Adam's, from swerve of shore to bend of bay, brings us by a commodius vicus of recirculation back to Howth Castle and Environs' (*FW* 1.1–3) – combines the family seat of an aristocratic Anglo–Irish family (also an acrostic for Here Comes Everybody, the central figure of the *Wake*) with the fall of man, a Dublin church near the Liffey and a pub once on the same site. A commode, and thus water cycles more generally, are associated with a circular river which is also a 'vicious cycle' and so 'connected' (whatever that might mean) to Commodious, a Roman Emperor noted for his tyrannical disposition and cruelty. The route of the river implies blood circulation but also Vico's *New Science* and its cycles of history (see below page 189), as well as following a local geography around Vico Road, Dalkey.

Here, then, allusiveness is caught up in a text so strange that many readers experience reading it as being analogous to learning a new language – it is famously comprised of some sixty-three languages, although the grammatical structures are mostly English – and there may be something to be said for approaching the *Wake* in that way. The various published annotations and word lists are an important resource in this respect (see the bibliographical section in 'further reading' for more detail), but no substitute for reading, discussing and thinking about Wakese in a more general way. A *Wake* reading group can be of real interest in this respect, an equivalent in terms of language learning to a trip abroad. There are some well-established ones, some based in the academy, others not, with around twenty-five currently being listed on the finneganswake.org website – including those based in Albuquerque, Antwerp, Berkeley (California), Buffalo (New York), Dublin, Vancouver and Zurich. Many more are not so listed, including the London group organized by the University of London and open to all. It is now in its fifth year. The sister *Ulysses* group is at the time of writing in its twenty-fifth year.

Many of the further problems – around tone, structure, identities and so on – often seem greater than they might be because of the expectations we bring to reading novels. The *Wake* toys with these, much of the engagement here taking place at, again, comic levels. It has been said many times before, but it bears saying repeatedly – the *Wake*, like *Ulysses*, is essentially comic and the comedy extends to the idea of reading. It is also wonderfully crude, with its vulgarity, as in *Ulysses*, often forming part of its critical engagement with the world. If you are easily offended by the 'obscene', you may struggle with the *Wake* – a text never far from 'the verge of selfabyss' (*FW* 40.23), indeed, seemingly over-indulgent to the extent of 'Three creamings a day' (*FW* 144.2–3). The book challenges contemporary sensibilities in this respect in ways that no longer apply to *Ulysses* on anything like the same scale. As I've argued elsewhere, 'filth' and 'vulgarity' – finding the right term for such material is not easy – are centrally important to the way the *Wake* works.[5]

For some readers it may help to come to the *Wake* with an idea. There are a huge number of threads to this text that might be exploited here – indeed it might be helpful to think of the *Wake* as a mechanism for bringing into contingency things that under normal circumstances are kept well apart. This is substantially what Joyce meant when he described himself as the 'engineer' of the *Wake*. Following just one thread will reduce the impact of that important dynamic greatly, but it may also provide the necessary focus to take you through, as I know from experience. After years of stops and starts, it was the perspective produced by looking at race and race discourse in the *Wake* which provided a platform from which to operate more confidently and widely across the *Wake*. Others have worked from different platforms – from languages (lexicons have been produced for such languages as German, Gaelic, Latin, Lithuanian, Sanskrit and Norwegian and so on), theatre history, geometry, Irish myth, and colonial politics through to insects. That ants, grasshoppers and earwigs have attracted particular attention will come as no surprise to readers familiar with the *Wake*, although even the most experienced might stumble over explaining critical interest in bees.

And, finally, for some readers the *Wake* will always be a grand illustration of modernism degenerating into gobbledegook. In fact, the *Wake* multiplies rather than destroys meaning. Tolerance for this multiplicity, not to say enjoyment of it, is crucial. It is a condition of 'the book of Doublends Jined' that 'every word will be bound over to carry three score and ten toptypsical readings' (*FW* 20.14–15). Reading the *Wake* is inevitably about handling that texture. Listening out loud will help, but not as much as is sometimes claimed, especially by those who imagine that the *Wake* operates somehow mystically. It does not.

How Was It Made?

The finished version of *Finnegans Wake* is six-hundred and twenty-eight pages long, but more than twenty-five thousand pages of its textual record have survived. These include some fourteen thousand pages of notes currently housed in the Poetry Collection at the University of Buffalo, State University of New York – which comprise the forty-eight Buffalo Notebooks – and the approximately nine thousand pages of manuscripts, typescripts and proofs that Joyce deposited with his benefactress Harriet Shaw Weaver. Weaver, the first Joyce archivist, donated her collection to the British Library in 1951 where it was worked on by David Hayman who produced *A First-Draft Version of Finnegans Wake* in 1963 and then by Danis Rose with the assistance of John O'Hanlon, who used it for the *James Joyce Archive* (1978–79). Even this large archive, supplemented by the discovery of new *Wake* manuscripts in 2006, is incomplete – there are absences in the early manuscript history in particular. Some notebooks have been lost and others are yet to be fully transcribed and annotated. Despite the gaps, the *Wake* archive together with the sequence of letters that Joyce sent to Weaver throughout the composition of the *Wake* from 1923 to 1939 has produced what appears to be a broad consensus among genetic critics about how the text was 'engineered'.[6] The story is fascinating in its own right, and in its more recent incarnation supports the idea that the decentred *Wake* is not simply a product of Derrida and deconstruction, but was, rather, built into the *Wake*'s design virtually from the beginning when the *Wake* existed as a series of distinct sites, or sketches.

In March 1923, Weaver received two pages from Joyce, 'the first', he claimed, 'I have written since the final *Yes* of *Ulysses*' (*Letters* I, 202).[7] This was the sketch of King Roderick O'Connor which was to resurface much later in the *Wake* as part of II.3. A series of further sketches followed, including the hagiographic pieces involving St Patrick and Bishop George Berkeley, St Dympna and St Kevin; a Tristan and Isolde sketch; the piece on the four old men or Mamalujo and an early Here Comes Everybody (HCE) sketch which of all the pieces had most in the way of legs and was to form the basis for Book I. Later that year Weaver received 'the revered letter', analysed in *Finnegans Wake* I.5 and eventually figuring in Book IV. The 'Anna Livia (ALP) piece' was 'finished' in March 1924 and several Shaun sketches, the 'watches' of Shaun, began to arrive around the same time (see *Letters* I, 212–3). These latter were to form the basis of Book III.

Whereas *Ulysses* developed progressively from such elements as the Homeric correspondence; very specific chronology; the imperative to represent Dublin and to incorporate other systems – colours, parts of the body and so on – the *Wake*'s growth appears to have been generated differently, developing outwards from the sequence of sketches described above. These produced what David Hayman has called a framework of 'nodality'.[8] The sketches became passages which not only expanded beyond recognition but also produced the 'intratextual echoes' eventually so important to holding the writing together. In his introduction to *How Joyce Wrote 'Finnegans Wake'* (2007), Sam Slote gives an explanation of this process:

> In order to get the *Wake* going Joyce needed to set up an initial chain of discrete textual events, the sketches, that would then, 'when they are more and a little older' [see *Letters* 1, 204], start to generate further swaths of text that would in turn generate more verbiage, and so on, and so on . . . Instead of proceeding from a story or from a single theme, the text proceeds from the *interactions* of various discrete passages . . . In a sense, the sketches were but the initiating spark for a perpetual motion text machine.[9]

In this way genetic criticism has confirmed the *Wake*'s innovation as a text designed with the sketches as its multiple points of origin. A linear narrative is dispensed with in favour of circularity, repetition and an 'intratexuality' that becomes operative in quite unique ways. Genetic criticism also helps position the *Wake* in terms of wider critical tradition where, far from representing reality and embodying old epistemologies, the text performs its own nature and the processes of its own making. As the metaphor of the machine suggests, this is a text unique in its capacity for engaging with the idea of meaning – all this confirming Samuel Beckett's insight that Joyce's writing is 'not about something; it is that something itself.'[10]

What were eventually to figure as Books I and III of the *Wake* comprised the early structure of the *Wake*, if structure is the right term – by November 1926 Joyce was clear that his new book, for all its complex planning, 'really has no beginning or end . . . It ends in the middle of a sentence and begins in the middle of the same sentence' (*Letters* I, 246). At the same time, Joyce was equally certain that he was working on two distinct large units, suggesting framework if not necessarily linearity. The question of how to join these sections together, the first circulating around the father and mother figures, HCE and ALP, and the third, turning on Shaun's rise and eventual fall, was not settled until 1926 when Joyce began work on 'three or four other episodes, the children's game, night studies, a scene in the "public", and a "lights out in the village"' (*Letters* I, 241).[11] Development of these episodes, beginning with II.2, was delayed while Joyce worked on I.1 and further sections of Books I and III – indeed Book II was not complete until 1938.

As early as June 1926, however, some 13 years before the *Wake*'s full publication, Joyce was claiming to have 'the book now fairly well planned out in my head' (*Letters* I, 241). By the same time Joyce also had versions of the *Wake* sigla worked out, the shorthand that not only stood for the individuals in the Earwicker family but also indicated dynamic relationships, like conflict, and which were sometimes combined, often to indicate complimentary.[12] He was also proficient in Wakese, which meant that first drafts from this point on were much more complex than the earlier first drafts which had been more standard in their English. Between 1926 and 1935 only three entirely new chapters were produced (I.6, II.1 and II.2), which gives some indication of just how much of the *Wake*'s compositional history was taken up with the extraordinary process of expansion that now characterized Joyce's writing technique.[13]

A particular strand of genetic criticism provides that history of text composition, so implying the self-generating dimensions of the *Wake*. Other strands work more closely with the idea of the *Wake*'s intertextuality, its dependency on material outside of itself – one key source here being other books by James Joyce. It is sometimes said, with some justification, that *Finnegans Wake* grew out of *Ulysses*. 'Scribbledehobble', the 'big' notebook containing some of the earliest *Wake* material, does indeed imply that Joyce's new work was conceived 'as an extension not only of *Ulysses* but of all his previous works'.[14] That 'big' notebook is divided into forty-seven parts, each one corresponding to previous works, including the eighteen chapters of *Ulysses*, which would appear to support Ellmann's description of the *Wake* as 'in many ways a sequel to *Ulysses*' (*JJ*, 545).

But the *Wake* also grew from thousands of pages of notes indicative of everything else – from biographies, histories, novels to newspapers, fanzines, encyclopaedias and so on. The notes were sometimes taken randomly from whatever came to hand, but there was frequently design to the sequences that Joyce took; groups of notes from books on anthropology, magic, sociology, history as well as copious notes taken from the *Catholic Encyclopaedia* and *Encyclopaedia Britannica*.

For genetic critics these notes form the foundation of the *Wake*. They are often seen as building blocks, the earliest stages of composition, 'harvested' (or not) for use in drafts and manuscripts where they become part of the extensive expansion of text characteristic of the *Wake*'s development. At the same time, however, the notebooks refer the *Wake* back to the wider culture in which it operates. The Brepols edition, a work in progress which has been under the editorship of Vincent Deane, Daniel Ferrer and Geert Lernout, indicates how important notebook research can be in this respect.[15] Already our notions about what the *Wake* is comprised of, formally substantially derived from Atherton's pioneering study *The Books at the Wake* (1959), have been radically challenged. We now know, for example, that as well as working with a huge number of literary works from the canon; with Vico and *New Science* and what Atherton calls 'the sacred books' – the Bible, the Book of the Dead, the Koran and so on – Joyce was also reading a huge range of other materials, so much so that Atherton's idea that there are books of 'structural' importance to the *Wake* can no longer be seriously maintained.

Among those other materials were newspapers, including the *Connaught Tribune*, the *Freeman's Journal*, the *Irish Statesman*, the *Irish Independent* and the *Leader*, as well as the *Daily Mail*, the *Daily Sketch*, the *Daily Express*, the *Evening Standard* and the *Times*. Joyce worked from guide books, biographies – notably the hagiological, but also from much less elevated material, S. M. Ellis's *The Life and Times of Michael Kelly: musician, actor and bon viveur* (1930) for instance. He used histories. Gibbons's *The Decline and Fall of the Roman Empire* was incorporated into *Wake* notes, as was Stephen Gwynn's *History of Ireland* (1923) and Benedict Fitzpatrick's *Ireland and the Making of Great Britain* (1922). There was a broad engagement with some of the central trends and controversies in European intellectual life – Jules Crepieux-Jamin's *Les éléments de l'écriture de canailles* (1923) (*The Features of the Handwriting of Scoundrels*); W. J. Perry's *The Origin of Magic and Religion* (1923) and J. B. S. Haldane's, *Daedalus or the Science of the Future* (1924) seem suggestive here.

Haldane, for example, was a radical scientist whose work strongly influenced Aldous Huxley's dystopia, *Brave New World* (1932) – with Haldane himself attacking the kind of naked social Darwinism that Huxley saw as being operated by the state of the future. Far from recommending eugenics, Haldane protested against those who 'having discovered the existence of biology . . . attempted to apply it in its then very crude condition to the production of a race of supermen . . . They [eugenicists] certainly succeeded in producing the most violent opposition and hatred amongst the classes whom they somewhat gratuitously regarded as undesirable parents'.[16] His comment that 'It took man 250,000 years to transcend the hunting pack. It will not take him so long to transcend the nation.'[17] was duly noted by Joyce at V1.B.1, 061(c) as '250,000 to transcend/hunting pack/ – nation.'

Also significant in this respect was Leon Metchnikoff's *La Civilisation et les Grandes Fleuves Historique* (1899). Metchnikoff was a radical social scientist, associated with anarchism and important to Joyce because of his work on I.8, the ALP and 'rivers' episode of the *Wake*. *Les Grandes Fleuves*, which Joyce was reading in 1924, was a work that examined rivers in terms of their social and cultural influence, but Metchnikoff was also a vociferous opponent of scientific racism. His book included a chapter entitled 'Race' (chapter 4) which demolished 'all possible arguments for racist theories by showing the inadequacies of classifications based on skin colour, on the form of the skull, or on language'.[18] Some of the passages that interested Joyce were as follows. The first was noted at V1.B.1, 075 (a) as 'races – hair/skull /hue/':

> Since the previous century, frequent attempts have been made to separate the human species into distinct and categorically defined groups. Some of these attempts were grounded on skin-colour and yet no-one would dream of determining which race a dog or horse belonged to on the basis of their fur-coat. Other classed men according to the cut of their hair . . . yet others according to the shape of their skull.[19]

This second was noted at V1.B.1, 075 (b) as 'change language/ – marry'.

> races were divided, dispersed, mixed and crossed in all proportions, in all directions, for thousands of centuries. Most of them abandoned their language for that of their conquerors only then to abandon that one for a third, if not a fourth.[20]

Notebook evidence is notoriously difficult to interpret, for many reasons. Not least, the nature of Joyce's notes, usually taken without any comment or contextual information, makes it impossible to know whether approval, disapproval or some entirely different mechanism is at work. At the very least, however, the notebooks confirm the importance of placing the *Wake* in a diversity of historical culture and, partly because of the many contemporary and European sources, greatly improve and problematize our sense of the cultural environment in which the *Wake* was written and which it addresses. The interest of the notebooks is only partly, then, that they help complete the picture of how the *Wake* was constructed. As we shall see, they also help us to position Joyce the intellectual and to develop responses to difficult matters, like the question of Joyce's 'politics', for example. Indeed, in the end they help us understand what the *Wake* actually is, what it comes out of but also what it writes to.

'In the beginning it came to pass' – What Happens(ed)?

In many ways the *Wake* sounds greatly familiar as a novel. Traditional storytelling is evoked from the first/last sentence. Scheherazade, teller of tales in *1001 Arabian Nights*, Hans Christian Anderson, Jacob and Wilheim Grimm are amongst those present in a construction of storyteller identities that lies behind much of the *Wake*'s framing. There is an obvious ambition, from whatever beginning one turns to, to set the scene, fix the time, establish the characters and tell the story – and there are a great many stories. One chapter, for example, 1.3, is structured almost entirely around a sequence concerning the fates of the citizens who eventually turn on HCE, including – A'Hara, Paul Horan, Sordid Sam, Langley, Father San Browne and Phislin Phil, the latter at one stage being 'asked by free boardschool shirkers in drenched overcoats overawall, Will, Conn and Otto, to tell them overagait, Vol, Pov and Dev, that fishabed ghoatstory of the haardly creditable edventyres of the Haberdasher, the two Curchies and the three Enkelchums in their Bearskin ghoats!' (*FW* 51.11–15).[21] Stories within stories are part of the familiar condition of the *Wake*, especially stories which attempt to arrive at origins. The first man; the first woman; the first copulation; building, city, flood and language – all are important reference points in the *Wake*, albeit points never reached.

Over and over the *Wake* invokes the conventions of storytelling, as in the opening to the story of Jarl van Hoother and the Prankquean – 'It was of a night, late, lang time agone, in an auldstane eld, when Adam was delvin and his madameen spinning watersilts' (*FW* 21.5–6). The frame that introduces one of many versions of HCE's crime in the park begins similarly 'They tell the story (an amalgam as absorbing as calzium chloereydes and hydrophobe sponges could make it) how one happygogusty Ides-of-April morning . . . he [HCE] met a cad with a pipe' (*FW* 35.1–11).[22] Resting points, end pieces, evoke the same traditions. These echo the sounds and rhythms of the conventional narratives that might be found in fairy tales, children's stories or other forms of popular narrative – the joke for instance. This, for example, concludes the story of 'Herr Betreffender' (*FW* 69.32), also known as 'Bully Acre' (*FW* 73.23), who at the end of 1.4 threatens HCE outside his pub 'from eleven thirty to two in the afternoon without even a luncheonette interval' (*FW* 70.33–4): 'And thus, with this rochelly exetur of Bully Acre, came to close that last stage in the siegings round our archicitadel which we would like to recall, if old Nestpor Alexis would wink the worth for us, as Bar-le Duc and Dog-an-Doras and Bangen-op-Zoom' (*FW* 73.23–7).[23]

The *Wake*, 'this scherzarade of one's thousand one nightinesses' (*FW* 51.4–5), also incorporates many stories outside its own through thousands of traces. Stories from the Bible, the Koran and the Book of the Dead, for example, are everywhere in the *Wake*. Narratives like Tristan and Isolde, Lewis Carroll's *Alice in Wonderland* (1865), Mark Twain's *Huckleberry Finn* (1884) or Sheridan Le Fanu's *The House by the Churchyard* (1863) are returned to repeatedly. Others, Walter Scott's *Rob Roy* (1817) or the Gertrude Page story *Paddy the Next Best Thing* (1916), have a more fleeting appearance.

Given all this activity around narrative, it is perhaps not surprising that readers have been tempted towards a summary of the *Wake*, just as they would be for any other novel, except that here, in face of the *Wake*'s astonishing linguistics, the imperative to establish some signposts towards narrative stability is particularly pressing. Many such summaries have been produced in the critical tradition – indeed, in the early years of *Wake* criticism synthesizing the narrative was high on the critical agenda, whole studies being devoted to not much more than reproducing a story of the *Wake*.[24] Now, however, we are much less concerned with narrative summary, partly because the critical frameworks have so changed but also because we have a narrative framework for the *Wake* which most would accept at some level – something like the following.

The *Wake* 'begins' (**pp 3–29**) with the death of a giant, a precursor, 'Bygmester Finnegan, of the Stuttering Hand' (*FW* 4.18). After some 'digressions', the corpse being admired at the wake starts to stir. The mourners pacify the sleeping giant, reassuring him that even in death he will be looked after with the Fenians bringing him gifts and sustenance, 'offering of the field' (see *FW* 25.1–5) such as 'hive, comb and earwax, the food for glory' (*FW* 25.6–7). Chapters 2 through 4 concern Finnegan's replacement/successor, the man 'ultimendly respunchable for the hubbub caused in Edenborough' (*FW* 29.35–6). Their focus is on 'the genesis of Harold or Humphrey Chimpden' (HCE) (*FW* 30.2–3), a figure especially associated in these early chapters with Anglo–Ireland and the Ascendancy, although his racial identity is by no means fixed. At 24.7–8, 'our ancestor most worshipful' has what appears to be a cod-African (or aboriginal?) identity as 'Unfru-Chikda-Uru-Wukru'; he is Gaelicised as 'Fionn Earwicker' (*FW* 108.21–2), although at his murder he becomes 'the unnamed non nonirishblooder' (*FW* 378.10–11). Hebraicised at 30.4, he is also subject to Germanicization at 532.6, for instance, when resurrected as 'Amtsadam . . . Eternest cittas, heil.' Most typically, however, his dimensions are Anglo–Saxon. He is a vassal elevated to the aristocracy as 'good Dook Umphrey' by the English king, but known 'to his cronies' everywhere by 'the nickname Here Comes Everybody' (*FW* 32.15–19).

Subsequent to this rise, rumours begin to spread about an ill-defined, or multiply-defined, crime(s) that HCE allegedly committed in Phoenix Park, observed by three soldiers. These rumours seem to be confirmed by HCE's highly defensive responses to the suspicious young man on the street who asks him the time in **I.2 (pp 32–47)**. From here on the rumours start to spread in earnest, culminating in the composition of 'The Ballad of Persse O'Reilly', a song demanding that the 'one time . . . King of the Castle' be sent off 'To the penal jail of Mountjoy!' (*FW* 45.7–10). **I.3 (pp 48–74)** opens with fog and the partial fading of both HCE and his accusers, although the gossip continues and the episode concludes with two conflicting stories, one where HCE is threatened by a man (the Cad reprieved) with a pistol, another where HCE is besieged at his home/pub by a man demanding drink after closing time and who shouts abuse at HCE. A fox chased by hounds, in **I.4 (pp 75–103)** Earwicker is traced to an underground retreat, and then tried in court by four judges, a jury and dozens of witnesses, some expert, some not – he appears to be prosecuted by one son (Shaun) and defended by the other (Shem). The evidence is unfathomable, and the judges fall to drinking and arguing about an obscure crime and a set of circumstances 'so very wrong long before when they were going on' (*FW* 96.8–9). By 'playing possum' in all this confusion, 'our hagious curious encestor bestly saved his brush' (*FW* 96.33–4), but the gossip and allegation continues and in **I.5 (pp 104–25)** attention turns to ALP's letter which seems to have a crucial bearing on the whole business of HCE's guilt/innocence. Instead of delivering the content, however, I.5 is taken up with a cod-scientific lecture which anthropologizes the letter as a 'proteiform graph' and a 'polyhedron of scripture' (*FW* 107.8), written in some distant past by 'naif alphabetters' (*FW* 107.8–9). Here the *Wake* becomes explicitly self-referential, with ALP's letter or litter taking on dimensions of the *Wake* itself where 'the traits featuring the *chiaroscuro* coalesce' (*FW* 107.29), a dynamic that continues in **I.6 (pp 126–68)**. This chapter functions as a kind of quiz – in a schoolroom-like environment, Shem quizzes Shaun. But equally this is a reader test involving our identification of the HCE identity in the response to the first question and ALP in the second – '2. Does your mutter know your mike?' (*FW* 139.15). Questions three and four both point to Dublin, with the fourth response divided into four, suggesting Mamalujo, or the four old men. Question five evokes the name 'Pore old Joe' or Sackerson, the Earwickers's man servant, and question six suggests Kate, their female servant. Seven involves the Murphies or the masses; eight the female Maggies who 'war loving, they love laughing, they laugh weeping' (*FW* 142.31–2) and nine ALP's (and Shem's) letter. Questions ten, eleven and twelve evoke Issy, Shaun and Shem respectively. If we recognize these references to the cardinal points of the *Wake*, we might be said to be making progress. In this sense, 1.6 is at much our test as Shaun's.

The conflict between Shem and Shaun, implied in the questioned/ questioner roles they adopt in 1.6, comes to the fore of **I.7 (pp 169–95)**, with Shaun this time taking the initiative, excoriating his brother as the despised other – the 'mental and moral defective' (*FW* 177.16) who writes with his own filth (see 183). With **I.8 (pp 196–216)** the gossipy narrative continues in newly explicit terms, now with two washer women washing HCE's clothes by the riverbank and taking particular interest in the narrative of ALP's rich sex life. She had, they say, 'aflewmen of her owen' (*FW* 202.5–6). There was 'Simba the Slayer' 'rubbing her up and smoothing her down' (*FW* 203.32, 34) and even before that the 'Two lads' who 'went through her . . . before she had a hint of a hair at her fanny to hide or a bossom to tempt a birch canoedler' (*FW* 204.5–9). Before that she was 'licked by a hound . . . while doing her pee' (*FW* 204.11–12).

II.1 (pp 219–59) is framed twice – as a play, *The Mime of Mick, Nick and the Maggies* (see *FW* 219.30–31) with all the Earwickers and their entourage playing parts, but with the central focus shifting to the conflict between Shem (Glugg) and Shaun (Chuff) and, in particular, their rivalry over the twenty-eight dancing girls (the Floras) and Issy (Izod). That competition is played out in the second frame which takes the form of a children's game, Angels and Devils, where the Devil player (Glugg) has to guess the colour of the Angels (here conflated with the colour of the Floras' underwear). Twice Glugg, the artist figure, guesses and twice he is wrong. The unimpressed girls turn their attention to Chuff, becoming his 'adorables' (*FW* 237.18) in an elevation that will continue from this point on until III.3. Glugg runs away in 'visible disgrace' (*FW* 227.23) to write *Ulysses*, 'his farced epistol to the hibruws' (*FW* 228.33–4), returning to fail yet again in his third and last guess.

Eventually the noise of the children's game disturbs HCE and the children are brought in to bed.

II.2 (pp 260–308), or Night Lessons, continues with the shift to the children and again focuses on the rivalry between brothers. Shem and Shaun (now named Dolph and Kev) prepare their lessons in a chapter that takes an academic form – a text with marginalia from Dolph and Dev and footnotes from Issy. The lessons begin with a version of theosophical philosophy and move to history, grammar and geometry where Dolph's facility puts Kev firmly in the shade. Appalled at the sight of his mother's 'muddy old triagonal delta . . . first of all usquiluteral triangles' (*FW* 297.24–7), Kev is brought to mock horror and fake panic. The chapter ends though with the three siblings in apparent harmony, or at least in concert as they send collective 'youlldied greedings' to their parents and all 'the old folkers below and beyant' (*FW* 308.17–19).

In contrast **II.3 (pp 309–82)** takes place in an adult masculine world, a public bar where men advanced in years tell stories and jokes and sing songs. The episode centres on the two stories told by the host (HCE). The first is ostensibly a story about the Norwegian sailor, a hunchback, who orders a made-to-measure suit. When the suit doesn't fit, the sailor refuses to pay. The tailor argues that it is the sailor's body that is out of shape and suggests he get a replacement. Alongside that, parable-like conflict between would-be husbands, fathers and daughters is registered. The second story invokes different kinds of masculinities. Buckley is a soldier in the Crimean War about to take a shot at a Russian General who takes that moment to defecate in a field. Moved by this human vulnerability, Buckley is unable to fire until, that is, the General wipes himself on a sod of turf, symbol of Ireland – at which point Buckley lets loose. That story moves into a more general sequence of guilt and confession which focuses on HCE's usurpation at the hands of his sons, especially Shaun. Eventually HCE calls time. His customers leave, reluctantly, cursing HCE as they go.

Book II concludes with a short Part **4 (pp 383–99)** in which the usurpation of HCE is completed and reformulated in terms of the Tristan and Isolde story. HCE as King Mark sleeps on while Shaun (as Tristan) sails off with his bride (Issy) 'kiddling and cuddling and bunnyhugging' (*FW* 384.20–1), being not just observed but acculturated through the frame of Mamaluju or the four annalists. These 'the big four, the four masterwaves of Erin' (*FW* 384.6) each in turn contribute to a new but at the same time very familiar historiography that begins 'on a lovely morning, after the universal flood, at about aleven thirty-two was it? (*FW* 388.11–13).

Book III continues the movement away from HCE towards Shaun – Joyce referred to the four sections in this part as the four watches of

Shaun (see *Letters* I, 224). In **III.1 (pp 403–28)** Shaun the post emerges as 'immense, topping swell for he was after having a great time of it' (*FW* 405.21–22). A 'walking saint' (*FW* 427.28), and at the head of a new republic, he deploys the story of the ant and the grasshopper to illustrate the virtues of his approach to life, his solid conformity and apparent stability. In response to questions about his brother, he reiterates the slanders of 1.7. Shaun ends III.1 in a barrel, with his undelivered letters, incomplete texts, floating down the Liffey (see *Letters* I, 214). **III.2 (pp 429–73)** continues with this elevation. Shaun presents himself before the rewards of his rise. The twenty-eight dancing girls and Issy are treated to a sermon, ostensibly about decent living according to conservative religious and social principles. Underneath the injunctions, however, there is the strong sense of a rising Don Juan, or Jaun as Shaun is now called, asserting his proprietorial rights over the young women of Ireland and being consumed by lust. The moral warnings ironically culminate in an uncontrolled outburst that imagines an incestuous orgy of 'reverse positions' – 'Lets have a fuchu all round, courting cousins! . . . Shuck her! Let him! What's he good for! Shuck her more!' (*FW* 466.4–16).

III.3 (pp 474–554) marks a further turning point, with Jaun (Yawn) becoming enlarged but at the same time utterly deflated as a vast baby in swaddling positioned somewhere near the centre of Ireland. Here he is subjected to the questioning of Mamalujo, now four republican senators, who turn events over and over seemingly to ascertain Yawn's true identity and status in the universe. The further motivation appears to be verification of his compliance with the historiographical, scientific and religious frameworks in which the four old men operate and from which they derive their authority. Yawn is invited to 'Name your historical grouns' (*FW* 477.35) and to confirm that he is 'in your fatherick, lonely one' (*FW* 478.28). He struggles to respond, but is confused ('I'm thinking to, thogged be thenked' – *FW* 487.7) and increasingly unable to satisfy their demands. His stories and explanations – about his family, historical events, the spirit world, the natural world and so on – become an 'Impassable tissue of improbable liyers' (*FW* 499.19), until at 532 the Yawn persona gives way to a resurrected HCE who proceeds to justify himself, or rather fails to justify himself, over thirty pages. During the course of this long monologue, HCE digs himself deeper, his crimes and misdemeanours becoming indistinguishable from his apparent achievements as a builder of cities and civilization. The son has become the dispossessed father, or, if we like, the usurper is put in his place by the return of the old king.

The sense of Shaun's rise being a temporary intervention, for some readers a dream within the wider dream of the *Wake*, seems supported by **III.4 (pp 555–90)**.[25] The *Wake* returns to night time at the

Earwickers' house, although the family is now renamed as the Porters. Issy, 'dadads lottiest daughterpearl' (*FW* 561.15), sleeps, dreaming of romance and lovers 'Of courts and with enticers' (*FW* 561.33). The twins Shaun and Shem (Kevin and Jerry) are also in bed with the 'audorable' Kevin being 'happily to sleep' (*FW* 562.33/24). Jerry, however, is 'a teething wretch', 'crying in his sleep' (*FW* 563.1–4) in a nightmare which features his father. Eventually ALP rises to comfort her distressed son. She returns to her room, where 'Albert', 'his goldwhite swaystick aloft ylifted' (*FW* 569.19), does his best to prove he can still sexually satisfy his laughing wife, now Victoria. They are watched by the four old men. The chapter ends with the three soldiers who similarly spied on HCE's misdemeanour in Phoenix Park attesting to HCE's status as 'our grainpopaw, Mister Beardall, an accompliced burgomaster, a great one among the very greatest' (*FW* 587.32–3) and marvelling at the depth of the fall which saw the collapse of his vast fortunes.

The final book, **book 4 (pp 593–628)**, has only one part. It begins with an invocation 'Calling all daynes to dawn' (*FW* 593.11) – to battle but also to resurrection (and insurrection) and renewal – quickly followed by an invitation to 'Pu Nuseht, lord of risings in the yonderworld' (*FW* 593.24) to 'speaketh'. The declaration that results, a hymn to a racial and historiographical return where 'european end meets Ind' (*FW* 598.15–16), is followed by two further stories. One is concerned with St Kevin the hermit of Glendalough, or, in Gaelic, Cóemgen, rendered as Coemghen (come again) in the *Wake*. The second, appropriately enough in this chapter of return and reruns, resurrects the Mutt and Jute encounter of I.1, with a meeting of Muta and Juva where invader meets native as St Patrick and the druid. The mysterious letter from ALP, which turns out to be hardly mysterious at all, is finally revealed at 615.12 and leads into the monologue that closes the book – ALP's death song as she flows out to the sea to the 'Finn, again' beginning with which she is joined (*FW* 628.14).

This, at some level, is what happens in the *Wake*. The account is able to take some measure of the *Wake*'s repetitions and ambiguities and also catches the importance of circularity in the *Wake*, implying Joyce's well-known deployment of Viconian cycles. This is the early Enlightenment world theory which divides human history into four periods – the divine age, the heroic age, the human age and the period of renewal – and which Joyce said was of structural as well as incidental importance to the *Wake* (see *Letters* I, 241), although with nothing like the force and highly-specified ingenuity that he insisted on the *Odyssey* as a framework for *Ulysses*.[26]

Nevertheless, this summary, like all others, is hugely reductive. It is, of course, greatly simplifying in terms of detail – the narrative above could be expanded many times over, although, it should be said, not completely rewritten so that it becomes, say, the story of a hunt for a great white whale. At the same time the summary misses the sheer extent of the slipperiness of things, the amalgamation of identities, for example, so that the story of HCE is somehow mixed up with the stories of Finn MacCool, Howth Head, Noah, Adam Kadmon, St Patrick, John Jameson, Arthur Guinness, St Peter, John Joyce, James Joyce, Roderick O'Connor, Henry VIII, Cromwell, Lewis Carroll, Mark of Cornwall, the Russian General, William I, William Gladstone, Prospero and so on – just as the story of ALP forms itself around such identities as Grace O'Malley, the Prankquean, Elizabeth I, Penelope, Molly Bloom, Nora Joyce, the river Liffey (and many other rivers), Eve and Mrs Noah.

Similar conflations are organized around space and time. The *Wake* is a place where a single paragraph can produce an 'amalgamation' of the Tudor court; nineteenth-century Fenians; vikings; 'Idahore shop-girls' (*FW* 504.22), along with old soldiers – 'killmaimthem pension-ers' – retired from service in the British empire (see *FW* 504.5 and the commentary on this passage below). Or it can conflate Middle Eastern Islam with Western Christianity; a twentieth-century luxury car (the Rolls Royce); Celtic monuments (at Carnac, Brittany); the modern press and legal institutions in classical Greece (see *FW* 4.14–36). None of which helps with the idea of narrative summary, indeed the *Wake* appears specifically designed to thoroughly undermine the very tradi-tions of storytelling that it evokes at every opportunity.

For all the awareness that the *Wake* is circular, such summaries as those given above also imagine a story retaining the dimensions of an unfolding and 'developing' narrative. In fact, the *Wake* is com-prised of endless twists and turns which make development let alone completion an impossible ambition. It is 'a meanderthalltale to unfurl' (*FW* 19.25–6) where 'every busy eerie whig' is just as likely to be 'a bit of a torytale to tell' (*FW* 20.23). The 'central' tale itself, the narra-tive of the Earwicker family – HCE, ALP, Shem/Shaun and Issy – is massively over-determined. Any 'truth' it might involve is indistin-guishable from the gossip, told over and over again, by members of the family, friends and enemies, and also by folklorists and other experts – people who knew and people who didn't. It evokes fear, hilarity, respect and disdain and at the same time is itself the subject of endless rumour. It generates multiple variations and is scrutinised in minute detail. Subjected to analysis (in I.5 for example), challenge, rectification and challenge again, it is minutely dissected and also cel-ebrated and turned into song (see I.2). It is also returned to endlessly throughout the *Wake*. One of the last chapters, III.3 for example, is essentially an interrogation of the stories of HCE and ALP and the fall of Finnegan in what turns out to be nowhere near the final attempt to get to the bottom of things.

Joyce fictionalizes not just this family tale and many others (including the tales of the meeting of Mutt and Jute; the Mookse and the Gripes; Buckley and the Russian General; the Norwegian sailor and the tailor and the fable of the Ant and the Grasshopper), but also the tale in terms of the cultural contexts that surround it, including the critical processes that annotate and explicate. One result is that the text appears to anticipate the Joyce industry in some ways, containing within itself echoes of the critical traditions that in reality would follow in the wake of the *Wake*. From producing epiphanies; short stories where little seems to happen in the way of 'go ahead plot'; impressionistic images of the artist at different stages of development and a huge one-day novel where story gives way to immediacy, Joyce in the *Wake* moves into a new and unique version of modernism which, far from being indifferent to story, is exhaustive in this respect. The *Wake* functions at narrative overdrive, where every possible dimension of story is activated – except completion of any kind. If at one level 'the tale rambles along' (*FW* 41.36; 42.1), it is just as typically unyielding to any forward motion or singularity. The 'Eyrawyggla saga . . . of poor Osti-Fosti' may be 'readable to int from and' (*FW* 48.16–19), but it is also astonishingly recalcitrant to what we normally understand as storytelling, not least because its language 'is nat language in any sinse of the world' (*FW* 83.12). Indeed it may be that 'from tubb to buttom', the *Wake* is 'all falsetissues, antilibellous and nonactionable and this applies to its whole wholume' (*FW* 48.17–20).

The idea of a key *Wake* narrative, then, may be functional for *Wake* readers but in constructing a singular structure all such accounts must be forced into resisting the way the *Wake* fundamentally works. However useful in mapping terms a synoptical account may be, it constitutes only a very partial initial opening up of the *Wake*, one that simplifies and operates at a cost in terms of resistance to how the *Wake* was designed and how it functions.

'I quizzed you a quid (with for what) and you went to the quod' – Meaning in the *Wake*

The appearance of reviews of *Work in Progess* produced at least one new critical cliché about Joyce's writing. To the charges that it was 'filthy' and self-indulgent a third was now typically added. It was, as many had always suspected, also completely meaningless. Mary Colum, an old friend of Joyce's and hardly unfavourably disposed to his work, initially asserted in the *New York Tribune* (1927) that no critic could conceivably allow *Work In Progress* into 'the domain of literature' (*CH*, 372) for this reason.[27]

For all these understandable complaints, repeated many times since, the *Wake* in fact makes an astonishing investment in cultures of rationality and processes of reasoning. It treats meaning very much as it does narrative. Just as it seems devoted to narrative procedures at every point, so critical examination, argument, controversy and apologetics are fundamental to the *Wake* – often linked to the idea of meeting, with meeting places and crossroads becoming centrally important sites. There are many such 'encounters' in the *Wake* – quite apart from HCE's fateful meeting with the cad and the central collision of the Mookse with the Gripes. The book is framed by the meeting of Mutt and Jute (figuring as a native/outsider; pagan/Christian; St Patrick/Bishop Berkeley) at 16–18, for example, which is revisited as a meeting of Muta and Java on 609–10. Each of these meetings, while being characterized by hilarious failures of understanding, nevertheless implies the dispersal of knowledge and subsequent processes of interpretation and interrogation.

It is partly against this context that the question seems so characteristic of the *Wake*, a narrative that often implies philosophical procedures, as in 'But in the pragma what formal cause made a smile of *that* to think?' (*FW* 56.31–2) and 'Isn't that effect?' (*FW* 322.26), and is frequently concerned with verification, authenticity – getting the facts right. Here, for example, the question concerns the facts of HCE's name ('nomen gentile' is latin for 'clan name') and thus his true place in 'anthropomorphic' ('andrewpaulmurphyc') chronologies (see *Annotations*, 31).

> – Comes the question are these the facts of his nominigentilisa-tion as recorded and accolated in both or either of the collateral andrewpaulmurphyc narratives. Are those their fata which we read in sibylline between the *fas* and its *nefas*? No dung on the road? And shall Nohomiah be our place like? Yea, Mulachy our kingable khan? We shall perhaps not so soon see. [28]
>
> (*FW* 31.33; 32.2)

There are many occasions when the narrative announces uncertainties – Herwho?' (*FW* 84.27); 'Why?' (*FW* 118.17); 'So?' (*FW* 126.1); 'Who? Anna Livia?' (*FW* 198.10); 'Which was said by whem to whom?' (*FW* 493.16) – but it appears to maintain a fundamental epistemological faith to the extent that asking continues throughout and, indeed, drives the *Wake* at fundamental levels.

Some questions seem to move the narrative forward, as in the first question raised in the *Wake*, concerned with the causes of Finnegan's fall from his ladder – 'What then agentlike brought about that tragoady thundersday this municipal sin business? (*FW* 5.13–14). Others reflect back on the authorship of the *Wake* ('So why, pray, sign anything as long as every word, letter, penstroke, paperspace is a perfect signature of its own? – *FW* 115.6–8) and the condition of its textuality. As Shaun is asked in III.3, 'Are we speachin d'anglas landadge or are you sprakin sea Djoytsch?' (*FW* 485.12–13) or, indeed, some other language, Hindi perhaps ('Cha kai rotty kai makkar, sahib?' – *FW* 54.12–13); Swedish ('Huru more Nee, minny frckans?' – *FW* 54.10–11) or Danish ('Hwoorledes har Dee det?' – *FW* 54.11).[29] Such questions often turn outwards as well as inwards, where the address is specifically to the reader attempting to make sense of the *Wake* world. 'So This Is Dyoublong?' (*FW* 13.4), the narrator asks at an early stage. 'Can you rede . . . its world ? It is the same told of all. Many. Miscegenations on miscegenations' (*FW* 18.18–20); 'You is feeling like you was lost in the bush, boy?' (*FW* 112.3); 'So what are you going to do about it?' (*FW* 117.8–9).

Typically in Joyce criticism it is the *Wake*'s strangeness that is seen as raising questions, but the *Wake* also literally asks a lot of questions. To put it another way, it has a questioning nature and carries a drive for epistemological order. It is no accident, then, that so much of this book is built around sites of knowledge acquisition, preservation and performance. I.1, for example, has a generally pedagogic frame. It attempts to articulate a history of events and includes a chronology (see *FW* 13–14). At one point it is positioned from within a 'museyroom' with the narrator becoming a tour guide. I.4, centred around a courtroom scene, involves forensic questioning, expert testimony and the maintenance of a demeanour appropriate to the serious business of truth building – thus the 'eye, ear, nose and throat witness' is 'sullenly cautioned against yawning while being grilled' (*FW* 86.32; 87.1). I.5 similarly concerns an expert examination of evidence, the letter which the 'hardily curiosing entomophilust' believes would once have been mistaken for the work of 'a purely deliquescent recidivist, possibly ambidextrous, snubnosed probably' (*FW* 107.10–13). I.6, as we have seen, works like an examination or quiz-game, and the responses seem to have encyclopaedic culture at their disposal, albeit in a strangely conflated form. Answering question one, the respondent describes HCE, 'a Colussus among cabbages', as 'Olaph the Oxman, Thorker the Tourable; you feel he is Vespasian, yet you think of him as Aurelius; whugamore, tradertroy, socianist, commoniser . . . Boomaport, Walleslee, Ubermeerschall, Blowcher and Supercharger, Monsieur Ducrow, Mister Mudson, master gardiner' (*FW* 132.17; 133.23).[30]

This kind of framing continues into Books II and III, shaping the conflict between Shem and Shaun and also the travels of Mamalujo

which, however voyeuristic they become in II.4, are ostensibly epistemological and linked to the *Annals of the Four Masters*, the medieval
chronicle which narrates Irish history from the flood to A.D. 1616. II.1
is structured around an extended game of riddling, with Shaun strug-
gling to find the correct answer which takes the form of a colour. Here
his guess is that the colour to be divined is yellow: '–Haps thee jao-
neofergs?/ –Nao./ –Haps thee mayjaunties?/ –Naohao./ Haps thee per
causes nunsibellies?/–Naohaohao (*FW* 233.21–6).[31] II.2, the classroom
episode, invokes pedagogic procedure and schoolboy engagement with
the classroom – 'Problem ye ferst, construct ann aquilittoral dryankle
Probe loom! . . . Can you nei do her, numb? asks Dolph, suspecting the
answer know. Oikkont, ken you ninny? asks Kev, expecting the answer
guess' (*FW* 286.19–28). III.2 performs like a homily, sermon or instruc-
tion book for manners and behaviour ('Sister dearest, Jaun delivered
himself with express cordiality, marked by clearance of diction and general delivery' – *FW* 431.21–2) and III.3 is an extended interrogation,
sometimes conducted with dark energy where Yawn is put under considerable duress to explain things clearly. His questioners are the 'four
claymen' who 'clomb together to hold their sworn starchamber quiry on
him. For he was ever their quarrel' (*FW* 475.18–19). This reference to a
judiciary (the Star Chamber) that, especially under the reigns of James
I and Charles II, became a byword for injustice and persecution, establishes a keynote to the interrogative nature of the episode.

Above all throughout the *Wake* there is a fascination with particular
essential and essentialist questions, thus the obsession with genealogy
and lineage, which derives from the fundamental concern with origins
to produce a 'book of breedings' (*FW* 410.1–2) and 'fornicolopulation'
(*FW* 557.17). At the beginning of I:2, for example, a broadly ethnographic
discourse tries to trace the origins of HCE's name 'in the presurnames
prodromarith period' and insists that there will be a 'discarding once
for all those theories from older sources which would link him back
with such pivotal ancestors as the Glues, the Gravys, the Northeasts,
the Ankers and the Earwickers' (*FW* 30.3–7). There is a closely associated frame of reference around race identity and classification and the
attempt to sort out the ethnographical confusions of such bizarre designations as 'Hispano-Cathayan-Euxine, Castilian-Emeratic-Hebridian,
Espanol-Cymric-Helleniky' (*FW* 263.13–15). That particular conun-
drum revolves around questions of race dispersal, formulated in part by
the many references to Noah and his sons, the patriarchal genealogy of
Judaeo–Christian myths. With HCE being associated with Noah, Shaun
is strongly linked to Japhet, by tradition the forefather of white Europe.
Shem is a composite of both Shem and Ham (see 'Mr Himmyshimmy' at
FW 173.27). The latter figure, subject of a curse, typically featured as the

progenitor of the 'black race'. In the *Wake* 'Sham' is aligned with a range of outcast racial configurations (including Irish), most aggressively so in 1:7 where 'this disinterestingly low human type' (*FW* 179.12–13) is racialized by his 'white' brother as 'a nogger amongst the blankards of this dastard century' (*FW* 188.13–14).

At the same time, Western challenges to this tradition, fundamentally shaped by Aryanism, are also incorporated into the *Wake* with allusions to Childeric, for example – reputed to have started the Germanic diasporas; Magog, the mythical son of Japhet and involved in so many European origin myths, including British ones; Olaf, founder of Dublin; Horsa and Hengest, legendary founders of the Anglo–Saxon race in England; 'Hebear and Hairyman' (Heber and Heremon, mythical fathers of the Irish race – *FW* 14.35–6) and so on. Firmly fixed 'Inn] the Byggning' (*FW* 17.22), at the first pub, 'here where race began' (*FW* 80.16)[32] in the 'garden of Erin' (*FW* 203.1) the *Wake* and its people are drawn to such ancestral schemas and driven by the search for origins.

The great range of potential ur-stories means that no single version has any more, or less, reliability than any other, indeed the *Wake* is an astonishing example of the entanglement of histories, again often racialised as in the composite – a 'cellelleneteutoslavzendlatinsoundscript' (*FW* 219.17) Nevertheless Shaun, as Yawn in III.3, appears to be asked throw light on the question of origins.

> – Remounting aliftle towards the ouragan of spaces. Just how grand in cardinal rounders is this preeminent giant, sir Arber? Your bard's highview, avis on valley! I would like to hear you burble to us in strict conclave, purpurando, and without too much italiote interfairance, what you know *in petto* about our sovereign beingstalk, Tonans Tomazeus. *O dite*!
>
> (*FW* 504.14–19)

Except, of course, that the question is actually far from exact. Behind the phrase 'ouragan of spaces' is the shadow of Darwin and the *Origin of the Species*, but it is the distortion, not our 'translation', that is on the page. What is invested in the 'disguise'? And why, if a scientific order is being invoked here, does that system of meaning become mixed with the world of myth and fairy tale suggested by the reference to the Jack and beanstalk story ('our sovereign beingstalk') and the mythological (Zeus the Thunderer lies behind 'Tonans Tomazeus' – see *Annotations*, 504)? The religious frame of reference only confuses things further. Along with references to science, myth and fairytale, the question invokes the scrutiny of conservative religious authority, implied initially in the references to the Vatican and the conclave of cardinals – in *Annotations*

Roland McHugh gives for 'purpurando' 'purpurandus', Vatican slang for 'one fit to be purpled, i.e. made a cardinal' (*Annotations*, 504). The question, then, is obscure as most questions are in the *Wake*, and the motives of the questioner impossible to unpick. Is he inviting confidence, speaking to an equal or seeking to trip up? For all the apparent desire to know, incompatible systems of thinking about the world jostle together in an astonishing clatter in the very framing of this enquiry. Yawn's response does little to clear things up.

> – Corcor Andy, *Udi, Udite*! Your Ominence, Your Imminence and delicted fraternitrees! There's tuodore queensmaids and Idahore shopgirls and they woody babies growing upon her and bird flamingans sweenyswinging fuglewards on the tipmast and Orania epples playing hopptociel bommptaterre and Tyburn fenians snoring in his quickenbole and crossbones strewing its holy floor and culprines of Erasmus Smith's burstall boys with their underhand leadpencils climbing to her crotch for the origin of spices and charlotte darlings with silk blue askmes chattering in dissent to them, gibbonses and gobbenses, guelfing and ghiberring proferring praydews to their anatolies and blighting findblasts on their catastripes and the killmaimthem pensioners chucking overthrown milestones up to her to fall her cranberries and her pommes annettes for their unnatural refection and handpainted hoydens plucking husbands of him and cock robins muchmore hatching most out of his missado eggdrazzles for him, the sun and moon pegging honeysuckle and white heather down and timtits tapping resin there and tomahawks watching tar elsewhere, creature of the wold approaching him, hollow mid ivy, for to claw and rub, hermits of the desert barking their infernal shins over her triliteral roots and his acorns and pinecorns shooting wide all sides out of him, plantitude outsends of plenty to thousands, after the truants of the utmostfear and her downslyder in that snakedst-tu-naughsy whimmering woman't seeleib such a fashionaping sathinous dress out of that exquisitive creation and her leaves, my darling dearest, sinsinsinning since the night of time and each and all of their branches meeting and shaking twisty hands all over again in their new world through the germination of its gemination from Ond's outset till Odd's end. And encircle him circuly. Evovae!

(*FW* 504.20–505.13)

Yawn's account of the tree of life or the tree of man leading back to our original ancestor is a carnivalesque articulation where the genealogical diagrammatic is brought to life, sexualized and conflated with early myths, so that it figures as Yggdrasil, as well as the tree of Eden and the hangman's tree (see *Annotations*, 504). Far from configuring human history according to Christian revelation, Aryanist historiography or an evolving Darwinist order – all implied in Yawn's account –[33] the tree schema is transformed into a strange confabulation which has no place at all for linearity or progressivism. Shopgirls mix with 'queenmaids'; criminalized Fenians; Eliot's massman 'Sweeney'; borstal boys and monkeys. 'Each and all' of the trees branches are 'meeting and shaking twisty hands' in the 'melting pot' of the New World. The tree itself is sexualized from the beginning where 'burstall boys with their underhand lead pencils' climb to the tree's 'crotch' to the wild culmination which involves an Issy-like girl-woman (as Eve) undressing herself from 'such a sathinous dress'. Here 'sinsinsinning' becomes both the cause of the Fall and the relish of Yawn's account. Thus the last word of this reply evokes 'evolution', but of a totally compromised kind. The allusion to 'Evoe', a cry of the Bacchantes (see *Annotations*, 505), imagines a wild, raucous kind of dynamic and a wanton world, a long way from both the sombre origins and destinies of Christian eschatology and the abstract mechanisms of Darwinism.

The passage, then, seems organized around opposing accounts of the world, secular versus religious and confabulations of race origins, but it points to other kinds of disagreement and disorder too – within the State and religious systems, between God and Satan, the Guelphs and Ghibellines, warring political factions in Dante, ('guelfing and ghiberring', see *Annotations*, 504) and so on – here order and linearity become entwined with, or thwarted by, chaos and conflict, a reasonable metaphor for the *Wake* as a whole.

But even this reading of epistemological disorder in the passage constitutes a considerable smoothing out of things as they are in the *Wake*. Why, for example, is there the reference to round and cardinal numbers at line 504.15? Why does interference become 'interfairance' at 18? What is the point of the reference to Greek settlers living in Italy in 'italiote' (18)? (see *Annotations*, 504). Does the word connect with Yawn addressing himself with strange familiarity to 'Andy' in his response, which might suggest St Andrew patron saint of Greece? Or is that a reach to far?

There are further puzzles. A reference to Erasmus Darwin might be expected. Erasmus, related to Charles Darwin, was himself a physician and natural philosopher who famously wrote poems about evolutionary processes. But why is that expectancy compromised in favour of the allusion to Eramus *Smith* (at 504.26)? This was the merchant adventurer who received huge Irish estates under the Cromwellian settlement, and who, in 1657 endowed grammar schools in Ireland for the exclusive education of Protestant children. As these and many other ambiguities and uncertainties indicate, the practice of critical 'translation', however sensitive to ambiguity, always reaches its limits in a destabilization specifically conditioned by the text as a result of the seemingly bottomless way in which Joyce gets allusiveness into his writing.[34] Or, to put it another way, the *Wake* may be, as is often pointed out, the exegete's dream text, but it is also his nightmare because it knows no limits and is so consistently and purposely disruptive of the idea of definitive interpretation.

Just as the *Wake* is a book that invests in storytelling, so it is a book that appears to want to establish meaning and to get to the truth. But just as its narrative is subject to the most severe disruptions and dislocations, so is its drive towards meaning. As virtually any phrase, sentence, paragraph or page will show, the capacity of the *Wake* for meaning is constantly under siege, at every level from the single word, to the sentence, passage, page, episode, and, indeed, the book. It is not that the book has no meaning, or that it produces from its bizarre amalgamations some version of superior meaning. The typical condition of the *Wake* is rather that it has over meaning, too many competing possibilities which run entirely counter to expectations raised by the will to knowledge, equally so characteristic of the *Wake*.

A Note on Conceptual Readings

This condition of the *Wake* text raises fundamental problems for critical exegesis. The *Wake* literally cries out for translation, but is entirely devoted to resistance. How to explain the meaning of a text that complicates meaning on such a spectacular scale? That difficulty surrounds meanings of individual words or passages in the *Wake*, but has an even deeper impact on attempts to read the *Wake* as a conceptual whole. In his 2007 book *Lots of Fun at Finnegans Wake: Unravelling Universals*, Finn Fordham draws up a list of some of the astonishing suggestions that have been thrown up in this respect. The 'reel of descriptions' with which Fordham opens his study includes the *Wake* as –

> a gigantic epiphany of mankind; an ark to all contain all human myths and types; a chaosmos of Alle; a polyhedron of scripture; a meandethalltale; thisnonday diary, this allnight's newseryreel; one of the boldest books every written; one of the most entertaining books ever written; one of the greatest works of twentieth-century architecture; nothing short of divine wisdom or a new cure for the clapp can be worth all [its] circumambient

peripherization; enormous, mad unreadable; a cold pudding of a book; a Wholesale Safety Pun factory; a dull mass of phony folk lore; a *divertissement philologique* ...

And so on. Of course, a good number of these descriptors are jokes that the *Wake* makes at its own expense; others are mischievous dismissals from the outside; some are vague and general back-of-the-dust-jacket observations ranging from the syrupy – the loathsome idea of the *Wake* as 'an Irish word ballet' for instance – to the frankly mad, like the notion of the *Wake* as 'a little Negro dance'. Others, however, belong to full-blown critical exegesis.[35] Francis Bolderoff's 1959 account, for example, *Reading Finnegans Wake*, rests on the idea that Joyce's book was composed in a secret language 'established a thousand years before in Ireland'.[36]

Not all these unfortunate attempts to so formulate the *Wake* belong to some outdated, innocent age of criticism. More recent, subtle and generally convincing accounts can easily fall into the same totalizing trap. What real evidence is there to sustain the view quite central to Thomas Hofheinz's postcolonial study, *Joyce and the Invention of History* (1985), that the *Wake* can be reconvened as the dream of a race stereotype, a drunken Irishman– 'a twentieth-century male subject disintegrating amidst its own dream, reflecting the fragmentation of Irish history in the neural trauma of alcoholic sleep'?[37]

It is not only the particulars of Hofheinz's account that are so problematic here. The general and much more mainstream concept of the *Wake* as a 'sleep story' or 'a protracted nightmare' is no less subject to the *Wake*'s systematic and stubborn 'openness'.[38] As long ago as 1989, Derek Attridge's seminal essay 'Finnegans Awake: The Dream of Interpretation' cast doubt on a critical tradition dominated by the idea of the *Wake* as a dream, in part through the strategy of tracing the idea to its rather humble and apparently singular origins. 'In the absence of evidence from any other source', Attridge concluded, 'one has to assume that the idea of the single dreamer's single dream, and the location of the whole book in one sleeping head in Chapelizod, is an invention of [Edmund] Wilson's dating from 1929.'[39]

More substantially, Attridge illustrated how the 'undecidable polysemic richness of the *Wake*' extended to its own self-image. The *Wake* might indeed see itself on occasion as a dream, although with nothing like the consistency that some critics maintained. But why should that one reference point be privileged over all the other possibilities available? The *Wake* also sees itself in terms of 'the letter, the manifesto, the midden, the illuminated page, the photograph, the ballad, the children's game, the television programme, the riddle, the radio broadcast, the bedtime story, the geometrical theorem, the anecdote, the quiz show, the lecture, the homily, the mailbag [. . .] the list could go on as long as the longest list in *Finnegans Wake*' and would include the idea of the *Wake* as novel.[40]

One suspects that Attridge was right in his general conclusion, that the longevity of the *Wake* as dream idea reflected more the necessity for a strategy in which what he termed 'conventional' criticism – here meaning criticism outside the deconstruction discourse – could achieve some kind of grip on the *Wake*, rather than any real condition of the text itself. As Attridge put it:

> While it is true that that one can find in the *Wake* equivalents of the processes of symbolization, condensation, and displacement identified by Freud in the dreamwork that turns latent into manifest content, and that Freud on occasion used puns and portmanteaux in his practice of dream-interpretation, no one has attested a real dream that uses these processes so richly and relentlessly. Freud's own concept of 'secondary revision' posits a narrativizing and character-constructing agency that produces something much closer to the traditional story than anything in *Finnegans Wake*.[41]

Whatever and for all Attridge's objections, the idea of the dreamwork *Wake* continues to make itself heard. Ignoring the criticisms – and deconstructive culture in its entirety – Philip Kitcher has produced in *Joyce's Kaleidoscope: An Invitation to Finnegans Wake* (2008) an account that restores a full, unreconstructed version to favour. He presents the *Wake* as the work of a singular dreaming subject, 'a set of fluid stories for the probing and exploration of questions that are hard – unbearably hard – to face directly'. 'If', Kitcher argues, 'we suppose that there is an enduring collection of urges, desires, and hopes, anxieties, fears and uncertainties, which are constitutive of the subject to whom this kaleidoscope is presented . . . then our principal interpretative project will consist in trying to discover the nature of this underlying psychological condition'.[42] In other words reading becomes analogous to the analytic process. The fact that such accounts of the *Wake* still find publishers, and apparently readers, is testimony to the long-standing need to reconcile the *Wake* to a recognizable framework of meaning, an episteme of some sort. If *only* the *Wake* could become organized around the centralized consciousness of an unconscious dreamer, a fundamental order would be restored alongside apparent chaos. Here the 'obscurity' of the *Wake* would not only become necessary and functional, but also, and despite Attridge's objections, significantly representational. As John Bishop put it in his 1986 account, 'if one operates on the premise that

Finnegans Wake reconstructs the night, the first preoccupation to abandon wholesale is that it ought to read anything at all like narrative or make sense as a continuous whole'.[43]

For all the great list of suggestions with which Fordham opens his account of the *Wake*, if we dispense with the totalizing dreamwork are we left with much of any substance by way of explanation – apart from the prospect of taking the complexity and obscurity *Wake* at its face value? Here meaning remains genuinely compromised, not just incapable of 'translation' but of resolving itself into any order – narrational, epistemological, teleological or whatever. The *Wake*, so much devoted to connecting things up, thus becomes a vast undoing of things. What would that signify for reading the *Wake*?

CHAPTER 6

The *Wake* and the 1920s and 1930s

The terms in which Joyce's fictions engage with the modern world are highly contestable, as we have seen, but no one seriously doubts that these texts do both reflect and address contemporaneity. The problem which affects the *Wake* much more so than any of the pre-*Wake* fictions, however, is that here the representational basis fundamental to the earlier fictions no longer exists in the same way. Evidencing a critical view, never easy for any Joyce text, now becomes extremely problematic indeed. The peculiar linguistic world of the *Wake* means that all and any explanations can usually be substantiated in some way. Equally, all and any can be wrecked. There is potential here for the *Wake* to be entirely relevant to modernity in some broad sense; equally, and at the same time, it might be constructed as completely self-contained, a vast 'game' or, as we have seen, more typically, as a 'machine'.

This ambiguity in respect of meaning and the associated radical withdrawal from any conventional mode of representational performance is not simply an abstract 'condition' of the *Wake* text. It is, rather, a strategy deployed, a specific working, which is calculated and precisely designed. On any level, from the single word to the whole book, meaning is specifically manipulated to be subverted by other meaning(s). Even in this highly self-referential linguistic world, there is a sense in which the presence of the real world is substantial then, if only as the mirror image which makes the *Wake* possible. The joke of the inability to produce clarity is transparent inasmuch as we are familiar with the forms of order to which the *Wake* writes. Put broadly, we laugh at the *Wake*'s endless attempts to tell stories because we know what a 'real' story should be like. The *Wake*'s attempt to construct patriarchal family at the centre of its world through the wildly dysfunctional Earwickers is hilarious because behind it are all the stereotypes of the 'sacramental family' so fundamental to cultures around the world. The *Wake*'s reputation for being a dark book of the night then, is misleading, not least because its configuration of chaos is a comedy sustained by the reverse image that informs it and which it 'fails', over and over, to reproduce. The strangeness of the *Wake*, far from representing a tragic collapse under a bleak universe, becomes a comic reaching and overreaching after a stability that we usually take for granted – the structures of meaning and terms of reference that at the highest level figure as the organizing principles of our reality.

Such a positioning produces a paradox that is central to the way the *Wake* operates – its failures of meaning are functional because of their relationship with meaning. One way of developing an understanding of this characteristic is through the *Wake's* relationship with the *Encyclopaedia Britannica* in its eleventh edition, not because this volume is somehow 'key' to any Wakean 'metameaning' but because in terms of its cultural ambition and the characteristically modern approach it takes to a universal and democratizing epistemology, the *Encyclopaedia Britannica* stands at the antithesis of the *Wake*. It is, of course, only one of a large number of texts with which the *Wake* is intertextual, but it has a particular significance precisely because it is so centralized on epistemological issues raised by and in the *Wake*. Its status here is as the text that above all achieves where the *Wake* 'fails'; it performs in ways the *Wake* simply cannot. For this reason it plays a precise part in framing what it is that the *Wake* gets at as it works off the knowledge the world claims to have of itself. The suggestion, it should be clear, is not that the *Wake* is a satirical version of the *Encyclopaedia Britannica*, but, rather, that set against the *Encyclopaedia Britannica* the satirical direction of the *Wake* becomes focused in particular and highly suggestive ways.

'In the search for love of knowledge through the comprehension of the unity in altruism through stupefaction' – *Finnegans Wake/Encyclopaedia Britannica*

Joyce used several encyclopaedias in the making of the *Wake* but it has long been known that he had a special relationship with the *Encyclopaedia Britannica*, 11th edition. Ready to hand and inexhaustible, it seems to have been particularly associated with the collaborative *Wake* where friends and family were inveigled into *Wake* composition, partly as a result of Joyce's eye problems which meant that at various stages he needed assistance but also because the idea of the *Wake* being in some sense the work of a collective appealed to Joyce. The Ellmann account has Stuart Gilbert and Helen Fleischman reading entries from a list of 30 cities,

> among them New York, Vienna, Budapest, Rio de Janeiro, Amsterdam and Copenhagen . . . At the names of streets,

buildings, parks and city-founders they paused to give Joyce time to think whether they could be brought by pun into his work. So Amsterdam became Amtsadam, references to Adam being appropriate to the universal man and Slottsgarten in Oslo became Slutsgarten to suit the gartered girls peeped on by Earwicker in the park'

(JJ, 628)

Such a practice was confirmed and extended with the publication of *Reflections on James Joyce: Stuart Gilbert's Paris Journal* (1993). Gilbert noted an occasion when five volumes of the *Encyclopaedia Britannica* were spread out on Joyce's sofa and wrote about the involvement of himself, Helen Fleischman, Padriac Colum and Paul Léon in the process of taking notes from them for later use in the *Wake*. He also suggests that words and phrases were selected by Joyce in terms of the potential for punning although it is now clear that in fact punning on the names of these parks, rivers, streets and so on was relatively rare in the notebooks.[1] There are some wild distortions that go well beyond punning but, as Geert Lernout points out, 'most of the time the names are transcribed literally' (*NBB*, VI.B.29, 5).

In his early study of the *Wake* and intertextuality, Atherton also recognized that *EB* 11 was of significance, claiming that Joyce worked from the articles 'Polar Exploration', 'Wax Figures' and 'The Kabballah' and using *EB* 11 to deflate some of the more pious conceptions of the range and depth of Joyce's knowledge. Atherton suggested, for example, that 'everything he [Joyce] uses in *Finnegans Wake* about the Cabbala seemed to be contained in the article on that subject in the eleventh edition of the *Encyclopaedia Britannica*,' although he gave no evidence for this view.[2]

In the unlikely event of there being a definitive account of the extent of Joyce's usage of *EB* 11 in the *Wake*, however, it is certain that the handful of articles identified by Atherton as being 'incorporated' will rise dramatically. Quite apart from the 30 odd cities – Prague, Stockholm, Tokyo, St Petersburg, Delhi, Edinburgh, London, Paris, Washington and so on – famously built into the 'Haveth Childers Everywhere' section (*FW* 532.44), there are less concentrated usages scattered throughout. A full exposition of the relationship between the *Wake* and *EB* 11 would involve numerous *EB* articles, many of them intersecting with the *Wake* at very suggestive points, with emblems and ideas that typify the *Wake* in various ways. Certainly notebook research, central to the identification of precise *EB* 11 usage in the *Wake*, has established that Joyce took notes from such *EB* articles as 'Herder', 'Geography', 'Ireland', 'Ramadan' 'Orkney Islands', 'River Brethren', 'Wales', 'River Engineering',

'Roman Law' and 'Rumania'. Thus in VI.B.24 at pages 209–16 a number of notes regarding Islam were taken, one sequence of which includes the words, 'privilege', 'sanctuary', 'caliphate', 'ha'jj' and 'Ka'ba'. This list of words appears in virtually the same order in the *EB* 11 article 'Mecca' (*EB* 11, 8: 950c/d), although the sequence does not appear in that order in the *Wake* itself and, indeed, was not harvested for *Wake* usage.

Other than precise identification in the notebooks, there are good reasons to believe that articles such as those on 'Funeral Rites', 'Ghazi', 'Giaour', 'Hegesippus', 'Heraldry', 'Koran', 'Mahomet', 'Mahommedan Religion', 'Nap', 'Napoleon', 'Orkney Islands', 'Pistol', 'Ulema', 'Wapentake', 'Waterloo Campaign', 'Zouave' and many more besides, also helped shape the *Wake*. Here in addition to precise verbal echoes, there may be relationships of style, tone, structure and even rhythm. Mistress Kate's tour around the 'museyroom' in I.i, for instance, utilizes many details from the *EB* article on the Waterloo Campaign (*EB* 11, 28: 371–81). 'Inimyskilling inglis' (*FW* 8.23), a reference to the Royal Iniskilling Fusiliers at Waterloo, draws on the *EB*'s comment: 'so desperate was the fighting that some 45,000 killed and wounded lay on an area of roughly 3 sq. m. At one point on the plateau 'the 27th (Iniskillings) were lying literally dead in square' (*EB* 11, 28: 381b). The article also has a reference to Wellington and Blucher meeting at 'La Belle Alliance' (*EB* 11, 28: 381b), echoed at *FW* 7.33 in 'this belles' alliance'. Joyce's references to Napoleon's General Gronchy (see *FW* 8.22) and to Blucher (*FW* 9.4) are broad enough but may similarly implicate the *EB* article. The most functional piece of intertextuality, however, may well consist not in verbal echoes of this kind but rather in the breathless rhythm of Kate Strong's tour of the 'museyroom'. This seems to get picked up from an excited narrative speed deployed in the 'Waterloo Campaign' article, a speed quite at odds with the careful and conservative restraint more typical of the *EB*.

More than all that, however, there is an overarching relationship here that derives from the particular status held by the *Encyclopaedia Britannica*. The first edition of the latter was produced by 'a Society of Gentlemen in Scotland' between 1768 and 1771. Based in part on principles developed by Dennis de Coetlogon, it was both a quintessential product of the Enlightenment and a hugely authoritative statement about Britain's status in the world. The 11th edition, from which Joyce worked, describes how the project was designed as a 'digest of general information', its purpose being nothing less than to 'give reasoned discussion on all great questions of practical and speculative interest' (*EB* 11, 1: vii). The *Wake*, positioned very differently at the tail end of the modern, is far from a digest and it reflects back on the encyclopaedic tradition in fascinating ways. To put it simply, *Finnegans*

Wake is a text that has apparently swallowed or 'digested' vast amounts of information only to return it in ways that seem contrary to reasoned discussion. From this perspective *The Encyclopaedia Britannica*, dedicated in its 11th edition 'by permission to His Majesty King George the Fifth King of Great Britain and Ireland and of the British Dominions Beyond the Seas Emperor of India and to William Taft President of the United States of America' (*EB* 11, 1: x), becomes exactly what the *Wake* is not in almost all respects. Both, it could be argued, are instruments 'of culture of world-wide influence' but Joyce's senses of instrumentality and culture are quite at odds with what the editors of the *Encyclopaedia* have in mind. Their goal is to make available to the public 'all extant knowledge' as it is discovered by the 'civilized world'. The ambition is educative, to produce 'a trustworthy guide to sound learning', but also celebratory. Above all the *Encyclopaedia Britannica* is testimony to the awesome power of the Western intellectual tradition, to its authority and universality. The editors have aimed for traditional order, of course, but also new levels of uniformity in construction. Dispensing with 'the old-fashioned plan of regarding each volume as a separate unit' they instead arrange their 'material so as to give an organic unity to the whole work' placing 'all the various subjects under their natural headings, in the form which experience has shown to be the most convenient for a work of universal reference' (*EB* 11, 1: vii–x).

It is hard to imagine anything more removed from the *Wake* project. Far from maintaining good relations with the empire and the wider 'English speaking world', the *Wake* undermines the very idea of English speaking. As opposed to formulating knowledge as an alphabetical and progressive coherency, the *Wake*, as we have seen, conflates, disintegrates and constitutes an astonishing refutation of any kind of epistemological order. Equally it refuses hierarchy, centricism and progressivism and seems specifically designed, not to extend knowledge to the ignorant but, rather, to render the idea of knowledge infuriatingly impossible. At some level the whole *Wake* enterprise – its language strategies, its subversion of narrative, character, structure and so on – collaborate in this dramatic enterprise, and so does the detail of Joyce's working of *EB* 11 and the individual encyclopedic unit, the article. Here in these local specifics are the signs of what many Wakeans now understand as Joyce's central engagement with modern epistemologies, with modern rationalism and universalism.

In the *Wake*, as in sections of *Ulysses*, interference with the encyclopedist traditions is in part a wicked mocking of second-rate intellectualism, but, more than that, it often operates at the fragile edges of epistemology where old knowledge becomes undermined not just by better science but by the internal contradictions collapsing 'knowledge' into crude ideology. At *FW* 1. v. for example, Shaun's assault on Shem involves a comic interference with the 'science' of craniometry, 'where the skulls of the higher and lower races are compared' and 'various sub-racial types such as the dark and fair Europeans are brought together for the purposes of comparison and contrast' (*EB* 11, 7: 372d–73a). Later at *FW* 422 in a comic backwoodsman stereotype, skull size is associated with still keeping. Shem has 'a lowsense for the production of consumption and dalickey cyphalos on his brach premises where he can purge his contempt and dejeunerate into a skillyton' (*FW* 422.6–9). The precise reference here is to Anders Retzius's 'cephalic' (with a play in Joyce's version on 'syphillis') or breadth index which measured the greatest width of a skull expressed as a percentage of the greatest length.[3] Shem appears to his brother to be 'Negroid', or 'dolichocephalic' ('dalicky'), as well as 'Samoyed' or 'brachycephalic'. The cephalic index of the former, as *EB* 11 tells us authoritatively, was 70 and of the latter 85; the ideal European skull apparently sitting in the middle with an index of 75 (see *EB* 11, 7, 373a–b). Such usages are put to the service of the *Wake* narrative but they point back to the traditions from which they derive to disrupt epistemological securities. The great potential interest of these interventions is only partly, then, that they help us to complete the picture of how the *Wake* was constructed. More importantly, they help us to position Joyce the intellectual in a complex modernity.

Equally suggestive usages play with *EB* 11's difficulties in handling forms of knowledge positioned not just on the shifting margins of contemporary currency but, one would have thought, well outside. Heraldry, for example, might be expected to have had little cultural value in the modern world of the early-twentieth century except as an example of redundancy. Reflecting a wide range of ideological sensitivities towards nation, race, aristocracy, conservative social order and so on, *EB* 11, however, produces a huge article on this subject – some 20 pages of double column print, illustrated by coloured prints. The astonishingly arcane procedures of 'blazoning' are faithfully reproduced with the *EB* article on heraldry describing the standard forms and giving many illustrations of how this strange practice was performed. On page 328b in Volume 13, it is pointed out how 'the description of the field is first set down, the blazoner giving its plain tincture or describing it as burely, party, paly or barry as powdered or sown with roses, crosslets or fleur de lys' – a sentence which would not look out of place in the *Wake*. In his hilariously contaminated versions of such practices, Joyce both follows these amazing injunctions and thoroughly ridicules them.[4]

Embedded just as deeply in the *Wake* are the interventions that poke fun at *EB* 11's attempts to articulate itself as a humanist project, where knowledge is constituted in terms of a progressive, civilizing dynamic, while at the same time indulging a less generous disposition that responds to conservative cultural nationalism. Here *EB* 11 finds itself operating across a spectrum of tones from the ostensibly generous to the patently narrow-minded, although the gaps between these extremes are not always as wide as one would think. As in the article 'Funeral Rites', which advises readers that to 'confine ourselves to the rites of a few leading races' would be to neglect 'their less fortunate brethren who have never achieved civilisation' (*EB* 11, 11: 329d), the former progressivism can often be just as toe-curlingly condescending and paternalistic as the latter narrow mindedness. Significantly, the same article, apparently in the spirit of inclusiveness, points out that 'a feast is an essential part of every primitive funeral and in the Irish 'wake' it still survives' (*EB*. 11, 11: 331c).

Joyce deals with such issues in a great number of highly inventive ways. Mostly obviously he has the *Wake* practise a kind of inverse appropriation, where causes most dear to patriotic hearts are reproduced in utterly wayward contexts. Here they become so hopelessly contaminated as to be virtually unrecognizable in culturally specific terms. The glorious Waterloo campaign, a product of Wellington's 'unswerving determination' and 'firmness' (which is why he figures as 'Willingdone' in the *Wake* incarnation) and 'the invincible steadfastness shown by the British troops and those of the King's German legion' (*EB* 11, 28: 381d), becomes predominantly an Irish victory in the *Wake*, not too great a stretch in that Wellington can be identified as Anglo–Irish. But it also becomes hopelessly conflated with a victory of the Spartan confederacy in 404 B.C.; an eighteenth-century defeat of the French by the Austrians; the Norman invasion of 1006; the Crimean War; the American War of Independence; Italian Unification and so on (see *FW*. 8–9). Elsewhere the *Wake* both takes on and outdoes the superior tones of *EB* 11, especially in relation to prestigious myths of origins. Here everything is first and foremost located as 'Irish' in invention. As we have seen, the first building; the first city; the first act of sex; the first writing; 'the first peace of illiterative porthery in all the flamend floody flatuous world' (this being claimed of the Prankquean tale at *FW* 23.9–10); even the first language, the first 'yew' and 'eye' (*FW* 23.36) – all are Irish.

Elsewhere again the *Wake* responds to such tones through massively overdone comic confirmation. Hence after Finnegan's funeral in I.i. the 'primitive' Irish not only have a wake where they commune with the dead in a funeral feast, they also assert the continued life of the dead by feeding the corpse with 'honey . . . hive, comb and earwax, the food for glory' (*FW* 25.5–7). They leave offerings, 'pouch, gloves, flask, bricket, kerchief, ring and amberulla, the whole treasure of the pyre' (*FW* 24.32–3), indicating that as 'primitive folk' they 'cannot conceive of a man's soul surviving apart from his body, nor of another life as differing for this, and the dead must continue to enjoy what they had done here' (*EB* 11, 11, 330b). They appease the dead to prevent a rising (see *FW* 24.6–26; 27.22–3) and see the dead in the stars. Tim Finnegan's 'heart is in the system of the Shewolf' and his 'crested head . . . in the tropic of Copricapron' (*FW* 26.11–13). In short, in this account Finnegan's Irish mourners display just about every kind of characteristic said to typify the response to death in *EB* 11 across 'primitive' peoples of the world, including practising suttee (see *FW* 253/*EB* 11, 11:330b) and eating the flesh of the departed (see *FW* 7.10–14), a practice not uncommon, *EB* 11 tells us, amongst primitives like the Uaupes of Amazonia (*EB* 11, 11: 331d).

Such examples point to just how suggestive *EB* 11 and the encyclopaedist principle is in terms of the *Wake* agenda. The evidence of Joyce working on the *Encyclopaedia* in these and many other disruptive ways are all over the pages of *Finnegans Wake* and show the limitations of the commonly held view that Joyce himself was a straight encyclopaedic borrower, sharing all the naïve confidence in the popular production of knowledge held by his lead character in *Ulysses*, Leopold Bloom. In fact, the *Wake*'s relationship with *EB* 11 is very much more interesting and it is fundamentally shaped by a thoroughgoing critical skepticism.

Joyce's working of the *Encyclopaedia Britannica* then, brings the larger perspective of the *Wake*'s engagement with progressivism and the modern world into sharper focus. His undermining of the encyclopaedia principle and the epistemology on which it is based also point to the many reasons why modern culture should have struggled, as it continues to struggle, with epistemological faith and why Joyce himself was so representative of modern culture in this respect. As a Catholic brought up and educated in a colonized culture and society, he was particularly positioned in relation to the specific authority – secular or spiritual – that defined itself in terms of the 'universal'. At the same time he was a rationalist, steeped in the Aristotelian tradition. The rise of pseudo-sciences, like eugenics, craniology and phrenology, and the cultural value attached to such irrationalist phenomena as theosophy rendered him likewise acutely sensitive to the limitations, ambiguities and downright impossibilities of the confident modern universalism that characterized the encyclopaedic tradition. The critical cultural travel of dangerous racist discourses across such fields of knowledge as anthropology, paleoanthropology, sociology, biology and historical linguistics for example – fields that were all simultaneously unravelling in the early decades of the twentieth century – again was crucial to the determination of a highly politicized response to the epistemology question. As the following sections illustrate, all these dynamics, and many more, are deeply embedded in the fabric of the endless 'openness' of the *Wake* text which so struggles for meaning.

The *Wake* and Eugenics – Jukes and Kallikaks

There are good reasons why the academy has typically understood Joyce's engagement with eugenics in Irish–English terms. A characteristically modern version of applied science, eugenics was significantly a product of England and had obvious implications for Irish–English relations in their racialized forms. English science and social science – Darwinism filtered through the social application of Herbert Spencer – figured largely in the development of eugenics and the crucial biometrical formulations were centrally the intellectual property of the English academy led by Francis Galton and Karl Pearson. Eugenics was clearly put to the service of imperial design and was considerably institutionalized in English society, especially in the Edwardian period. Legislation like the Alien Immigration Act (1905) and the Mental Deficiency Act (1913) responded to the eugenist climate, as did the widespread concern over 'national efficiency' and the condition of the English army recruit as exposed by the Report of the Physical Deterioration Committee (1904).[5] Above all, eugenics had a profound impact on English intellectual life. G. R. Searle has shown how virtually the whole of the British biology establishment had joined the Eugenics Education Society by 1909 and how 'pathologists and experts in mental deficiency and abnormality' were much active on its behalf. Similarly infant British sociology 'seemed taken over entirely by eugenicists' and there was strong representation amongst psychologists and the religious establishment. Cambridge had its own Eugenics Society and in 1913 the Oxford University Union carried by 105 votes to 66 a motion that 'this house approves of the principles of eugenics.'[6] Given this degree of embedding and the resonance of eugenics as an English science used to underpin traditional racisms, it is easy to see how the comic derision that Joyce gets from this subject in the *Wake* must have been shaped from an Irish perspective.

At the same time eugenics raised wider issues about the West and modernity. However much England may have signified here, the *Wake* implies a broader and more diverse world, where once more the kind of epistemological view underpinning eugenics gets linked up to larger debates frequently contextualised in terms of Enlightenment historiography. Part of the very self-conscious modernizing of Joyce's territory in the *Wake* is this location in the wider Western scene – a process much exemplified by the cultural contemporaneity of references in the *Wake* and by the strong investment in new cultural forms like television, radio and film.[7] Eugenics in the *Wake*, then, is Europeanized – as is suggested by allusions to figures like André Retzius; Jules Crepieux-Jamin; the German anatomist and anthropologist Gustave Schwalbe and the early sociologist and ethnographer from France, Lucien Lévy Bruhl. They are also Americanized. Indeed the most frequently used signifier of eugenics in the *Wake* is located in New World social science and its study of the two families of degenerates, the Jukes and the Kallikaks.[8]

Neither of these families, the Jukes nor the Kallikaks, existed in reality. The names were invented and, in any case, the problems of individual families were not the focus of interest here. The 'science', or 'moral science', on which the two studies were based pointed not to any isolated case of 'degeneracy' but to a perceived widespread social condition. R. L. Dugdale, author of *The Jukes: A Study in Crime, Pauperism, Disease and Heredity, also Further Studies of Criminals* (1877; revised in 1915) emphasized that 'there was not one "Jukes" family alone in the state . . . the Jukes family is the type of a great class.'[9] Likewise Henry Herbert Goddard's, *The Kallikak family – a Study of the Heredity of Feeble-Mindedness* (1912) warned that 'there are Kallikak families all about us'. Both accounts were classically eugenist. They used a combination of statistics, Lamarckian biology and 'careful observation' to 'prove' how criminality, 'harlotry' and 'feeble-mindedness' were inherited characteristics. In the case of the Kallikaks it was shown how the original family were of 'good stock', until in the late-eighteenth century one Martin Kallikak, at the age of 15, had sex with a 'feeble-minded' girl who became pregnant. Martin never married the girl, but she gave her child the Kallikak name and from there a 'bad' Kallikak line began. The result, according to Goddard, was 480 direct descendants – 26 were illegitimate; 31 'sexually immoral persons, mostly prostitutes' with a further 8 keeping 'houses of ill-fame'; 24 were 'confined alcoholics'; 3 were epileptics; and 82 died in infancy. Many more were 'indeterminate' – that is to say, Dugdale's field workers knew that they were not 'normal', but could not ascertain whether they carried the bad 'germplasm' which would mark them out as 'feeble-minded'.[10] The history of the Jukes told the same sorry tale, with the family becoming 'so despised by the reputable community that their family name had come to be used generally as a term of reproach.' Again 'fornication' was focused on as the cause of degeneration, an association of sex and immorality implied in the *Wake*'s tale of the ant and the grasshopper where the 'Ondt', 'spizzing all over him like thingsumanything in formicolation' (*FW* 417.24–7) is 'jucking Vespatilla jukely by the chimiche' (*FW* 417.30–1). The Jukes 'lived in log or stone cabins similar to slave-hovels, all ages and sexes, relations and strangers "bunking" indiscriminately'.[11]

A classic biological determinism made the idea of any liberal social intervention into the lives of the Jukes and the Kallikaks utterly pointless. According to Goddard 'if all the slum districts of our cities were removed tomorrow and model tenements built in their places, we would still have the same slums in a week's time, because we have these mental defective people who can never be taught to live otherwise than they are living.' The Kallikaks and those like them formed a separate species or type and the racial implications were emphatic. Thus the 'idiot' was not 'our greatest problem' because he rarely bred, but the 'moron type' was different, because he continued 'the race with a line of children like himself'. Chillingly, the 'lethal chamber' was ruled out as a reasonable solution, but only because progressivist modern sensibilities would not allow such a course of action – 'humanity is steadily tending away from the possibility of that method'. Goddard considered sterilization as a possible response, but, in the end, recommended education so that men like Martin Kallikak were persuaded to realize the 'consequence of their immorality'; for the existent 'defectives' he advocated 'segregation and colonisation'.[12]

This kind of material is incorporated into the *Wake* in a variety of ways. According to his detractors, themselves eugenically unsound as members of 'an imperfectly warmblooded race', HCE is 'a great white caterpillar' (a homosexual, this being the phrase that Lady Campbell used to describe Oscar Wilde), 'capable of any and every enormity in the calendar recorded to the discredit of the Juke and Kellikek families' (*FW* 33.21–4). Interestingly, there are certain 'wisecrackers' who believe him to be suffering 'from a vile disease' (*FW* 33.16–18). The associations between syphilis, homosexuality, and eugenics – all contextualized in the hysteria of a paranoid mob – constitute a clear indictment of the Juke and Kallikak material, one that is entirely missed in an annotative literature which simply lists the Jukes and Kallikaks as 'degenerate American families'.

But the associations between the Earwickers and Jukes/Kallikaks does not stop at I.3 and Earwicker's 'crime'. Shem's contruction as 'a moral and mental defective' (*FW* 177.16), a 'hybrid' made up of 'an adze of a skull, an eight of a larkseye, the whoel of a nose' and 'one numb arm up a sleeve' (*FW* 169.11–13), is clearly shaped by eugenist literature of the Juke/Kallikak kind, as is the suggestion that his activities, if allowed to continue unchecked would have the effect of wiping every 'english spooker . . . off the face of the erse' (*FW* 178.6–7).

Other members of the Earwickers, besides Shem, are also associated. Indeed at II.2 the whole family become Kallikaks and Jukes, with ALP visualized sewing up the torn clothing of 'big Kapitayn Killkook and the Jukes of Kelleiney' (*FW* 295.fn.1). In some ways the Earwickers, like the Jukes and Kallikaks, are scapegoated (see *FW* 375.3–4 – 'And kick kick killykick for the house that juke built!'), but with the important difference that they are also centralized, not as the freaks and misfits of the modern world, but rather as the mock prototypes/stereotypes. This is the real point about the association, that with it the condition of the Jukes and the Kallikaks becomes not 'their' condition, but ours. In this context it is hard to tell the 'defectives' from the 'heroes', presumably the point about the many associations between 'Dook Weltington' (*FW* 371.36) or the 'artful Juke of Wilysly' (*FW* 137.11) and the Jukes and of other similar conflations that seem otherwise incomprehensible – like those between Chuculain and the Kallikaks at 137.12 ('Kukkuk Kallikak') and the Jukes and Napoleon (see 'Jukoleon' at 367.20). One of the relatively minor but highly symptomatic transformations of *Finnegans Wake* is that here the outcasts and rejects of contemporary social science get so profoundly repositioned, not just at the cultural centre but at new margins of myth, history and romanticism.

There are many further contexts where eugenics is utilised by Joyce, almost always with the effect of ridicule. The beginning of I.4, for instance, articulates HCE's 'most besetting of ideas' – the elimination of crime 'from all classes and masses' by breeding out the offending gene into a specific 'criminal stratum', thereby producing 'a distinguished dynasty of his posteriors, blackfaced connemaras not of the fold' (*FW* 75.24–76.7). The eugenist commitment to civic responsibility is laughed at in the idea that HCE's new burial chamber will include rooms for 'useful councils public' where such bodies as 'the Breeders' Union' can meet (*FW* 77.21–3). The great eulogy to Finn Macool in I.6 refers to his clearing out of 'three hundred sixty five idles to set one all khalassal for henwives hoping to have males' (*FW* 128.31–3). Shem's failure to fulfil the 'wious pish' of his 'cogodparents' and 'repopulate the land of your birth and count up your progeny by the hungered head and the angered thousand' is also contextualized in eugenics, in part by the intervention of his godparents, who present him at his birth with the 'handsome present of a selfraising syringe and twin feeders' (*FW* 188.29; 189.1). Yaun's proprietorial stand on Issy and the twenty-nine dancing girls is riddled with eugenist discourse, sometimes advocating eugenic practice, as in the exhortation to 'Hold, flay, grill, fire that laney feeling for kosenkissing disgenically' (*FW* 436.9–10), but elsewhere speaking quite to the contrary, advocating both incest and buggery – 'Love through the usual channels, cisternbrothelly, when properly disinfected and taken neat in the generable way upon retiring to roost in the company of a husband-in-law or other respectable relative of an apposite sex, not love that leads by the nose as I foresmellt but canalised love, you understand, does a felon good' (*FW* 436.14–19). Above all, however,

III.2 takes it eugenist dimensions from Yaun's protection of the race from 'the black fremdling' and other 'strangers' (see *FW* 442.1) and in III.4 HCE and ALP's last attempt at copulation is, again, contextualized by eugenics – not just by the references to birth control which, as Mary Lowe-Evans has shown,[13] conflate with ideas about 'population', but also by the sporting metaphor which takes the eugenicists' obsession with race discourse and literalizes it in a variety of ways:

> By the queer quick twist of her mobcap and the lift of her shift at random and the rate of her gate of going the pace, she thinks at a time, her country I'm proud of. The field is down, the race is their own. The galleonman jovial on his bucky brown nightmare. Bigrob dignagging his lylyputtana. One to one bore one! . . . One to one on!
>
> (*FW* 583.5–13)

So much, even so, does not constitute the limit of the *Wake*'s comic dispersal of eugenist thinking – there are many further examples – but it does indicate just how much the *Wake* is involved in debunking this most modern version of much older prejudices. As *EB* 11 points out in a relatively a short and curt entry, eugenics was not new in itself but rather a contemporary reformulation, 'the modern name given to the science which deals with the influences which improve the inborn qualities of a race, but more particularly with those which develop them to the utmost advantage, and which generally serves to disseminate knowledge and encourage action in the direction of perpetuating a higher racial standard' (*EB* 11, 9: 885). The *Encyclopaedia Britannica* was surely right to insist on a containment of what often appeared to be an upstart, pretentious and derivative project. But equally, it is a mistake to imagine, as some Joyceans have, that eugenics was just population studies revisited, a traditional extension of regulation into the family. It was political in other ways, too, most obviously in terms of how it constructed class and race as 'natural' realities and social and cultural life as a conflict where the old biblical antipathies of good and evil became transferred into scientific terms. The *Wake* is fully alive to these meanings of eugenics, and, for all its seemingly infinite open-endedness, clear in terms of where it positions itself in relation to them.

'No such race' – The *Wake*, Aryanism and Totalitarianism

As we have seen in earlier chapters, race has been a primary site in historicized accounts of the Joyce's fiction for some time. In the overview that follows race retains its impact in terms of relations between

England and Ireland, a dynamic shaped with particular emphasis on formulations of the 'Celt'. The primary interest here, however, is not in Irish, Anglo–Irish and British identities *per se* but in a race history that again operates on a different scale and thus places Joyce in a wider context, and a very different political environment. Here race remains important in terms of the romanticized identities of both decolonizing radicals and the conservative state, but also becomes disastrously positioned at the heart of the extreme right. Joyce's engagement with race, certainly a product of colonial dispossession, also figures in the context of a wider disputation with rationalism and modernity. From this perspective, *Finnegans Wake* features not as an Irishman's assault on the English language as a critic like Declan Kiberd has it, but once more becomes a very particular and specifically targeted engagement with the Enlightenment.[14]

Race discourse, as indicated in an earlier chapter, is fundamental to *Finnegans Wake*. This is true of the detail in Joyce's 'book of breedings' (*FW* 410.1–2) and 'fornicolopulation' (*FW* 557.17), where HCE, most usually seen in Anglo–Saxon or Anglo–Irish terms, is also a 'Ruddy blond, Armenian' (*FW* 559.24–5). ALP, typically white and European, on one occasion has the distinction of a 'Nubian shine' (*FW* 559.28). Shem is both a 'pure blood Jebusite, centy procent Erserum spoking' (*FW* 240.28) and 'a nogger among the blankards' (*FW* 188.13), whereas Wyndham Lewis's notion of a dull, methodical Joyce is reproduced in Shaun, who, by his own admission, is also a 'slav to methodiousness' (*FW* 159.30–1). Race is also important to the wider scheme of things. Vincent Cheng is one of a number of critics who have argued that standard strategies of racism are defeated by *Wake* aesthetics, 'all attempts to assert the Self by denying the Other are problematized and unstable in the multipleness of *Finnegans Wake*.'[15]

'Neo-grammarian' historical linguistics become much implicated here at this most general level of the *Wake*'s cultural practice, because this linguistics provided the essential scientific basis once underpinning knowledge about race. The astonishing language strategies which produce *Wake* speak ('cellelleneteutoslav- zendlatinsoundscript' – *FW* 219.17) constitute a sharply comic representation both of an 'original' language from which all other languages can be taken to have descended, and of language 'contamination' where a prototype language, spread through migrations and conquest, merges with the languages of the conquered or assimilated tribes and peoples. It imagines, in fantastically grotesque and comic forms, both the pure language of Aryanist eulogy, 'a language of heroes existing for and by itself', and the corrupted languages of Aryanist scorn, the 'patched up' languages which are like a 'harlequin's coat'.[16]

At the same time, there is the *Wake* obsession not just with the first language but with other imagined originary states. Again, as we saw in the preceding chapter, racial progenitors appear by the dozen in the *Wake*. Firmly fixed 'Inn the Byggning' (*FW* 17.22), at the first pub, 'here where race began' (*FW* 80.16), the *Wake* and its people migrate from the 'himals' (the Himalayas of the Aryan myth – *FW* 5.1), but in reverse direction – 'craching eastuards, they are in surgence' (*FW* 17.25), and 'Miscegenations on miscegenations' (*FW* 18.20) follow. The first race appears to be Aryan/Irish or 'Arioun' (*FW* 75.2), indeed Irish/Aryan identities are interchangeable in the *Wake*, producing such conflations as 'Eirenesians' (*FW* 25.17); 'Aaarlund' (*FW* 69.8); 'Airyanna (*FW* 275.14); 'grain oils of Aerin' (*FW* 338.36); 'Ayerland' (*FW* 347.11); 'dawnybreak in Aira' (*FW* 353.32–3); 'Eironesia' (*FW* 411.12); 'gan greyne Eireann' (*FW* 503.23) and 'Eryan's isles' (*FW* 580.34).

But while it thoroughly exploits passions for lineage, the *Wake* is also infamous for its expression of 'the secrest of . . . soorcelossness' (*FW* 23,19), an important message in the 1920s and 30s. For *Finnegans Wake* was constructed and published not just during a critical phase of Ireland's colonial and post-colonial history but also at a turning point in the history of both the modernizing project and of racism. The most grotesque manifestation of the modern spirit, the industrially organized death camp, was in close chronological proximity to the writing and publication of the *Wake*. Racial identity had never been more vital, nor the consequences of being of the 'wrong' race more grave. As Leon Poliakov put it, 'the most important differentiation between the inhabitants of Europe was that between Aryans and Semites: the former were permitted to live, the latter condemned to die.'[17]

This polarization and its corollary, the rise of Nazism, affected Joyce in close and personal ways. It brought new urgencies to already difficult family circumstances, determining the final move from Paris to Zurich and compelling Joyce to explain at the Swiss border that he was not in fact '*juif de Judée mais aryen d'Erin*' (*JJ*, 736). At least one of Joyce's friends, Paul Léon, was murdered by the Nazis for his race and, as is well-known, Joyce used his contacts in Paris to help some sixteen Jews escape from the country he invariably referred to at this time as 'Hitlerland' (*JJ*, 708).

Even without these personal dimensions, however, it is hard to imagine any significant cultural intervention of this period, let alone the book supposed to include everything, not taking position on the race issue in its most modern European form. It is unsurprising, then, that at one level illustration of the *Wake*'s engagement with race politics is a relatively straightforward matter. The *Wake* registers many references to German race pride and Nazism, almost all of them insulting – like 'erst curst Hun' (*FW* 76.32); 'Achdung' (*FW* 100.5); the reference to 'Finn MacCool' being 'evacuated at the mere appearance of three germhuns' (*FW* 127.13), and the splendid mockery of the Nazi slogan 'Heil Hitler! Ein volk, ein Reich, ein Führer' in 'heal helper! one gob, one gap, one gulp and gorger of all' (*FW* 191.7–8). The Nazi salute is darkly mocked in 'Seek hells' (*FW* 228.6); the Nazi leader cult diminished and made childish to the rhythm of 'Ten Men Went to Mow' in 'hun men wend to raze a leader' (*FW* 278.21). Storm troopers, the Gestapo, the Strength Through Joy movement, Hitler's road building programme and so on, are all meted out a similar treatment.

If the *Wake*'s participation in race politics was restricted to these lively insults, however, it would be of limited interest. The argument here is more complex and substantial. Far from being so self-referential as to be apolitical, the *Wake* locates ideas of racial origin and language classification in terms of the Enlightenment and the Western intellectual tradition and interrupts these with a subversion that is astonishingly original in its form. Notions of pure racial identity, for example, so much at the heart of scientific racism, are thoroughly disposed of in quite unique ways. Hilarious versions of race origin, race dispersal and race meeting, often seen as being somehow just Irish, become parodic assaults on an academy that for over two hundred years had tried to establish race as an essential condition; to classify, scientifically, racial difference and similarity and, most importantly, to chart history in racial terms. In this kind of context the treatment of race in the *Wake* cannot be limited to 'allusiveness' to the Nazis. On the contrary it goes to the very heart of the *Wake* and the kind of radical cultural practice in which it engages.

The *Wake* assaults this kind of 'reasoning' by reconvening it as unreason. In terms of its specific response to Aryanism, and its variants, Anglo–Saxonism, Germanism, Teutonism and Celticism, it appropriates, conflates, confuses and complicates. 'Scientific racism' is ridiculed, not just through 'allusions', but as a product of the *Wake*'s monstrous language; inveterate, hopelessly confused story telling and the disastrously uncertain identification of its characters. The notorious difficulty of the *Wake* reflects outwards, then, on the absurdities of 'rationalism' gone badly wrong, becoming a vast comic parody of the European imperative to establish itself as the prototype society of the first race. In this sense, the *Wake* is designed as a monstrous 'failure', a failure to concoct 'pure', original language, to find racial origins and to construct the dimensions of racial identity, which also means that the famous circularity of the *Wake*, often noted for its apparent lyricism, has a sharp satiric edge too. It is especially for this reason, for its willingness to expose through massively overdone deployment, the utter absurdities at the heart of race discourse and the parallel discourses of such *fin de siècle* 'sciences' as criminology, eugenics, phrenology and craniology that the *Wake* can be read as a thoroughly politicized text of the inter-war years.

A number of important dimensions converge in Joyce's handling of the Aryan myth. These are Irish and European; post-colonial and global; political and cultural; historical and contemporary to the 1920s and 30s. It is not possible to say how much of the *Wake* can be 'explained' in terms of the Aryan myth, but, clearly, the encounter with Aryanism and its variants is important to the *Wake* at a number of levels. It shapes *Wake* identities. It also figures centrally in the *Wake's* extraordinary aesthetics, and especially in the cavalier vitality with which it 'corrupts' language. Configuring Germanism as the 'hundering blundering dunderfunder of plundersundered manhood' (*FW* 596.2–3), Joyce identifies its most radical manifestation in the Aryan myth as a wider European fascination both ridiculous and dangerous. This becomes fundamental to the politics of the *Wake*, producing among many other effects a comic rhetoric that damns 'Errian copulation' (*FW* 525.6) and an erasure of the race science that divides, like 'Aerian's [Hadrain's] Wall' (*FW* 379.11). Through this aesthetics the *Wake* realizes the madness of an ideology that leaves 'Shivering William' having 'his teeth . . . shaken out of their suckets by the wrang dog, for having 5 pints 73 of none Eryen blood in him abaft the seam level' (*FW* 507.35–508.3).

These treatments of eugenics, the Aryan myth, the modern academy and fascism throw the *Wake* back into the precise conditions of the modernity it reconvenes in powerfully subversive ways. It should be emphasized that the focus on European context in the above account in no way implies Ireland is somehow unimportant to the *Wake*. As should be clear, the Joyce agenda, throughout his fiction, is centrally concerned with repositioning Ireland at the centre and nowhere is this more thoroughly achieved than in the *Wake* where 'the history of the whole world is mapped onto Ireland'[18] – a history that 'begins' with the death of a Celtic hero and 'continues' in I.2 with 'yer maggers', 'William the Conk' (*FW* 31.10/14), handing the supervision of his Irish lands over to his 'vassal', 'Humme the Cheapner' (*FW* 29.18). More contemporary Ireland is no less important to the *Wake* than its ancient history or establishment as the first modern colony. As a number of critics have argued, the setting up of the Irish Republic is crucially implicated in the *Wake*. In *Joyce and the Invention of Irish History*, Hofheinz sees the final section of the *Wake* opening with 'dawn breaking over Ireland, an Ireland linked to modernity by a cluster of references to the first fifteen years of the Irish Free state'. Hofheinz continues 'The dream of a free and united Ireland seems to be coming true in this page, but the dream's "truth" materialises in the coldly comprised terms of the Irish

Free State', an Ireland where Catholicism and the State move into new contingent relationships and the nation becomes formally Celticized. In this sense, for Joyce, the Republic shades off into other kinds of authoritarianism. Hofheinz points out that:

> Joyce's crowning ironic reference to the persistently British nature of the Irish Free State appears in an addition to the *Wake*'s galley sheets in 1938: the Church of England's thirty-nine article map insidiously onto De Valera's deeply Catholic 'reconstitution' of the Free State constitution in 1937 ('articles thirtynine of the reconstitution').[19]

My own account in *Joyce Race and Finnegans Wake* is a development from Hofheinz's. It makes even more explicit how the formation of the Irish Republic shadows one of the great cycles of the *Wake*, HCE displacement by his sons, especially Shaun who is the voice of the conservative Republic in the *Wake*. Indeed, in this cycle Joyce's handling of modern Irish history and its defence of 'traditional and Catholic familial and social values', its rising 'Celtic fundamentalism',[20] is specifically linked to his exposure to right-wing nationalism and totalitarianism in Europe.

Neither does the above account constitute anything like the full extent of the *Wake*'s engagement with what was once the modern world, indeed it is difficult to visualize what a definitive account would look like in this respect. The *Wake* works off world histories, topographies, popular novels, modern psychology, contemporary politics and so on and so on. Far from having nothing to say, it speaks very loudly across a great range of culture. The epistemological issue, however, quite apart from positioning us at the centre of the *Wake* and its language, also leads to the dominant authoritarian political formations of Joyce's day. Fascism was the most powerful and extreme manifestation of right-wing political ideology ever to emerge in the history of the West. If the Joyce text really is politically engaged and shaped by 'history' as this introduction to Joyce has maintained, it must be that the engagement with fascism is somewhere at the centre of the *Wake*'s agenda. This is not to dispute the fact that defining the *Wake*'s historical dimensions is a difficult and slippery business. Many 'histories' are evoked by the *Wake* – Irish histories, French histories, British histories, 'Prooshian' histories as well as Slavonic, African and Australasian ones. At the same time its 'periodisation' is, at one level, non-existent. It is just as appropriate, or inappropriate, to articulate the *Wake* in terms of its 'medievalist' dimensions as it is to recover it as eighteenth century, or designate its prehistorical fabric. The *Wake* maintains a condition which is not just multi-layered but utterly cross-contaminated, where historical periods are routinely conflated and hybridized – this is presumably one reason why some critics have thought of the *Wake* in universalist terms.

But these multiple histories and 'times' reconvened in the *Wake* in such playful ways are the product of aesthetic design. The history of the 1920s and 30s was particular in that these decades constituted Joyce's lived experience during the writing of the *Wake*. They formed the only reality for which he could be held in any way accountable. Whether Joyce takes position on the issue of Bonapartism, or sides in the Spanish War of Independence, or any other historical issue is of no *necessary* importance to the question of what used to be called 'Joyce's politics' or, in an earlier critical tradition, to the idea of the writer's 'commitment'.[21] The issue of where he is positioned in relation to fascism, however, is hugely significant. Indeed, it is difficult to see how Joyce can hold any serious status as a radical writer, politically engaged with his society and culture, if he ignores or is indifferent to fascism. This means that fascism is central to the agendas operating in this account of the *Wake* – to the general understanding of a literature that is 'political' and crucially influenced by historical contexts. That observation does not constitute anything like a 'key' to the *Wake*, nor make the *Wake* any easier to read. It does, however, allow us to register its significance in more meaningful ways.

CHAPTER 7

'I Do Not Like That Other World' – Joyce's Publics

Texts and Contexts began with an overview of some of the difficulties associated with formulating an introduction to Joyce, one of them being how to handle the critical culture surrounding the Joyce text in a project substantially implicating the 'ordinary reader' – a further one identifying who that latter abstraction might be. As the book approaches its end, it becomes even clearer, whatever the difficulties, that Joyce's fiction is tightly bound up with critical history and the academy – not just for the Joyce 'expert' but for any reader. Whether implicitly or explicitly, an introduction to Joyce inevitably rests on critical tradition, not least because the expectancies we bring to reading books like *Ulysses* have been so thoroughly mediated by such cultures. Put more strongly, discourses outside the academy will struggle to 'introduce' this kind of literature with any authority because 'Literature' is so deeply an institutional product.

That said, it should be equally clear that Joyce criticism is hardly a stable commodity. The Joyce text is a much contested site, as we have seen repeatedly. There is, admittedly, a tradition which insists otherwise – presenting the much maligned 'Joyce industry' and its associated institutions as an ecumenical authority that welcomes and celebrates variety, but this is very much an outward-facing presentation of things. The more insiderly perspective will also be highly conscious of the shifting trends and patterns – which of the critical schools are 'in' and which 'out' – as well as the divisions and conflicts that constitute the rough end of politics in the academy.

These may be trivial and insular in the larger scheme of things but every now and then they burst into more exposed public domains, indicating the stakes that can appear to be in play in academia. They did so when Derrida, speaking before the Ninth International James Joyce Symposium in Frankfurt in 1984, delivered his highly entertaining interrogation of the very notion of the Joyce expert[1] and again in 1988 when the dispute between John Kidd and Hans Walter Gabler over the authorized *Ulysses* text 'exploded' in the so-called 'Joyce wars' – the 'scholarly equivalent of a barroom brawl'.[2] Ten years later a similar furor was prompted by Danis Rose's attempt to produce a more reader-friendly *Ulysses*, a 'people's version' which, in Rose's own fighting words, had been 'smuggled out of the ivory tower of the academics and put squarely in the marketplace'. This dramatic-sounding escapade involved some 10,000 changes to the text, 'including perhaps 7000 that do not appear in any manuscript or edition'. According to the Joyce estate, the result was so radical that the author of this *Ulysses* was held to be 'Danis Rose, not James Joyce'. Representatives of the estate demanded that if a second edition were to appear the name 'James Joyce' should be 'stripped from cover, spine and title page'.[3]

However inextricable from these cultures of criticism the Joyce text has become, it is also clear that while we might like to imagine a genuine community of interest existing between the Joyce academy and the 'ordinary' reader, the realities are rather different. Indeed it is an obvious and demonstrable fact that the professional Joyce world generally ignores the wider constituency of Joyce readers, and vice versa. The average academic book on Joyce, even one published by one of the prestigious academic publishers, is lucky to sell many more than 1000 copies. A journal article will be read by an even smaller audience. Joyce academia substantially writes to itself and works to agendas often irrelevant outside the academy. The example of genetic studies in Joyce illustrates the point, although no trend, strand or tradition is immune from the point being made here.

There can be no doubt that genetic studies generally, from being a fairly marginal activity in the Joyce academy, is now at the ascendant. Ownership of the 'raw materials' that went into producing the Joyce text determines the location of scholarly activity to a significant extent and those who work the field have become elevated into something of a corps according to Jasmine Lellock who refers to the 'the power-point wielding cadre of geneticists' present at 21st International James Joyce Symposium in 2008. That conference included Ilaria Natali on 'the textual development of *A Portrait*'; Christopher Whalen on the Gabler edition of *Ulysses* and a panel entitled 'collaborators and anti-collaborators: new genetic readings in Joyce'.[4] Both the Trieste and Dublin Summer Schools regularly include practical sessions in genetic criticism – the 2009 Trieste Summer School held 'genetic seminars Monday to Friday' and Dublin usually holds similar workshops at the National Library of Ireland. The North American James Joyce Conference, 2009 took place at the University of Buffalo, New York – 'the epicentre of genetic Joyce scholarship over the last fifty years'. Unsurprisingly it was a celebration of this version of expertise in Joyce studies. The plenary was given by the geneticist Luca Crispi on the re-cataloguing of the Joyce archive at Buffalo and Gabler, Groden and Christopher Whalen ran a series of workshops on 'Working with the making of *Ulysses*' which 'surveyed and modelled the theoretical and methodological premises of genetic studies'.[5]

Precisely what the full outcomes of these efforts will be is difficult to predict– unfortunately the project which appeared to be of most general value, the Brepol editions of the *Wake* notebooks, seems to have stalled, although there are signs that it will be resumed. But for many hard-core geneticists, outcomes of an applied kind are not really the point. Geneticist criticism, it is argued, has it own self-evident value and rationale, which is fortunate because the idea of a fully stable text – one obvious aim, one would have thought, of genetic study – is, for most geneticists, no more than chimerical. If textual critics can subscribe to any single principle, it is ironically enough that these texts, from the earliest notes through to the manuscripts and proofs and the published editions, can never be completed. They remain, always, works in progress.[6]

It is hard to imagine, most 'ordinary' readers being much bothered about all this activity around what might reasonably be constructed as so much minutiae with so little in the way of end result. Most, one would guess, will be quite indifferent to the idea of textual incompletion and will, for very good reasons, accept the finality of the product they buy from Waterstones or Amazon.com; just as, for all the talk of the death of the author, they will accept the notion of a subject who wrote it – always assuming, that is, that the general reader of Joyce really exists outside the academy, an issue, again, raised at the very beginning of this account.

One problem with conceptualizing the relationship between the academy and the 'everyday' Joyce reader in such ways is that we actually know very little about the latter – although we do now know quite a bit about the *historical* readership of the later Joyce texts and we also have sophisticated frameworks for understanding what the idea of reception might entail.[7] In the case of *Ulysses*, for example, first published in a high-brow journal and then in an expensive first edition, the initial market appears not to have much involved the conventional academy. Some of the earliest readers would have been literature professionals, but this readership was more substantially comprised of an even more exclusive elite. Many of the subscribers were known to Joyce personally and actively recruited by Sylvia Beach. The first printing was also highly sought after by collectors in the know as an investment and sometimes sent out in brown packages marked 'private'. Some subscribers thought they were buying pornography – 'enquiries – from England and the United States . . . sent accompanying notes stating that they required it [*Ulysses*] for psychological or medical research, even including "my prior qualifications, as proofs of my bona fides."'[8]

Clearly this book, and certainly the *Wake*, was always going to have a difficult relationship with the 'ordinary' reader to whom, as one commentator puts it with some understatement, neither text is 'affable'. Quite apart from the matter of their 'obscenity', a signifier of a dangerous and, at that time, almost out-of-reach desirability, there is what John Nash regards as their 'apparent narcissism' and the endless demands made on reader time – just as apparent to earlier readers, and to Joyce himself, as they are now.[9] H. G. Wells, somewhat disingenuously representing himself as a 'typical common reader', represented this constituency forcefully when he complained that with *Work in Progress* Joyce had turned his back 'on common men, on their elementary needs and restricted time and intelligence' (quoted in *JJ*, 620–1).

Again, we know quite a lot about the general public reception of these texts from review cultures. In relation to *Ulysses*, reviewers tuned into the myth correspondence issue, as we have seen, but also focused on the perceived realism and 'filth', as they had with *Dubliners*, *A Portrait* and *Exiles* . Writing to Sylvia Beach in response to an invitation to subscribe to the first edition, Shaw famously described the sections he had read of the serialized *Ulysses* as 'a revolting record of a disgusting phase of civilisation; but . . . a truthful one' (*CH*, 189). For others its representation of 'our most secret and unsavoury private thoughts' (*CH*, 191) placed *Ulysses* well and truly beyond the pale. Shane Leslie, writing in the *Dublin Review* of 1922, blasted *Ulysses* as the work of a decadent – an 'abomination of desolation' and 'so much rotten caviare' (*CW*, 203). 'In this work', he wrote, 'the spiritually offensive and the physically unclean are united' (*CH*, 201). A related strain of criticism made the familiar connections between the 'immorality' of *Ulysses* and its potential political radicalism. S. P. B. Mais writing in the *Daily Express* in 1922, for example, compared reading Joyce to 'making an excursion into Bolshevist Russia: all standards go by the board' (*CH*, 191). In a more interesting account in *Nation and Athenaeum*, John Murray took issue with Larbaud's sense of *Ulysses* representing 'European' culture by arguing for the book as being 'many things: it is very big, it is hard to read, difficult to procure . . . extraordinarily interesting to those who have the patience (and they need it) . . . But European? That we would have thought is the last epithet to apply to it.' After a long description of the European virtues, Murray identified *Ulysses* as 'the work of an egocentric rebel *in excelsis*, the arch-esoteric. European! He is the man with the bomb who would blow what remains of Europe into the sky', an anarchist, but one whose 'excess' makes him, fortunately, 'socially harmless'. For all its 'transcendental buffoonery . . . [the] sudden uprush of the *vis comica*', Murray wrote, the book had the 'curse of nimiety, of toomuchness', which puts it out of reach of the 'ordinary reader' (*CH*, 195–7).

Early reviews of the *Wake*, again as we have seen, focused much more on the question of its unreadability. In an article entitled, 'The cruelty and beauty of words', (*Virginia Quarterly Review*, 1928) Sean O'Faolain described the language of *Work in Progress* as coming from nowhere, and going nowhere – 'it is not part of life at all. It has one reality only – the reality of the round and round of children's scrawls in their first copybooks, zany circles of nothing' (*CH*, 392). A not so affable 'Affable Hawk' (Desmond McCarthy) was simply exasperated. The 'deformation of word and sentence' that characterized *Work in Progress* should not provoke laughter, he wrote, 'It should disgust. The taste which inspired it is taste for cretinism of speech, akin to finding exhilaration in the slobberings and mouthings of an idiot . . . When will it strike Mr Joyce that to write what it is a physical impossibility to read is possibly even sillier than to write what it is mentally impossible to follow?' (*CH*, 376). An unsigned review appearing in the *Times Literary Supplement* (1930) gave Joyce the benefit of the doubt in this respect – clearly this was not the work of charlatan – but, quite reasonably, its author refused to play, on the grounds that 'an understanding of his works asks more of our erudition and understanding then we are prepared to give' (*CH, 384*)

To what extent do such conditions survive? It is clear that the reification of the Joyce text has been sustained by an academy to which – it hardly needs emphasizing – this current account is very much connected. Insisting, over and over, on the insurmountable difficulty of the Joyce text, the critical establishment joins hands with a very lively antiquarian market to confirm Joyce's highly-privileged position in an aristocracy of culture. The value of first editions of Joyce's texts have soared over what they were thirty years ago and similarly so with secondary materials. Copies of the three volumes of letters in the first edition, for example, are now quite expensive – some £600 for a clean copy. The full run of *transition* will now cost in excess of £6000 and any Joyce manuscript goes pretty much off the scale. A single letter written by Joyce to the publishers Heinemann in 1905 achieved the value of £32,265 in 2004. In the same year, a rare copy of Joyce's satirical poem 'The Holy Office' fetched £28,680 and one of the 25 copies of the poetry collection *Pomes Penyeach* in the Obelisk Press edition sold for £26,290.

At the same time, the secret reader of *Ulysses* has disappeared and no one could now construct the *Wake* as pornography, however much it may evoke the obscene. While accounts of the impossibility of the

Wake will still resonate, few readers these days would now identify the radicalism of *Ulysses* in terms of a representation of human nature that is 'bitter' and satirical. Culture has changed radically since the 1920s. As a result, most would probably identify more with the early assessment by Holbrook Jackson that found *Ulysses* simply open and courageous in this respect, 'naked: naked and unconscious of shame' (*CW*, 918).

More importantly still, the readership of the Joyce text has hugely widened. As I say, our knowledge is badly underdeveloped here – how ironic that there should be such a cult of the expert around Joyce's books and yet we know virtually nothing about those who read them. But there can be no doubt that while the Joyce industry hammers home its insistence on the monstrous unreadability of these texts, Joyce's writing has entered the consumerist world of mass markets.

Dubliners and *A Portrait* are sustained in part by featuring so largely on school and university curricula, a precisely institutionalized version of the mass market. But neither *Ulysses* nor the *Wake* are widely taught in the academy, certainly not at undergraduate level. Indeed there are good reasons to suppose that there will be less and less opportunity for undergraduates to work on texts like this, not least because of the time they consume. Yet between the first trade edition (1936) and the first Penguin edition of 1968 just over 250,000 copies of *Ulysses* were sold and that is only one edition of many worldwide. It is thought that *Ulysses* now sells some 100,000 copies a year and these quite simply cannot all be going to the members of the academy. As Julie Sloan Brannon points out in *Who Reads Ulysses?*, 'the university . . . plays a role in Joyce's reputation, but there are other forces at work.'

The worldwide web is one obvious place to appreciate the point. There is now a high volume of traffic in Joyce material on the web, so much so that Michael Groden on behalf of the *James Joyce Quarterly*, one of the earliest and most prestigious journals devoted to Joyce studies and very much part of the institutionalized Joyce, is now attempting to 'track the enormous amount of internet activity that Joyce and his works have inspired' – presumably an innocent enterprise but conceivably construable as a kind of cultural surveillance. Whatever, it is clear that while many of the sites and discussion groups belong to professional academic communities – like the James Joyce Mailing list set up by the Joycean Karen Lawrence – others do not. The *Finnegans Wake* Astrology Discussion List; the Joyce Luck Club; the James Joyce Campfire and the James Joyce Yahoo! Club or its French version, the French James Joyce Yahoo! Club, to name but a few, all appear to be located outside the professional academy. Indeed some are specifically set up in opposition – 'to rescue Mr J's work from the swamp of academia', as the JamesJoyce OneList puts it. Under these conditions, boundaries between experts, amateurs, aficionados and 'ordinary' readers are simultaneously reaffirmed and blurred as the web – like the national library or the research centre – becomes a new site of contest for ownership of Joyce and the Joyce text. As with digitized and hypertext versions of Joyce's writing, such developments often imply a democratizing dispersal. They also confirm that reading Joyce, in whatever way, implicates all Joyce readers, professional or not, in a contemporary politics of culture.

The Joyce text has been dispersing in other ways through modern cultures and technologies. There have, for example, been quite a few film versions of Joyce's texts, the earliest one being Mary Ellen Bute's 'reaction' to the *Wake*, *Passages from Finnegans Wake* filmed in 1966. Joseph Strick's 1967 *Ulysses* starring Milo O'Shea was more mainstream, as was the same director's version of *A Portrait* made 20 years later in1987. The American director John Houston made a critically acclaimed film of *The Dead* in 1977 and a new film of *Ulysses*, directed by Stephen Walsh and staring Stephen Rea, appeared in 2003. With *Nora*, written by Brenda Maddox from her own biography, Joyce's own life has made the transition to the big screen – again the Joyce estate stepped in with this project, refusing to grant permission for any Joyce text to be quoted by the film. Nevertheless, the film got made and it stars a real live matinee-idol – Ewan McGregor no less – who performs in the part of Joyce. Needless to say, many of these films are now available on DVD. We do not even have to go to the trouble of making a visit to the cinema to appreciate them; we can now have them at home and play them as often as we like.

There have also been many attempts to bring Joyce's fiction texts to the stage. Bute's film inspired by the *Wake* was based on a play of the same name devised by the actor Burgess Meredith and written by the Irish playwright Mary Manning Howe. It was first produced in 1955 and there have been later versions, one on the West End in 1959; a Broadway revival in 1974 and a production at the Abbey in 1990. There was also a 1975 production staged by the Broome Community College in Binghampton, New York, which apparently involved the use of photographic images of Adolf Hitler, Richard Nixon and starving Biafran children as a backdrop. Recalling the production, Patrick A. McCarthy commented that although the 'production was successful in conveying certain key aspects of Joyce's book', this attempt at 'updating' was a mistake. From another perspective however, far from being tricksy, the setting of this play against images of monolithic authority might seem much consistent with fundamental principles of Joyce's book.[10]

The 'Circe' episode has been performed several times and there have been many stage recreations of the Molly Bloom soliloquy, including a notorious musical version performed at the Edinburgh Festival in 2000. Stephen Joyce, Joyce's grandson, again tried to get the production banned on behalf of the estate, apparently indifferent to the fact that his grandfather had spent a life-time fighting censorship and oblivious to the wonderful ironies implicated in his protest that this show, if it went ahead, would turn the 'masterful' work of *Ulysses* into a 'circus act'. A spokesman rightly declared the Festival a platform for free speech – 'we understand that the production is perfectly legal and the permission of the Joyce estate is not needed' – and the show did go ahead. Anna Zapparoli was at its centre, draped across a piano which served as bed. Reclining from this position she sung such songs as 'Song of the Big Hole'; 'Rap of Spunk'; 'Rap of Hip Bones' and the 'Song of Sucking'. Here the Joyce text became appropriated as 'cabaret', just as Stephen Joyce feared it would, simultaneously making a partial entry into the world of adult entertainment (it was an adult-only show).[11]

The extension of the Joyce text into music has also had a long history, sometimes with Joyce's knowledge and personal involvement. With the American composer Edmond Pendleton, he wrote a setting for his own poem 'Bid Adieu' and in 1932 the Irish composer Herbert Hughes coordinated the musical settings of all thirteen poems of *Poems Penyeach*. Contributors included E. J. Moeran, George Anteuil, Albert Bax, Herbert Howells, a young Roger Sessions and Albert Roussel. After the war, the American composer Samuel Barber set 'Sleep Now, Rain has Fallen' and 'I Hear an Army' to music and later, in 1947, used lines from *Finnegans Wake* in his *Nuvoletta*, 'a kind of mock operatic scene . . . based upon a waltz'.[12]

It is, however, in more contemporary music that the Joyce influence on music really comes to life. The French avant-gardist Pierre Boulez never set a Joyce text to music, but he was greatly influenced by *Ulysses* and the *Wake*. John Cage sent him a copy of the latter, and Boulez wrote back explaining how despite the difficulties – reading it was 'slower than slow' – the book became for him 'almost a totem'.[13] His 1960 essay, 'Sonaté, que meveux' (Sonata, what do you want of me?), draws emphatically on *Ulysses* and *Finnegans Wake* in explanation of the aesthetic behind his own third piano sonata.[14] Cage himself, 'obsessed' by *Finnegans Wake*, wrote several compositions which incorporated the Joyce text in various ways, including *Roaratorio: an Irish Circus on Finnegans Wake*. This was an hour-long reading of Cage's 'writing through *Finnegans Wake*', spoken against a version of traditional Irish music juxtaposed by a barrage of urban sounds. The composer Stephen Albert has used Joyce texts, both in song cycles and 'a Pulitzer prize-winning symphony'; Matthew Rosenblum has written a piece entitled 'Maggies' which, again, utilizes the *Wake* and so on.[15]

Such examples only scratch the surface of Joyce's influence on modern music. The Italian composer and key figure in the development of *musique concrete*, Luciano Berio, recorded *Thema: Omaggio a Joyce* in 1958 – an 8-minute piece consisting of the manipulated sounds of Cathy Berberian reading from the opening of the *Sirens* chapter of *Ulysses*. In 1965 the composer André Hodeir wrote a piece entitled 'Anna Livia Plurabelle', a jazz piece with lyrics derived from the *Wake* and first recorded in 1966. Another 'jazz suite' based on *Ulysses*, this one by Louis Stewart, was first performed at the Cork Jazz and Blues Festival in 1982. It was filmed by RTE and later broadcast on Irish television.

But it is not only musicians and composers in classical and avant-garde traditions who have worked on Joyce texts or used them and their author for inspiration and aesthetic innovation. In other music cultures, too, Joyce has figured largely. Syd Barrett, the influential figure from Pink Floyd who composed such classics as 'Arnold Layne', 'See Emily Play' and 'Bike' also wrote a musical accompaniment to 'Poem V' from *Chamber Music* entitled 'Goldenhair'. It was recorded on his 1969 solo piece *The Madcap Laughs*. On their 1967 recording *After Bathing at Baxter*, the West Coast band Jefferson Airplane, one of the first 'psychedelic' bands to achieve mainstream success, included the song 'Rejoice'. It contains such lines as 'Molly's gone to blazes/Boylan's crotch amazes' and 'Mulligan stew for Bloom/the only jew in the room'. The cover of this album, incidentally, is famous. It features a Heath-Robinson type flying machine, modelled on a typical Haight-Ashbury district house soaring above 'the chaos of American commercial culture.'[16]

Other figures in 60s counter culture also drew on Joyce – Joan Baez, or instance, sang the poem 'Ecce Puer' (renamed 'Of the Dark Past') on her 1968 recording *Baptism* – and so have writers, composers and performers in different traditions. The punk-folk band, the Pogues, for instance, featured a picture of Joyce on the back cover of their 1987 recording *If I Should Fall From Grace With God*. The degree of identification involved is worth emphasizing. Here the heads of the band members are superimposed on a well-known picture of Joyce posing in hat and typically sharp dress. Joyce himself figures at their centre, as a ninth member of the band – not surprising that the Pogues should want to so implicate the great literary iconoclast with their own ground-breaking celebration/subversion of 'Irish' kitsch.

A year later a very different kind of performer, Kate Bush, became yet another victim of the Joyce estate when she was refused permission to use words from 'Penelope' for her song 'The Sensual World' on the album of the same name. She made an adaptation. More recently the folk group Nickel Creek included a song called 'Eveline', based on *Dubliners* story, on their 2005 recording 'Why Should the Fire Die?'.

From American bluegrass to Irish heavy metal music, James Joyce and his works have become a compelling and often irreverent point of reference, sometimes in really quite unexpected ways. The song 'Potato Junkie', for example, is an anthem for the Irish metal band Therapy. It includes the line, repeated over and over, 'I'm bitter, I'm twisted/ James Joyce is fucking my sister', lines which a loyal fan base apparently roar with great enthusiasm wherever this song is performed. This year (2010) the band tours, among other places, Turkey and Russia, where presumably the fans will continue the tradition.

Attempts by the James Joyce estate to maintain control over Joyce's work and reputation have been damaging to real scholarship and artistic endeavour. They have also sometimes been absurd. Even if one disagrees with it, it is quite possible to understand the logic behind wanting to stop Molly the musical. It is not so easy to appreciate the rationale that refused the Irish composer David Fenessey permission to use just eighteen words from *Finnegans Wake* in a choral piece. Such interventions seem pointless, not least because they swim so much against the tide. The movement of Joyce through contemporary culture is unstoppable and here the fate of the Joyce image itself, so much manipulated by Joyce in life, is highly suggestive.

Thousands of images that were taken of him or inspired by him flow into the mainstream culture of commercial life everywhere quite indifferent to any version of authority. Here Joyce, far from being remote and detached, is made available in all sorts of guises – on coffee mugs (one bears his death mask), buttons, badges, posters, t-shirts, diaries, notebooks, mouse mats and so on. There are statues on the streets of a number of cities – in Dublin, Trieste, Zurich – and, of course, a huge number of James Joyce and Finnegans Wake food and drink outlets, especially pubs which appear to operate on something of a global franchise. James Joyce pubs exist in such places as Baltimore, Calgary, Paris, Atlanta, Zurich, Tampa, Athens, Prague, Illinois, Brussels, as well as in Ireland of course. One of them sells Nora Barnacle ribs ('the way to a man's heart') and has devised a James Joyce club sandwich.

The issue here is sometimes about the tourist dollar, but not, by any means, always so. For Joyce kitsch has been institutionalized at the highest levels of government and sometimes overlaps with a wide range of cultural and nationalist agendas. If the commemorative stamp issued by in the Irish Republic manages to escape the peat smoke, the famous image issued by the Irish Central Bank in September 1993, showing a benign, grandfatherly Joyce smiling down from the back side of an Irish ten pound note, surely does not.

This evocation of a more demotic Joyce needs to be strongly registered, not as the romanticised antidote to a dry and insular academy but as a reminder that the fascinating texts produced by Joyce belong not only to professional Joyceans – nor to collectors, the estate, research centres, libraries or other national bodies. There is a much very wider constituency, one which includes the website '*Ulysses* for Dummies' – a series of one-line cartoons accompanied by brief explanations of a *Ulysses* narrative – and the public polls that named Joyce as one of the most important people of the twentieth century and ranked his books *Ulysses, A Portrait* and, yes, even the *Wake*, at position 1, 3, and 77 respectively on the lists of 'the 100 best English language novels of the twentieth century'. Of course, such polls are quite meaningless at most levels, but they do point to the wider culture where Mel Brooks names the Gene Wilder character in his film *The Producers*, Leo Bloom in honour of Joyce and composer Gilberto Mendes writes a musical composition entitled 'Ulysses in Copacabana Surfing with James Joyce and Dorothy Lamour'. This, of course, is a world that held particular fascination for Joyce himself, figuring in his work not just as part of its representational brilliance but also in the avant-gardism that connects Peggy Lee, Paul Robeson, Mickey Rooney, Ivor Novello, Dutch Schultz, a one-time English cricket team, the Zurich General Post Office and so on to the linguistic strangeness of the *Wake*.

Our knowledge of *Ulysses* and the *Wake* operating in such domains outside the academy may be limited. Although there clearly are short-cuts that can be taken with these books, there is also no disputing the demands of reading Joyce – the academy's self-indulgent respect for the 'impossibility' of Joyce is unhelpful in many respects, but not based on thin air. At the same time, Anthony Burgess, perhaps the most inveter-ate proselytizer of *Ulysses* and the *Wake* – he wrote abridged versions of both and *The Blooms of London*, a 'musical-hall opera' written for the BBC (1992) – clearly had an important point to make. We cannot iso-late *Ulysses* and *Finnegans Wake* from their challenges, but nor can we cut them off from their insistent and continuing articulation with the extraordinary world of the 'ordinary'.

Notes

Chapter 1

1. The following account is from the Wikipedia entry for Whiteboys at en.wikipedia. org – 'The Whiteboys (Irish: *Buachaillí Bána*) were a secret Irish agrarian organization in eighteenth-century Ireland which used violent tactics to defend tenant farmer land rights for subsistence farming. Their name derives from the white smocks the members wore in their nightly raids, but the Whiteboys were as usually referred to at the time as Levellers by the authorities, and by themselves as "Queen Sive Oultagh's children", "fairies", or as followers of "Johanna Meskill" or "Sheila Meskill", all symbolic figures supposed to lead the movement. They sought to address rack-rents, tithe collection, excessive priests' dues, evictions and other oppressive acts. As a result they targeted landlords and tithe collectors. Over time, *Whiteboyism* became a general term for rural violence connected to secret societies. Because of this generalization, the historical record for the Whiteboys as a specific organisation is unclear. There were three major outbreaks of Whiteboyism: 1761–4; 1770–6; and 1784–6'.
2. For a fuller account of this radical tradition, including the O'Connell link, see Peter Costello, *James Joyce: The Years of Growth 1882–1915* (West Cork: Roberts Rinehart, 1992), 1–53.
3. The Christian Brothers were a lay order of the Catholic Church providing education for those who could not afford it, for ' – Paddy Stink and Mickey Mud', as Simon Dedalus colourfully puts it in *A Portrait* (*P*, 59).
4. Ellsworth Mason and Richard Ellmann, *The Critical Writings of James Joyce* (London: Faber and Faber, 1959), 149–52.
5. Yeats's first meeting with Joyce apparently concluded with Joyce declaring his age as twenty and asking Yeats how old he was. 'I am afraid I said I was a year younger than I am', Yeats explained in an account of the meeting. 'He said with a sigh, "I thought as much. I have met you too late. You are too old" . . . The younger generation is knocking at my door'. (*JJ*, 103)
6. Revivalism, conceived as cultural nationalism predates Yeats's birth by about a century and evolved not from a national consensus but, ironically enough, out of Catholic demands for equality of political and social rights. By the 1840s however, it was taken over by the Protestant Ascendancy under threat from Catholic Emancipation and the slow liberalizing of Irish society. From this perspective, Joyce's scorn at Celticism is hardly surprising and far from unique. For a history of cultural nationalism in Ireland see J. Hutchinson, *The Dynamics of Cultural Nationalism: The Gaelic Revival and the Creation of the Irish Free State* (London: Allen and Unwin, 1987).
7. In later life, Joyce claimed that *The Book of Kells* was 'the most purely Irish thing we have, and some of the big initial letters which swing right across a page have the essential quality of a chapter of *Ulysses*' (*JJ*, 545).
8. Nora was to remain hostile to the Republic and pro-British until the end of her life. After Joyce's death in 1950, there were moves made to house Joyce's manuscripts in the National Library of Ireland. Sean MacBride, then Irish minister for external

affairs, wrote to Nora 'to tell her that the Irish Government was proud to claim James Joyce, "one of the greatest Europeans of all time," as also a son of Ireland' (*N*, 488). Nora was unimpressed, apparently preferring that the British Museum hold Joyce's papers, which is where they eventually went.

9. Stanislaus Joyce, perhaps the first to realize what his brother might be capable of, was brought out to Trieste in 1905 and spent the next 9 years playing 'Sancha Panza ... to James's Don Quixote' (*MBK*, 21). See Ellmann's account in his introduction to *MBK*, 15–25.

10. Both these terms, 'technic' to describe the styles of Ulysses and 'hallucination' to indicate the particular style of the 'Circe' episode, come from the columnar schemes that Joyce sent to his friends, including to Herbert Gorman, Joyce's first biographer and the Italian critic Carlo Linati. They have been published in many accounts of *Ulysses*, but appeared first in Stuart Gilbert, *James Joyce's 'Ulysses': A Study* (London: Faber and Faber, 1930). For a reproduction see *JJ*, 152

11. See Senia Pašete, *Thomas Kettle* (Dublin: University College Dublin Press, 2008), 10–11.

12. See John Nash, *James Joyce and the Act of Reception: Reading, Ireland, Modernism* (Cambridge: Cambridge University Press, 2006), 109.

13. G. V. L. Slingsby, 'Writes a Common Reader' in Samuel Becket and others, *Our Exagmination Round His Factification for Incamination of Work in Progress* (1929; London: Faber and Faber, 1972), 190.

14. For an account of these institutions and how they steered contemporary art literature into the 'public sphere' see Lawrence Rainey, *Institutions of Modernism: Literary Elites and Public Culture* (New Haven, Conn.: Yale University Press, 1998).

15. Eugene Jolas, 'Transition: An Occidental Workshop (1927–1938)' in Eugene Jolas (ed.), *transition workshop* (New York: Vanguard Press, 1949), 13–18 (16).

16. Stuart Gilbert, 'Transition days' in Jolas (ed.), *transition workshop*, 19–25 (20).

17. See *A Portrait* 163–67 where Stephen Dedalus refuses to sign McCann's petition for 'universal peace'.

18. Eugene Jolas, 'Manifesto: The Revolution of the Word' in Jolas (ed.), *transition workshop*, 173–4. The manifesto was signed by Kay Boyle, Whit Burnett, Hart Crane, Caresse Crosby, Harry Crosby, Martha Foley, Stuart Gilbert, A. L. Gillespie, Leigh Hoffmann, Eugene Jolas, Elliot Paul, Douglas Rigby, Theo Rutra, Robert Sage, Harold J. Salemson and Laurence Vail.

19. James Joyce, *Ulysses* (Oxford: Oxford University Press, 1993), ix.

20. *Sydney Morning Herald*, 6 September 1997, 9.

21. Julia Sloan Brannon, *Who Reads 'Ulysses'?: The Rhetoric of the 'Joyce Wars' and the Common Reader* (New York and London: Routledge, 2003), xii.

22. Unfortunately Brannan is unable to answer this question with any substantive detail, and, instead, focuses on the dispute between John Kydd and Hans Walter Gabler over the status of Gabler's corrected *Ulysses* text.

23. Brannon, *Who Reads 'Ulysses'?*, xvii.

24. See Sam Slote, 'Structuralism, Deconstruction, Post-structuralism' in John McCourt (ed.), *James Joyce in Context* (Cambridge: Cambridge University Press, 2009), 65–75 (67).

25. Harry Levin, *James Joyce: A Critical Introduction* (London: Faber and Faber, 1959), 16.

26. Finn Fordham, 'Biography' in McCourt (ed.), *James Joyce in Context* (17–26).

27. Erika Mihálycsa, '"Lots of Fun at *Finnegans Wake*" – The Eleventh Annual Trieste Joyce School, 1–7 July 2007', *James Joyce Quarterly*, 44/3, Spring 2007, 432–6 (433).

28. Richard Ellmann and Charles Feidelson, Jr., (eds), *The Modern Tradition* (New York: Oxford University Press, 1965), vi.

29. See, for example, more recent Lacanian readings of *Dubliners* which see the stories less in terms of realism and more in terms of the kind of postmodern performance that others would attribute to the later texts. Wolfgang Wicht writing on '"Eveline" and/as "A Painful Case": Paralysis, Desire, Signifiers', claims that 'the

state of paralysis [in *Dubliners*] is not confined to its representational and symbolic quality but must be taken as a moment of artistic presentation that immediately sets free aspects of the Other (dreams, visions and desires), and is to be related to the politics of gender and to processes of deconstruction and to the *difference* of meaning, which the Joycean texts perform'. See Wicht's essay in Ulrich Schneider and Mary Power, *New Perspectives on Dubliners* (Amsterdam-Atlanta: Rodopi, 1997), 115–42 (117).

Chapter 2

1. Aingeal Clare, '"Trieste Ate I My Livre": The Nineteenth Annual Trieste Summer School', 28 June–4 July 2009, *JJQ*, 46/2, 207–10 (209).
2. *United Irishman*, led by Arthur Griffiths and William Rooney, was the newspaper of Sinn Féin between 1898 and 1906 when it collapsed under a libel suit. The newspaper was reformed as *Sinn Féin*, which continued until 1914 when it was suppressed by the British government.
3. A number of critics have suggested that Joyce was a pacifist. There is little to support such an assertion, unless one assumes that Bloom's famous outburst against force in the 'Cyclops' episode of *Ulysses* speaks for Joyce. See *U* 12.1481.
4. Peter Costello, *James Joyce: The Years of Growth 1882-1915* (West Cork: Roberts Rinehart, 1992), 8.
5. 'Accursed be the day . . . when the invaders first touched our shores. They came to a nation famous for its love of learning, its piety, its heroism [and] doomed Ireland to seven centuries of oppression . . . In my daydreams I revive a brighter period of Irish history when Erin was the cradle of saints and science.' *The Correspondence of Daniel O'Connell* edited by M. O'Connell, vol. iv (Shannon: Irish University Press, 1974), 87–8.
6. See W. B. Yeats, *Uncollected Prose by W.B. Yeats*, edited by John P. Frayne, vol. 1 (London: Macmillan, 1970), where Yeats describes Mangan's poetry as a 'brute cry form the gutters of the earth' (177) and compares his intense but essentially feeble introspection with the combative vigour Yeats thought typical of the O'Grady/ Ferguson strain of Gaelicism.
7. 'Ireland at the Bar' (1907) deals with the trial of Myles Joyce 'a bewildered old man, left over from a culture which is not ours' (*OCPW*, 146) who did not know English. He was found guilty of agrarian outrage and hung. In Joyce's account the trial 'presents the image of Ireland in the dock and unable to defend itself against the charges of the international press and popular opinion' (*OCPW*, 325).
8. Mason and Ellmann (eds.), *The Critical Writings of James Joyce* , 38.
9. See Barry's notes to this sentence – 'Pierre Corneille (1606–84), French dramatist; Metastasio, pseudonym of Pietro Trapassi (1698–1792), Italian poet and creator of *opera seria*; Pumblechook, a fawning character in Dickens's *Great Expectations*; Pedro Calderón de la Barca (1600–81), Spanish dramatist and poet' (*OCPW*, 292).
10. See for example, Garry M. Leonard, *Reading Dubliners Again: A Lacanian Perspective* (Syracuse: Syracuse University Press, 1993) and Gerald Doherty: *Dubliners' Dozen: The Games Narrators Play* (Madison N.J.: Fairleigh Dickinson University Press, 2004).
11. See *Letters* II, 111, for Joyce's explanation of the structure of *Dubliners* in these terms.
12. See the comment in Joyce's essay, 'Oscar Wilde: The Poet of "Salome"', 'What Dorian Gray's sin was no one says and no one knows. He who discovers it has committed it' (*OCPW*, 151).
13. For glosses on some of these allusions see *JA*, 49.
14. The phrase belongs to Stanislaus Joyce who wrote in *My Brother's Keeper*:

> The life which he found in novels was not the life that passed before his steel-blue eyes and unblinking gaze in the streets of Dublin; the emotions which he found in poetry were not those he found in his own heart, but sumptuous

exaggerations to which the poets rose by dint of leading haughty and elaborate lives ... His refusal to compromise with the truth had begun. Some of the poorest nations in the world – Armenia, Greece, Ireland – have given birth to some of the world's richest men. The most secretive race in Europe, the Irish, whose literature has never dared to express any but academic ideas on anything, gave birth to one of the most ruthless realists in literature.

(*MBK*, 106–7)

15. See *JA*, 81. The Tristan and Isolde story is important not just in 'A Painful Case' but in *Exiles, Ulysses* and especially *Finnegans Wake*. For a short account of the story see *Brewer's Dictionary of Phrase and Fable*, revised edn (London: Cassel, 1963), 913.
16. Mason and Ellmann (eds.), *The Critical Writings of James Joyce*, 150.
17. For an account of the development of the *A Portrait* text see Hans Walter Gabler, 'The Seven Lost Years of *A Portrait of the Artist as a Young Man*', in Thomas F. Staley and Bernard Benstock (eds), *Approaches to Joyce's 'Portrait': Ten Essays* (Pittsburgh: University of Pittsburgh Press, 1976).
18. For a discussion of the *bildungsroman* and Joyce's part in it see J. H. Buckley, *Season of Youth: The Bildungsroman from Dickens to Golding* (Cambridge, MA.: Harvard University Press, 1974).
19. Jenny Holt, *Public School Literature, Civic Education and the Politics of Male Adolescence* (Farnham: Ashgate, 2008), 58.
20. See Patrick Parrinder, *James Joyce* (Cambridge: Cambridge University Press, 1984) which sees Stephen following 'a typically romantic quest, inherited by the symbolists and decadents of the late nineteenth century and passed on to early modernists' (92).
21. See Holt, *Public School Literature*, 56.
22. The word 'egoist', although it echoes throughout *Stephen Hero*, never appears in *A Portrait* which refers instead to Stephen's 'pride'. For a discussion of Joyce and egoism which has significant bearing on the account here see Jean Michel Rabaté, *James Joyce and the Politics of Egoism* (Cambridge: Cambridge University Press, 2001), where identifying Joyce as an egoist becomes 'an effort to link his literary and political position to a much older debate hinged around the claims of the "individual" fighting against repressive systems, claims that were often refuted as being either "egoistic" or "anarchistic"' (24). Drawing on David Weir's thesis in *Anarchy and Culture: The Aesthetic Politics of Modernism* (Amherst: University of Massachusetts Press, 1997), Rabaté sees modernism as an aesthetic following on from the political failure of anarchism, much as revivalism developed out of the failure of Parnellism (see *Politics of Egoism*, 25).
23. See Hugh Kenner, *Dublin's Joyce* (London: Chatto and Windus, 1955), 109–33.
24. Parrinder, *James Joyce*, 78.
25. Esau was the dispossessed son of Issac. See 'Genesis' 25–7
26. Harry Levin, *James Joyce: A Critical Introduction*, (London: Faber and Faber, 1954), 33–4.
27. William York Tyndall, *A Reader's Guide to James Joyce* (London: Thames and London, 1959), 106.
28. Kenner, *Dublin's Joyce*, 81.
29. Kenner, *Dublin's Joyce*, 93.
30. Michael Billington writing in *The Guardian*, 3 August 2006. He went on to suggest that the play's unresolved ending 'reminds us that Joyce anticipated Pirandello, Beckett and Pinter in allowing spectators the dignity of choice'.
31. Nicholas de Jongh, *Evening Standard*, 3 August 2006.
32. See, for example sections 202–04 of *Beyond Good and Evil* (1886) where Nietzsche writes that 'the democratic movement is not only a form of the decay of political organisation but a form of the decay, namely the diminution, of man, making him mediocre and lowering his value.' *Beyond Good and Evil: Prelude to a Philosophy of the Future*, translated with a commentary by Walter Kaufmann (New York: Vintage, 1966), 117.

Chapter 3

1. The chapters or episodes of *Ulysses* were originally known by their Homeric titles.
2. See Hans Walter Gabler, 'Joyce's Text in Progress' in Derek Attridge (ed.), *The Cambridge Companion to Joyce*, first edition, (Cambridge: Cambridge University Press, 1990), 223.
3. Michael Groden, *'Ulysses' in Progress* (Princeton: Princeton University Press, 1977), 4.
4. Groden, *'Ulysses' in Progress*, 7
5. Stacey Herbert, 'Composition and Publishing History of the Major Works: an Overview', in McCourt (ed.), *James Joyce in Context*, 10.
6. Quoted in Walton A. Litz, *The Art of Ulysses: Method and Design in 'Ulysses' and 'Finnegans Wake'* (Oxford: Oxford University Press, 1961), 12.
7. The one printed in Chapter 3 on 50–1 is derived from the 1977 book *James Joyce: Citizen and Artist* and was compiled by Charles Peake from the Linati and Gilbert copies of the plan.
8. In the Linati scheme, the phrase 'Telemaco non soffre ancora il corpo' is inserted in the 'Organs' column. Translating this as 'Telemachus does not yet bear a body', Ellmann writes that, as yet, Stephen remains 'abstract' and only potentially 'corporeal'. See Richard Ellmann, *Ulysses on the Liffey* (London: Faber and Faber, 1972), 31.
9. See, for example, Joyce's account of his incorporation into *Ulysses* of 'moly', the herb which Hermes gives to Odysseus as protection from Circe's magic:

   > *Moly* is a nut to crack. My latest is this. Moly is the gift of Hermes, god of public ways and is the invisible influence (prayer, chance, agility, presence of mind, power of recuperation) which saves in case of accident. This would cover immunity from syphilis .. . . Hermes is the god of signposts: i.e. he is, specially for a traveller like Ulysses, the point at which roads parallel merge and roads contrary also. He is an accident of Providence. In this case his plant may be said to have many leaves, indifference due to masturbation, pessimism congenital, a sense of the ridiculous, sudden fastidiousness in some detail, experience.
   >
   > *(Letters* I, 147–8)

10. These titles were removed in the first edition of the full text and replaced by numbers.
11. T. S. Eliot, *Selected Essays* (London: Faber & Faber, 1932), 15
12. T. S. Eliot, '*Ulysses*, Order and Myth', *The Dial* LXXV (1923), 480–3; reprinted in Seon Givens (ed.), *James Joyce: Two Decades of Criticism* (1948; New York Vanguard Press, 1963) and many other places.
13. A common enough phrase, but used to great effect by an eminent figure in classical studies. See Gilbert Murray, *The Rise of the Greek Epic* (1907; Oxford: Oxford University Press, 1934), 3.
14. Mulligan's idea is borrowed from Matthew Arnold's *Culture and Anarchy* (1867). See Stephen's subsequent fantasy about Oxford, a city that by 'her ineffable charm, keeps ever calling us nearer the true goal of all of us, to the ideal of perfection'. See Matthew Arnold, 'Oxford' (1865), reprinted in *Arnold: Poetry and Prose*, introduction and notes by E. K. Chambers (Oxford: Oxford University Press, 1939), 51
15. *The Odyssey of Homer: Done into English Prose* by S. H. Butcher and A. Lang (London: Macmillan, 1893), 26. This was the version used by Joyce in the writing of *Ulysses*.
16. For an early example see Seamus Deane, 'Joyce and Stephen: The Provincial Intellectual' in his *Celtic Revivals: Essays in Modern Irish Literature* (London: Faber and Faber, 1985), 75–91. Later examples include Vincent Cheng, *Joyce Race and Empire* (Cambridge: Cambridge University Press, 1995), 152–62 and Len Platt, *Joyce and Anglo-Irish*, 48–59.
17. Prefatory note to *The Encyclopaedia Britannica*, eleventh edition (Cambridge: Cambridge University Press, 1911), ix. The precise linking of *Ulysses* with modern popular culture remains an incomplete project of Joyce studies. Among the work

that has been done along these lines see Cheryl Herr, *Joyce's Anatomy of Culture* (Chicago: University of Illinois Press, 1986); R. B. Kershner *Joyce, Bakhtin and Popular Culture: Chronicles of Disorder* (Chapel Hill: University of North Carolina Press. 1989) and Garry Leonard, *Advertising and Commodity Culture in Joyce* (Gainesville: University Press of Florida, 1998).

18. For an account of this aspect of 'Wandering Rocks' see Clive Hart, 'Wandering Rocks' in Clive Hart and David Hayman (eds), *James Joyce's 'Ulysses': Critical Essays* (Berkeley and Los Angeles: California University Press, 1974).

19. The list is particularly important in 'Cyclops' and 'Ithaca'. In his essay '"Ithaca": Portrait of the Chapter as a Long List', Fritz Senn writes that 'With its startling novel narrative mode, 'Ithaca' comes as close to a catalogue as anything in literature ever will.' See Andrew Gibson (ed,), *Joyce's Ithaca* (Amsterdam-Atlanta: Rodopi, 1996), 31–77 (31).

20. Dujardin explained in a preface to the 1923 reissue of his novel, a product of Joyce's championing, how in *Les Lauriers* 'the reader finds himself established, from the first lines, in the thought of the principal personage, and the uninterrupted rolling of that thought' (see *JJ*, 519).

21. This head once adorned the Salvation Army Hostel in Townsend Street.

22. See Clifford Geertz, '"Thick Description": Towards an Interpretative Theory of Culture' in *The Interpretation of Cultures:Selected Essays* (New York: Basic Books, 1973), 3–30.

23. Walton A. Litz, 'Joyce's Notes for the Last Episodes of *Ulysses*', *Modern Fiction Studies*, IV (1968), 16. According to Joyce, the word 'yes' in 'Penelope', becomes a 'female word'. Moreover, the female is represented in the four words, 'because', 'bottom', 'woman' and 'yes', these words apparently diagrammatizing woman because they somehow stand-in for the physical reality of 'the female breasts, arse, womb and cunt'. The 'numerology' of the episode, much of it concerned with the number eight, number of infinity and figure of a woman at rest, is a further demonstration of an apparent overindulgence in arch stereotyping (see *Letters* I, 170).

24. See David Hayman, '*Ulysses'and the Mechanics of Meaning* (Englewood Cliffs: Prentice-Hall, 1970).

25. See James H. Maddox. *Joyce's 'Ulysses' and the Assault on Character* (Hassocks: Harvester Press, 1978).

Chapter 4

1. However much Britain may have been perceived as an important site of modernism between the 1880s and the 1920s, it played a relatively minor part in the critical elevation of modernism post-1945. Indeed in Britain the critical term 'had little more than a walk on part . . . and could easily be written into the category "modern" or dismissed by Larkin's kind of provincial snobbism'. See Peter Brooker, *Modernism/Postmodernism* (Harlow: Longman, 1996), 8–9.

2. Richard Ellmann and Charles Feidelson, Jr., (eds), *The Modern Tradition* (New York: Oxford University Press, 1965), ix, viii, 685.

3. Harry Levin, 'What was modernism?' in *Refractions: Essays in Comparative Literature* (New York: Oxford University Press, 1966), 284–5.

4. Ellmann and Feidelson, *The Modern Tradition*, 7.

5. Hugh Kenner, *The Pound Era* (Berkeley and Los Angeles: University of California Press, 1971), 8, 27.

6. Ezra Pound, 'The new sculpture', *Egoist*, 16 February 1914, 67–8

7. Irving Howe, *The Decline of the New* (London: Victor Gollancz, 1971), 17.

8. Jacques Derrida, '*Ulysses* Gramophone HEAR SAY YES IN JOYCE', in Derek Attridge (ed.), *Acts of Literature/Jacques Derrida* (New York and London: Routledge, 1992), 281.

9. James Fairhall, *James Joyce and the Question of History* (Cambridge: Cambridge University Press, 1993), 9.

10. Margot Norris, 'The Critical History of *Finnegans Wake* and the *Finnegans Wake* of Historical Criticism' in Mark A. Wollaeger, Victor Luftig and Robert Spoo (eds), *Joyce and the Subject of History* (Ann Arbor: University of Michigan Press, 1996), 177–93 (178).

11. Lyn Pykett, *Engendering Fictions: The English Novel in the Early Twentieth Century* (London: Edward Arnold, 1995), 3.

12. Enda Duffy, *The Subaltern 'Ulysses'* (Minneapolis and London: University of Minneapolis Press, 1994), 1, 10.

13. See Deane, *Celtic Revivals*. Deane was one of the first to point out how as an Irish journalist in Trieste Joyce had 'staunchly defended Griffith's [Sinn Fein] line of argument on key issues', 139. See also Cheng, *Joyce Race and Empire*, xv.

14. Andrew Gibson and Len Platt, 'Introduction' in Gibson and Platt (eds), *Joyce, Ireland, Britain* (Gainesville: University Press of Florida), 11.

15. Cheng, *Joyce Race and Empire*, 2.

16. Luke Gibbons, *Transformations in Irish Culture* (Cork: Cork University Press, 1996), 3.

17. 'Dialogue with Jacques Derrida' in Richard Kearney, *Dialogues with Contemporary Continental Thinkers* (Manchester: Manchester University Press, 1985), 116.

18. Gibbons, *Transformations in Irish Culture*, 5–6.

19. Emer Nolan, *James Joyce and Nationalism* (London: Routledge, 1995), 28, 31.

20. Nolan, *James Joyce and Nationalism*, 57–8.

21. Gibbons, 6.

22. Nolan, 95.

23. Ibid., 130.

24. See Thomas Hofheinz, *Joyce and the Invention of Irish History: 'Finnegans Wake' in Context* (Cambridge: Cambridge University Press, 1995) and Len Platt, *Joyce, Race and Finnegans Wake* (Cambridge: Cambridge University Press, 2007).

25. It seems clear also that the juxtaposition of the genteel cultural nationalism of Anglo–Ireland against the cynical narrow mindedness of the I-narrator frames the bigotry of the citizen, producing a three-cornered assault on conservative cultural nationalism, although, not on republicanism itself. For an alternative view see Nolan, *James Joyce and Nationalism*, 85–119.

26. See Andrew Gibson, *Joyce's Revenge: History, Politics and Aesthetics in Ulysses'* (Oxford: Oxford University Press, 2002), 171–82.

27. Gilbert Seddes writing specifically about 'Oxen' in a review of *Ulysses* published in *The Nation* in 1922.

28. Joyce claimed not to have read Freud and had 'a distaste' for his ideas. See *JJ*, 546.

29. Peake, *James Joyce: the Citizen and the Artist*, 287.

30. Gerald L. Burns, 'Eumaeus', in Hart and Hayman (eds), *James Joyce's 'Ulysses'*, 369.

Chapter 5

1. Joseph Campbell and Henry Morton Robinson, *A Skeleton Key to 'Finnegans Wake'* (London: Faber and Faber, 1947), 11 and 13.

2. Margot Norris, *The Decentred Universe of 'Finnegans Wake': A Structuralist Analysis* (Baltimore: Johns Hopkins University Press, 1974), 7.

3. See Finn Fordham, *Lots of Fun at 'Finnegans Wake': Unravelling Universals* (Oxford: Oxford University Press, 2007).

4. Weldon Thornton, *Allusions in Ulysses: A Line by Line Reference to Joyce's Complex Symbolism* (1961; New York: Touchstone, 1973), 11.

5. See Katherine Mullin's work in this area in *James Joyce, Sexuality and Social Purity* (Cambridge: Cambridge University Press, 2003) and chapter 7 of Platt, *Joyce, Race and Finnegans Wake*.

6. The analogy between writing and engineering, now commonplace, was apparently first suggested by Weaver herself. 'I am glad you liked my punctuality as an engine

driver,' Joyce replied to her in April 1927. 'I have taken this up because I am really one of the greatest engineers, if not the greatest, in the world besides being a music-maker, philosophist and heaps of other things. All the engines I know are wrong. Simplicity. I am making an engine with only one wheel. No spokes of course. The wheel is a perfect square. You see what I am driving at, don't you?' (*Letters* I, 251).

7. As Danis Rose and John O'Hanlon have shown, VI.B.10, dated late October 1922, contains notes used for the earliest drafts and is thus the earliest surviving record of the *Wake*. See Danis Rose and John O'Hanlon, 'A Nice Beginning: On the *Ulysses*/*Finnegans Wake* Interface', in Geert Lernout (ed.), *'Finnegans Wake': Fifty Years* (Amsterdam: Rodopi, 1990), 165–73.

8. See David Hayman, *The 'Wake' in Transit* (Ithaca: Cornell University Press, 1961), 33–55

9. Luca Crispi, Sam Slote and Dirk van Hulle, 'Introduction' in Luca Crispi and Sam Slote (eds), *How Joyce Wrote 'Finnegans Wake'* A Chapter-by Chapter Genetic Guide (Madison: University of Wisconsin Press, 2007), 3–48 (14–15). In *The Textual Diaries of James Joyce* (Dublin: Lilliput, 1995), Danis Rose argues differently that the sketches were ideas for a book to be called *Finn's Hotel*. That project was abandoned when the HCE sketch developed, as Rose sees it, into the *Wake*. The other sketches later appear, but they were incorporations of detritus rather than fundamental. Slote argues that recently discovered manuscripts do not support Rose's ideas in this respect (see the introduction to *How Joyce Wrote 'Finnegans Wake'*, 15).

10. Samuel Beckett, 'Dante . . . Bruno. Vico . . . Joyce' in Samuel Beckett and others, *Our Exagmination Round his Factification for Incamination of 'Work in Progress'* (1929; London: Faber and Faber, 1961), 14.

11. 'Public' here refers to the public bar, earthier than the lounge or the saloon and usually reserved for men only in Joyce's day.

12. The sigla changed over time and were used with great inventiveness by Joyce. The essential designations, however, are:

    E (used in rotated forms) HCE
    Δ ALP
    ⊏ Shem
    ∧ Shaun

    ⊏ Shem and Shaun
    I Issy
    T Tristram
    X Mamalujo (the four old men)

    ⪦ Snake
    P Patrick
    K Kevin or Kate
    O the Twelve (jurors)

    O the Maggies (dancing or rainbow girls)
    □ the Book

13. For an engaging account of the development of the text through the various stages of composition see Fordham, *Lots of Fun at 'Finnegans Wake'*.

14. *James Joyce's Scribbledehobble: The Ur-Workbook for 'Finnegans Wake'* edited with notes and an introduction by T. E. Connolly (Evanston: Northwestern University Press, 1961), ix.

15. Published by Brepols, volumes have now appeared for notebooks 1, 3, 5, 6, 10, 14, 16, 25, 29, 32, 33 and 47.

16. J. B. S. Haldane, *Daedalus, or the Science of the Future* (London: Kegan Paul, 1924), 57–8. For an account of Joyce's usage of this text in the notebooks see Geert Lernout (ed.), *The Finnegans Wake Notebooks at Buffalo* (Turnout, Belgium: Brepols, 2001), V1.B.1, 5–6.

17. Haldane, *Daedalus*, 84–5.

18. Geert Lernout's introduction to *Notebooks at Buffalo*, V1.B.1, 7.
19. See Lernout, *Notebooks at Buffalo*, V1.B.1, 075 (a). The translations in this and the following extract are Lernout's.
20. See *Notebooks at Buffalo*, V1.B.1, 075 (a)
21. The names of these supplicants suggest the verbs 'will', 'can' and 'ought' in English and French. See *Annotations*, 51.
22. Calcium chloride absorbs moisture; whether 'hydrophobe sponges' do is a moot point. See *Annotations*, 35.
23. This passage concerns sieges. It alludes to Balfe's opera, *The Siege of Rochelle*; Bar-le-Duc, the town in France that was the staging post for the siege of Verdun in 1916, and Bergen-op-Zoom, the town in southwest Holland that was frequently besieged. See *Annotations*, 73.
24. For examples of early accounts see Campbell and Robinson, *A Skeleton Key*; William York Tindall, *A Reader's Guide to James Joyce* (London: Thames and Hudson, 1959), 237–96 and Adaline Glasheen, *Third Census of Finnegans Wake*: *An Index of Characters and Their Roles* (Berkeley: University of California Press, 1977), xxiii–lxxi.
25. See, for example, *Lots of Fun at 'Finnegans Wake'* where Fordham writes that at III.1, 'It is now night – midnight or later, and while everyone is sleeping we move into a dream world, or a dream within the larger dream of the whole novel' (14).
26. In this 1926 letter to Harriet Shaw Weaver, Joyce indicated that the 'theories' of Giordano Bruno and Vico were important to the *Wake*. 'I would not pay overmuch attention to these theories,' he wrote, 'beyond using them for all they are worth, but they have gradually forced themselves on me through circumstances of my own life'. Since then a full-length study on Joyce and Vico has appeared as well as a collection of essays and numerous individual essays and articles on the subject. One of the latter, Beckett's 'Dante . . . Bruno. Vico . . . Joyce' is perhaps the single most well-known essay on the *Wake*. Despite these efforts, however, there is no consensus on precisely what the importance of *New Science* is to the *Wake* and, indeed, some critical frustration on the issue. In his study, *Joyce and the Invention of Irish History* (Cambridge: Cambridge University, 1995), Thomas Hofheinz's argues that the *Wake* is not modelled on *New Science* at all but constitutes, rather, a fundamentally parodic dismantling of Vico's 'patriarch paradigm'. Here the *Wake* assaults what Hofheinz sees as 'Vico's primary axiomatic weakness . . . the purity of the transcendent patriarchy he portrayed, a purity absolutely necessary for any professedly orthodox Catholic interpretation of history' (141).
27. Mary Colum was a revivalist who later became a generalist literary critic. She knew Joyce over a long period of time. See her reminiscences, assembled posthumously by her husband Padraic Colum as *Our Friend James Joyce* (London: Victor Gollancz, 1959).
28. See *Annotations*, 31–2 for further explanation of this passage.
29. See *Annotations*, 54 for glosses on these questions. The first roughly translates as an offer of tea with bread and butter. The second suggests the phrase 'how are you, my young ladies?' and the third 'how are you?'
30. Amongst the figures alluded to here are Vespasian and Marcus Aurelius (both Roman Emperors); Napoleon Bonaparte; the Duke of Wellington (Wellesley); General Blucher (a Prussian general who fought at Waterloo) and Andrew Ducrow. The latter was a horseman who performed at the Theatre Royal, Dublin as 'The Napoleon of Equestrians'. See *Annotations*, 132–3.
31. The French word for yellow, 'jaune', is implied here, and jaundice – and the season Spring, which might be thought of in yellow terms. See also *Annotations*, 233.
32. This version of the start of things is accompanied by a string of Sanskrit words and other Hindu references and is for that reason particularly evocative of the Aryan myth.
33. For Darwin see 'origin of species'; 'charlotte darlings', suggesting the song 'Charlie is my Darling', and 'chattering in dissent' which in this context alludes to Darwin's *The Descent of Man*. Christian revelation is suggested in the references St Jerome

the hermit and to the fall (see *Annotations*, 504–5), and Aryanism in the diagrammatic which purported to account for racial superiority/inferiority.

34. 'Translation' characterized much of the early work on the *Wake*, the pioneering concordances and lexicons of *Wake* literature – Helmut Bonheim's *A Lexicon of German in 'Finnegans Wake'* (1967), for example; Adaline Glasheen's *The Census of 'Finnegans Wake'* (1963,1977); Clive Hart's *A Concordance to Finnegans Wake* (1963); Lewis O. Mink's *A 'Finnegans Wake' Gazetteer* (1978) and *A Wake Newslitter* (1962–1984) initially edited by Clive Hart and Fritz Senn. This kind of scholarship, although it has had to face criticism, also had an important impact on the culture of Joyce scholarship. While it has been displaced by different kinds of *Wake* expertise, it remains significant in terms of contemporary *Wake* reading practices, for obvious reasons – the *Wake* is a text that cries out for explication. For many readers, then, the most indispensable companion to the *Wake* remains Roland McHugh's *Annotations to Finnegans Wake* (1980, 1991, 2006), a compilation of annotation.
35. Fordham, *Lots of Fun*, 11.
36. Francis Motz Boldereff, *Reading Finnegans Wake* (Pennsylvania: Classic Non-Fiction Library, 1959), 2.
37. Thomas C. Hofheinz, *Joyce and the Invention of Irish History: 'Finnegans Wake'* (Cambridge: University of Cambridge Press, 1995), 121.
38. Fordham, *Lots of Fun*, 11.
39. Edmund Wilson was an influential critic of his day. See Derek Attridge, 'Finnegans Awake: The Dream of Interpretation', *James Joyce Quarterly*, vol. 27 no. 1 (1989), 11–29 (21)
40. Attridge, 'Finnegans Awake', 17, 26.
41. Attridge, 13.
42. Philip Kitcher, *Joyce's Kaleidoscope: An Invitation to Finnegans Wake* (Oxford and New York: Oxford University Press, 2007), 18, 51.
43. John Bishop, *James Joyce's Book of the Night: 'Finnegans Wake'* (Madison: University of Wisconsin Press, 1986), 27.

Chapter 6

A version of the material on the *Encyclopedia Britannica* first appeared in the *James Joyce Quaterly*, Vol. 47 (fall 2009), and appears here by permission of the *JJQ*.

1. Thomas F. Staley and Randolph Lewis, *Reflections on James Joyce: Stuart Gilbert's Paris Journal* (Austin:University of Texas Press, 1993), 20–1; 26–7.
2. James S. Atherton, *The Books at the Wake: a Study of Literary Allusions in James Joyce's 'Finnegans Wake'* (1959; Mamaroneck, NY: Paul Appel, 1974), 87, 47. Actually there is no article on polar exploration in *EB* 11, although there is one on 'polar regions'.
3. Retzius (1796–1860) was a professor of anatomy at the Karolinska Institute in Stockholm.
4. See, for example, *FW* 5.6–9, which explains that Tim Finnegan was the first 'to bare arms and a name', the first to roll up his sleeves as the first builder, the first to bear military arms and the first to possess a coat of arms: 'His crest of huroldry, in vert with ancillars, troublant, argent, a hegoak, poursuivant, horrid, horned. His scrutchum fessed, with archers strung, helio, of the second. Hooch is for husbandman handling his hoe.'
5. The Mental Deficiency Act of 1913 created 'mental defectives' categorized as 'imbeciles', 'idiots' or 'the feeble-minded'. The latter included those of average intelligence who were nevertheless deemed 'socially inefficient'. The Alien Immigration Act, much shaped by Edwardian anti-Semitism, was designed to prevent paupers and criminals from entering the UK. The Report of the Physical Deterioration Committee (1904) was set up in response to a document by the Director General of

the Army Medical Services in which he claimed that recruitment for the Boer War was being hindered by the lack of physically adequate men. National efficiency became a board-based movement the primary aim of which was to address the perceived issue of a decline in the quality of racial stock.

6. G. R. Searle, *Eugenics and Politics in Britain 1900–1914* (Leyden: Noordhoff International Publishing, 1976), 12–13.

7. See *Joyce and the Invention of Irish History* where Hofheinz writes of 'Joyce's internationalization of Ireland in *Ulysses*' which 'paves the way for a more radical effort in *Finnegans Wake*', 42.

8. It is not known whether Joyce knew the books about these 'families'. *Notebooks at Buffalo* V1.B.10 states at 108 that a note about the Jukes 'presumably has its source in an article [discussing Goddard's book] which appeared in 1913', but there is no indication as to why this view is held.

9. R. L. Dugdale, *The Jukes: A Study in Crime, Pauperism, Disease and Heredity, also Further Studies of Criminals* (1877; London: G. P. Putnam, 1891), viii. In Edward Larson's *Sex, Race and Science – Eugenics in the Deep South* (London and Baltimore: John Hopkins Press, 1995), Dugdale is described as a pioneer 'in the genealogy of degeneracy' (19).

10. Henry Herbert Goddard, *The Kallikak Family – A Study in the Heredity of Feeble-Mindedness* (New York: Macmillan, 1912), 71, 55, 18.

11. Dugdale, *The Jukes*, 13, 8.

12. Goddard, *The Kallikak Family*, 101–3, 70–1. Goddard was an important figure in American eugenics. In Larson's *Sex, Race and Science*, he is referred to as the 'architect' of plans to segregate the 'feeble-minded' (26).

13. Mary Lowe-Evans, *Crimes Against Fecundity: Joyce and Population Control* (Syracuse, NY: Syracuse University, 1989), 90–9.

14. 'The moment when Joyce wrote in English, he felt himself performing a humiliating translation of a split language choice. In his writings he seeks to express that sundering; and, eventually, in *Finnegans Wake* he would weave the absent texts in the space between standard Irish and standard English.' Declan Kiberd, *Inventing Ireland: The Literature of the Modern Nation* (London: Jonathan Cape, 1995), 332.

15. Cheng, *Joyce, Race and Empire*, 269.

16. This is Leon Poliakov, referring to and quoting from Grimmelshausen's seventeenth-century text *Teutschen Michael*. See *The Aryan Myth: A History of Racist and Nationalist Ideas in Europe* (London: Sussex University Press in association with Heinemann, 1974), 92.

17. Poliakov, *The Aryan Myth*, 1.

18. Hofheinz, *Joyce and the Invention of Irish history*, 186.

19. Hofheinz, 36–7.

20. Hutchinson, *The Dynamics of Cultural Nationalism*, 137. See also R. F. Foster who writes that the Free State, highly sensitive to notions that it had sold out was later to develop an 'obsession with enforcing public modes of "Irishness"'. Although 'liberal rights were ostensibly guarded in the constitution, the new government was authoritarian; the new regime showed its derivation from Sinn Féin, never unduly fastidious about democratic procedure . . . [it] believed in "strong" not to say, ruthless, government.' *Modern Ireland, 1600–1972* (Harmondsworth: Penguin, 1988), 518–19, 521.

21. For an early account of Joyce's politics see Dominic Manganiello's book of that name, *Joyce's Politics* (London: Routledge and Kegan Paul, 1980).

Chapter 7

1. Reprinted as 'Ulysses Gramophone HEAR SAY YES IN JOYCE', in Derek Attridge (ed.), *Acts of Literature* (London: Routledge, 1992).

2. Julia Sloan Brannon, *Who Reads 'Ulysses'?*, xi.

3. See John Kidd, 'Making Joyce the Wrong Way', *New York Review of Books*, September 25, 1997. Online at www.nybooks.com/articles/archive/1997/sep/25making-the-wrong-joyce/

4. Jasmine Lellock, '"Too full for words": A Reflection on the XXIst International James Joyce Symposium in Tours, France, 15–20 June 2008', *James Joyce Quarterly*, 45/2, Winter 2008, 209–12 .

5. Leah Culligan-Flack, ' "Coming Home to Joyce": A Report on "Eire on Erie", the North American James Joyce Conference, 13–17 June, 2009'. *JJQ*, 46/2, Winter 2009, 201–4 (201–2).

6. Although all genetic critics use similar methods, Geert Lernout has argued that there are at least three versions of genetic criticism each with quite distinct cultural agendas and each with different expectations as to what genetic criticism can achieve. See Lernout's account 'The *Finnegans Wake* Notebooks and Radical Philology' in David Hayman and Sam Slote (eds), *Probes: Genetic Studies in Joyce* (Amsterdam: Rodopi, 1995).

7. Despite its title, Julia Sloan Brannon's 2003 book is primarily about the 'Joyce wars' as opposed to the question of who reads *Ulysses*. William Powell Jones's book, *James Joyce and the Common Reader* (1955, reprinted in 1997) is also disappointing on this score.

8. Nash, *James Joyce and the Act of Reception*, 101.

9. Nash, *James Joyce and the Act of Reception*, 98, 109.

10. See Patrick A. McCarthy, 'Finnegans Wake on Film' online at www.flashpoint-mag.com/pmfilm.htm and Michael Allen's posting on 'Grumpy Old Bookman' at http://grumpyoldbookman.blogspot.com/2004/09/ulysses-in-nighttown.html.

11. See Kate Watson-Smythe, 'Joyce's Grandson Tries to Keep Explicit Molly Bloom off Stage', *Independent on Sunday*, 3 July, 2000, online at www.indepedent.co.uk

12. Scott W. Klein, 'James Joyce and Avant–Garde Music' (2004) online at http://cmc.ie/articles/article850.html.

13. Quoted in Klein, 'James Joyce and Avant–Garde Music'.

14. Reprinted in Pierre Boulez, *Orientations: Collected Writings* edited by Jean-Jacques Nattiez and translated by Martin Cooper (London: Faber, 1986), 143–54.

15. For a listing of some of these works see the 'Bronze by Gold' section of the 'James Joyce the Brazen Head' at www.themodernword.com/joyce.music.html

16. See http://en.wikipedia.org/wiki/jefferson_airplane'

Further Reading

For full bibliographical details of items cited in the text, including the editions of Joyce's texts used in this volume, see Abbreviations. The following is a highly selective sample of some of the secondary material published on Joyce since the 1930s – although some of the titles in the Irish history and culture section go back earlier. This material is classified under the following headings:

- Bibliographical
- Annotations, Concordances
- Archival/Genetic Studies
- Biographical
- Criticism subdivided into the following categories – General Accounts, Critical and Political Writings, *Dubliners*, *A Portrait of the Artist as a Young Man*, *Exiles*, *Ulysses*, *Finnegans Wake*
- Irish History and Culture
- Journals Devoted to Joyce

Bibliographical

The most complete bibliography of Joyce texts and critical material is the ongoing record being compiled by William S. Brockman as the 'Current JJ Checklist' and published in the *James Joyce Quarterly*. This has been running since 1964, previously as the 'Supplemental James Joyce Checklist'. Checklists are cumulated on line at http://research.hrc.utexas.edu/jamesjoycechecklist/ See also:

Deming, R. H. *A Bibliography of James Joyce Studies*. Boston: G. K. Hall, 1964, 1977.

Slocum, J. J. and Cahoon, H. *A Bibliography of James Joyce, 1882–1941*. New Haven: Yale University Press, 1953: reprinted, Westport, CT: Greenwood, 1971.

Staley, T. F. *An Annotated Bibliography of James Joyce*. Brighton: Harvester, 1989.

Annotations, Concordances

The standard annotations to Joyce's work are Don Gifford, *Joyce Annotated: Notes for 'Dubliners' and 'A Portrait of the Artist as a Young Man'*, (2ⁿᵈ edn). Berkeley: University of California Press, 1982; Weldon Thornton, *Allusions*

in 'Ulysses'. Chapel Hill: The University of North Carolina Press, 1961; Don
Gifford and R.J. Seidman, *'Ulysses' Annotated: Notes for James Joyce's 'Ulysses'*,
(2nd edn). Berkeley: University of California Press, 2008; Roland McHugh,
Annotations to 'Finnegans Wake' (3rd edn). Baltimore: The Johns Hopkins
University Press, 2005. See also:

Glasheen, A. *Third Census of 'Finnegans Wake': An Index of the Characters and
Their Roles* (3rd edn). Berkeley and Los Angeles: University of California
Press, 1977.
Hart, C. *A Concordance to 'Finnegans Wake'*. Minneapolis: University of
Minnesota Press, 1963. This retains value, even in the age of the searchable
electronic text.
Hart, C. and Knuth, L. *A Topographical Guide to James Joyce's 'Ulysses'* (revised
1986). Colchester, Essex, England: A Wake Newslitter Press, 1975. Includes
maps and lists of addresses.
Schutte, W. M. *Index of Recurrent Elements in James Joyce's 'Ulysses'*.
Carbondale: Southern Illinois University Press, 1982.
The following are helpful to an understanding of the materials that went into
the making of Joyce's fiction:
Atherton, J. S. *The Books at the 'Wake': A Study of Literary Allusions in James
Joyce's 'Finnegans Wake'*. 1959; New York: Paul P. Appel, 1979. Now much
out of date but a classic study nevertheless.
Bowen, Z. *Musical Allusions in the Works of James Joyce: Early Poetry through
'Ulysses'*. Albany: State University of New York Press, 1975.
Connolly, T. E. *The Personal Library of James Joyce*. University of Buffalo
Studies, Monographs in English, No. 6. Buffalo, NY: The University of
Buffalo Press, 1955.
Ellmann, R. *The Consciousness of Joyce*. London: Faber and Faber, 1977. See
especially the appendix, a full list of Joyce's library up to 1920 and the
move to Paris.
Hodgart, J. C. and Worthington, M. *Song in the Works of James Joyce*. New
York: Columbia University Press, 1959.
Mink, L. O. *A 'Finnegans Wake' Gazetteer*. Bloomington: Indiana University
Press, 1978. A guide to place-names in the *Wake*.

Archival/Genetic Studies

For prepublication material and accounts of the making of Joyce's works see –

Connolly, T. E. (ed.) *James Joyce's Scribbledehobble: The Ur-Workbook for
'Finnegans Wake'*. Evanston, IL: Northwestern University Press, 1961.
Crispi, L. and Slote, S. (eds) *A Genetic Guide to Finnegans Wake*. Madison:
University of Wisconsin Press, 2004.
— *How Joyce Wrote Finnegans Wake*. Madison: University of Wisconsin
Press, 2004.
Deane, V., Ferrer, D., Lernout, D. and G. (eds) *The 'Finnegans Wake' Notebooks
at Buffalo*. Turnout, Belgium: Brepols, 2001. Groundbreaking work on the
Wake notebooks.

Groden, M. *'Ulysses' in Progress*. Princeton: Princeton University Press, 1977.

Groden, M., Gabler, H. W., Hayman, D., Rose, D. and O'Hanlon, J. (eds) 63 volumes. *The James Joyce Archive*. New York and London: Garland, 1977. This important resource is comprised of facsimiles of notebooks, drafts, manuscripts, typescripts and proofs.

Hayman, D. *The 'Wake' in Transit*. Ithaca, NY: Cornell University Press, 1990.

Hayman, D. and Slote, S. (eds) *Probes: Genetic Studies in Joyce*. Amsterdam: Rodopi, 1995.

Herring, P. F. (ed.) *Joyce's 'Ulysses' Notebooks in the British Museum*. Charlottesville: University Press of Virginia, 1972.

Higginson, F. H. *Anna Livia Plurabelle: The Making of a Chapter*. Minneapolis, MN: University of Minneapolis Press, 1960.

Litz, A. W. The *Art of James Joyce: Method and Design in 'Ulysses' and 'Finnegans Wake'*. London: Oxford University Press, 1961.

Rose, D. *The Textual Diaries of James Joyce*. Dublin: Lilliput, 1995.

Scholes, R., and Kain, R. M. (eds) *The Workshop of Dedalus: James Joyce and the Raw Materials for A Portrait of the Artist as a Young Man*. Evanston, IL: Northwestern University Press, 1965 – contains examples of the original epiphanies, some of which were incorporated into chapter two of *A Portrait*; the aesthetic theories later used in chapter 5; the first version of *A Portrait* and many other interesting items.

Slote, S. and Van Mierlo, W. (eds) *Genitricksling Joyce*. Amsterdam: Rodopi, 1999.

Biographical

The standard biography remains Richard Ellmann's *James Joyce*, although it has attracted controversy over the years and been challenged on a number of grounds. Brenda Maddox's *Nora* is a fascinating companion piece. The three volumes of Joyce's letters, although not particularly well edited by comparison to, say, the Oxford edition of Yeats's letters, are an important source for further Joyce study. There are, besides these classics, a great many additional biographies and personal reminiscences.

Byrne, J. F. *The Silent Years: An Autobiography with Memoirs of James Joyce*. New York: Farrar, Straus and Young, 1953.

Costello, P. *James Joyce: The Years of Growth 1882–1915*. West Cork, CO: Roberts Rinehart, 1992.

Gilbert, S. *Reflections on James Joyce: Stuart Gilbert's Paris Journal*. Edited by Thomas F. Staley, Thomas F. and Lewis, Randall. Austin. University of Texas Press, 1993.

Gorman, H. *James Joyce: A Definitive Biography*. London: John Lane, The Bodley Head, 1941. The first and only authorized biography.

Jackson, J. W. and Costello, P. *John Stanislaus Joyce: The Voluminous Life and Genius of James Joyce's Father*. London: Fourth Estate, 1997.

Joyce, S. *The Dublin Diary*. Edited by George Harris Healey. London: Faber and Faber, 1962. A firsthand account and important companion to *My Brother's Keeper*.

McCourt, J. *The Years of Bloom: James Joyce in Trieste, 1904–1920*. Dublin: Lilliput Press, 2000.

Power, A. *Conversations with James Joyce*. Edited by Clive Hart. Dublin: Lilliput, 1999.

Scloss, C. L. *Lucia Joyce: To Dance in the 'Wake'*. London: Bloomsbury, 2004.

Sullivan, K. *Joyce Among the Jesuits*. New York: New York Columbia Press, 1958.

Criticism

(i) General Accounts

A very large number of critical volumes have covered a full range of Joyce's writing. This is a wide category covering everything from general introductions to specialist studies. It includes at the early end of things Harry Levin's *James Joyce: A Critical Introduction* (London: Faber and Faber, 1941), pioneering in its day and still of some interest, both historical and otherwise; Colin McCabe's, *James Joyce and the Revolution of the Word* (London: Macmillan, 1978), which marked the 'turn to theory' in Joyce studies and Jean Michel Rabate's *James Joyce and the Politics of Egoism* (Cambridge: Cambridge University Press, 2002), a Lacanian account of how 'textuality' became the central ground in Joyce's studies. See also :

Attridge, D. (ed.) *The Cambridge Companion to James Joyce* (2nd edn). Cambridge: Cambridge University Press, 2004. This edition differs substantially from the first published in 1990.

Attridge, D. and Ferrar, D. (eds) *Post-Structuralist Joyce: Essays from the French*. Cambridge: Cambridge University Press, 1984.

Attridge, D. and Howe, M. (eds) *Semicolonial Joyce*. Cambridge: Cambridge University Press, 2000.

Brown, R. *James Joyce and Sexuality*. Cambridge: Cambridge University Press, 1985.

Cheng, V. J. *Joyce, Race and Empire*. Cambridge: Cambridge University Press, 1995.

Fairhall, J. *James Joyce and the Question of History: 'Finnegans Wake' in Context*. Cambridge: Cambridge University Press, 1993.

Froula, C. *Modernism's Body: Sex, Culture and Joyce*. New York: University of Columbia Press, 1996.

Gibson, A., and Platt, L. (eds) *Joyce, Ireland Britain*. Florida: University Press of Florida, 2006.

Henke, S. *James Joyce and the Politics of Desire*. London: Routledge, 1990

Herr, C. *Joyce's Anatomy of Culture*. Urbana and Chicago: University of Illinois Press, 1986.

Kenner, H. *Dublin's Joyce*. London: Chatto and Windus, 1955. This set some important agendas, especially in relation to Joycean irony in *A Portrait* and remained a standard text until the 1970s.

— *Joyces Voices*. London: Faber and Faber, 1983.

Lowe-Evans, M. *Crimes Against Fecundity: Joyce and Population Control*. Syracuse, KS: Syracuse University Press, 1989.

Manganiello, D. *Joyce's Politics*. London: Routledge and Kegan Paul, 1980.

McCormack, W. J. and Stead, A. (eds) *James Joyce and Modern Literature*. London: Routledge and Kegan Paul, 1982.

Mullin, K. *James Joyce, Sexuality and Social Purity*. Cambridge: Cambridge University Press, 2003.

Nash, J. *James Joyce and the Act of Reception: Reading, Ireland and Modernism*. Cambridge: Cambridge University Press, 2006.

Nolan, E. *James Joyce and Nationalism*. London: Routledge, 1995.

Parrinder, P. *James Joyce*. Cambridge: Cambridge University Press, 1984.

Peake, C. *James Joyce: The Citizen and the Artist*. London: Edward Arnold, 1977.

Rabaté, J. M. *James Joyce, Authorized Reader*. Baltimore: Johns Hopkins University Press, 1991.

Riquelme, J. P. *Teller and Tale in Joyce's Fiction: Oscillating Perspectives*. Baltimore: John Hopkins University Press, 1983.

Seidel, M. *James Joyce: a Short Introduction*. Oxford: Blackwell, 2002.

Spoo, R. *James Joyce and the Language of History*. Oxford: Oxford University Press, 1994.

Valente, J. *James Joyce and the Problem of Justice*. Cambridge: Cambridge University Press, 1995.

Critical and Political Writings

Relatively little has been devoted specifically to Joyce's critical and political writings, although they have frequently been used in many general accounts. Kevin Barry's introduction to *Occasional, Critical and Political Writing*, and his notes to the pieces, are excellent. See also Jeanne A. Flood, 'Joyce and the Maamtrasna Murders', *JJQ*, 28/4 (Summer 1991), 879–88 and L. H. Platt, 'Joyce and the Anglo-Irish Revival: The Triestine Lectures', *JJQ*, 29/2 (Winter 1992), 259–66.

Dubliners

There have been many memorable essays on *Dubliners* including Brewster Ghiselin's much anthologized, 'The Unity of *Dubliners*', which first appeared in *Accent*, Spring and Summer 1956, and Ellmann's 'The Backgrounds of "The Dead"', which first appeared in the 1959 edition of *James Joyce*. Both these pieces are featured in the useful 1973 collection edited by Morris Beja, *'Dubliners' and 'A Portrait of the Artist as a Young Man': A Casebook* (London: MacMillan). John Michel Rabate's 'Silence in *Dubliners*' in Colin McCabe (ed.), *James Joyce: New Perspectives* (Brighton: Harvester Press, 1982), has been influential, as has John Paul Riquelme's Lacanian reading, 'Joyce's "The Dead": The Dissolution of the Self and the Police', which first appeared in *Style*, 25 (1991). Two editions of the *JJQ* (in 1991 and 2000) have been devoted to the *Dubliners* stories, as has a 1995 edition of *Studies in Short Fiction*.

Many single-authored books and collections on *Dubliners* have appeared over the years. The following have, for various reasons, made particular impact:

Beck, W. *Joyce's 'Dubliners': Substance, Vision and Art*. Durham, NC: Duke Press, 1967.

Garrett, P. K. (ed.) *Twentieth Century Interpretation of 'Dubliners'*. Englewood Cliffs, NJ: Prentice-Hall, 1968.

Hart, C. *James Joyce's 'Dubliners': Critical Essays*. London: Faber, 1969.

Since the 1990s a spate of interesting new criticism has appeared on this early work, some of it informed by Lacanian perspective. See:

Doherty, G. *'Dubliners' Dozen, The Games Narrators Play*. Madison, NJ: Fairleigh Dickinson University Press, 2004.

Frawley, O. (ed.) *A New and Complex Sensation: Essays on Joyce's 'Dubliners'*. Dublin: Lilliput Press, 2004.

Leonard, G. *Reading 'Dubliners Again: A Lacanian Perspective*. Syracuse, NY: Syracuse University Press, 1993.

Norris, M. *Suspicious Readings of 'Dubliners'*. Philadelphia, PA: University of Pennsylvania Press, 2003.

Schneider, U., and Power, M. (eds) *New Perspectives on 'Dubliners'*. Amsterdam-Atlanta: Rodopi, 1997.

For a post-colonial reading of Dubliners see:
Murphy, S. P. *James Joyce and Victims: Reading the Logic of Exclusion*. Chapter 2. Madison, NJ: Fairleigh Dickinson University Press, 2003.

A Portrait of the Artist as a Young Man

For the early critical debates on irony in *A Portrait* see:

Kenner, H. 'A Portrait in Perspective' and Booth, W. C. 'The Problem of Distance' in *A Portrait of the Artist'*, both reprinted in Beja, *'Dubliners' and 'A Portrait of the Artist as a Young Man': A Casebook*.

As with *Dubliners* and the critical writings, most generalist works on Joyce will have sections on *A Portrait*. Charles Peake, *James Joyce: The Citizen and the Artist* is noteworthy for its attempt to relate Stephen Dedalus's aesthetic theories in *A Portrait* to the formal design of the novel itself. Patrick Parrinder's *James Joyce* gives an interesting overview which is particularly strong on *A Portrait* and aestheticism.

The many collections of essays on *A Portrait*, include:

Schutte, W. M. *Twentieth-Century Interpretations of 'A Portrait of the Artist as a Young Man'*. Englewood Cliffs, NJ: Prentice-Hall, 1968.

Staley, T. and Benstock, B. (eds) *Approaches to Joyce's 'Portrait': Ten Essays*, containing Breon Mitchell's useful essay, 'A Portrait and the Bildungsroman Tradition'. Pittsburg, PA: University of Pittsburg Press, 1976.

Wollaeger, M. (ed.) *James Joyce's 'A Portrait of the Artist as a Young Man'*. Oxford: Oxford University Press, 2003. Among the many interesting contributions here are Maud Ellmann's stylish piece 'The Name and the Scar: Identity in *The Odyssey* and *A Portrait of the Artist as a Young Man*' and Michael Levenson's 'Stephen's Diary in Joyce's *Portrait* – The Shape of Life'.

Exiles

J. MacNicholas, *James Joyce's 'Exiles': a Textual Companion*. New York: Garland Press, 1971, is useful. For the most part, criticism on *Exiles* will be found in the more general accounts of Joyce's work. See, for example, E. Brandabour, *A Scrupulous Meanness: a Study of Joyce's Early Work*. Urbana: University of Illinois Press, 1971. Among essays on *Exiles* see S. R. Britvic, 'Structures and Meaning in Joyce's *Exiles*', *JJQ*, 6, 1968 and B. W. Schaffer, 'Kindred by Choice: Joyce's *Exiles* and Goethe's Elective Affinities', *JJQ*, 26, 1989.

Ulysses

Collections of essays and individual studies on *Ulysses* include:

Attridge, D. (ed.) *James Joyce's 'Ulysses': A Casebook*. New York: Oxford University Press, 2003.

Duffy, E. *The Subaltern 'Ulysses'*. Minneapolis, MN: University of Minneapolis Press, 1994.

French, M. *The Book as World: James Joyce's 'Ulysses'*. Cambridge, MA: Harvard University Press, 1976.

Gibson, A. *Joyce's Revenge: History, Politics and Aesthetics in 'Ulysses'*. Oxford: Oxford University Press: 2002.

Gilbert, S. *James Joyce's 'Ulysses'* (revised edition), (1930). London: Faber, 1952.

Goldberg, S. L. *The Classical Temper: a Study of James Joyce's 'Ulysses'*. London: Chatto and Windus, 1961.

Hart, C. and Hayman, D. (eds) *James Joyce's 'Ulysses': Critical Essays*. Berkeley and Los Angeles: California University Press, 1974.

Hayman, D. *'Ulysses' and the Mechanics of Meaning*. Englewood Cliffs, NJ: Prentice-Hall, 1970.

Kenner, H. *'Ulysses'* (revised edition), (1980). Baltimore, MD: Johns Hopkins University Press, 1987.

Kershner, R. B. (ed.) *Joyce and Popular Culture*. Miami: University Press of Florida, 1996.

Lawrence, K. *The Odyssey of Style in 'Ulysses'*. Princeton, NJ: Princeton University Press, 1981.

Maddox, J. H. *Joyce's 'Ulysses' and the Assault on Character*. Hassocks, Sussex: Harvester Press, 1978.

Norris, M. (ed.) *A Companion to James Joyce's 'Ulysses'*. Boston: Bedford Books, 1998.

Platt, L. *Joyce and the Anglo-Irish: a Study of Joyce and the Literary Revival*. Amsterdam-Atlanta: Rodopi, 1998.

Sherry, V. *James Joyce: 'Ulysses'*. Cambridge: Cambridge University Press, 1994.

Sultan, S. *The Argument of 'Ulysses'*. Columbus: Ohio State University Press, 1964.

Finnegans Wake

Beckett, S., and others *Our Exagmination Round his Factification for Incamination*, 1929. London: Faber, 1972.

Bishop, J. *Joyce's Book of the Dark: 'Finnegans Wake'*. Madison: University of Wisconsin Press, 1986.

Campbell, J. and Morton, H. *A Skeleton Key to Finnegans Wake*. London: Faber and Faber, 1947.

Dalton, J. P. and Hart, C. (eds) *Twelve and a Tilly*. London: Faber and Faber, 1966.

Deane, S. 'Introduction', *Finnegans Wake*. London: Penguin, 1992.

DiBernard, B. *Alchemy and 'Finnegans Wake'*. Albany: State University of New York Press, 1980.

Fordham, F. *Lots of Fun at Finnegans Wake: Unravelling Universals*. Oxford: Oxford University Press, 2007.

Hart, C. *Structure and Motif in 'Finnegans Wake'*. London: Faber and Faber, 1962.

Hofheinz, T. C. *Joyce and the Invention of Irish History*. Cambridge: Cambridge University Press, 1995.

McHugh, R. *The Sigla of 'Finnegans Wake'*. London: Edward Arnold, 1976.

Norris, M. *The Decentred Universe of 'Finnegans Wake'*. Baltimore: Johns Hopkins University Press, 1974.

Platt, L. *Joyce, Race and 'Finnegans Wake'*. Cambridge: Cambridge University Press, 2007.

Rose, D. and O'Hanlon, J. *Understanding 'Finnegans Wake': A Guide to the Narrative of James Joyce's Masterpiece*. New York: Garland, 1982.

Solomon, M. C. *Eternal Geomater: The Sexual Universe of Finnegans Wake*. Carbondale: Southern Illinois University Press, 1969.

Tyndall, W. Y. *A Reader's Guide to 'Finnegans Wake'*. London: Thames and Hudson, 1969.

Verene, P. (ed.) *Vico and Joyce*. New York: State University of New York Press, 1987.

Verene, P. *Knowledge of Things Human and Divine: Vico's 'New Science' and 'Finnegans Wake'*. New Haven, CT and London: Yale University Press, 2003.

Irish History and Culture

Boyd, E. *The Irish Literary Renaissance* (revised edition). London: Grant Richards, 1922.

Brannigan, J. *Race in Modern Irish Literature and Culture*. Edinburgh, Scotland: Edinburgh University Press, 2009.

Brown, M. *The Politics of Irish Literature: from Thomas Davis to W. B. Yeats*. London: Allen and Unwin, 1972.

Cairns, D. and Richards, S. *Writing Ireland: Colonialism, Nationalism and Culture*. Manchester: Manchester University Press, 1988.

Cleary, J. *Literature, Partition and the Nation State: Culture and Conflict in Ireland, Israel; and Palestine*. Cambridge: Cambridge University Press, 2001.

— *Outrageous Fortune: Capital and Culture in Modern Ireland*. Dublin: Field Day, 2007.

Cleary, J. and Connolly, C. (eds) *The Cambridge Guide to Modern Irish Culture*. Cambridge: Cambridge University Press, 2005.

Deane, S. *Celtic Revivals: Essays in Modern Irish Literature*. London: Faber and Faber, 1985.

— *Strange Country: Modernity and Nationhood in Irish Writing Since 1790*. Oxford: Clarendon Press 1997.

Duffy, C. G. Sir, Sigerson, G., K. C. M. G. and Hyde, D. *The Revival of Irish Literature*. London: T. Fisher Unwin, 1894. See especially Douglas Hyde's contribution 'The Necessity for De-Anglicizing Ireland'.

Dwan, D. *The Great Continuity: Culture and Nationalism in Ireland*. Dublin: Field Day, 2008.

Eglinton, J. *Literary Ideals in Ireland*. Dublin: Maunsel, 1899.

— *Anglo-Irish Essays*. Dublin: the Talbot Press, 1917.

— *Irish Literary Portraits*. London: Macmillan, 1935.

Fallis, R. *The Irish Renaissance*. Syracuse, NY: Syracuse University Press, 1977.

Foster, R. F. *Modern Ireland 1600–1972*. Harmondsworth, England: Penguin, 1988.

Gibbons, L. *Transformations in Irish Culture*. Cork, Ireland: Cork University Press, 1996.

Graham, C. *Deconstructing Ireland: Identity, Theory, Culture*. Edinburgh, Scotland: Edinburgh University Press, 2001.

Hutchinson, J. *The Dynamics of Cultural Nationalism; The Gaelic Revival and the Creation of the Irish Free State*. London: Allen and Unwin, 1987.

Kiberd, D. *Inventing Ireland: The Literature of the Modern Nation*. London: Jonathan Cape, 1995.

Leersson, J. *Mere Irish and Fíor-Ghael: Studies in the Idea of Irish Nationality, its Development and Literary Expression Prior to the Nineteenth Century*. Cork, Ireland: Cork University Press in association with Field Day, 1996.

Lloyd, D. *Anomolous States: Irish Writing and the Post-Colonial Moment*. Dublin: Lilliput, 1993.

— *Irish Times: Temporalities of Modernity*. Dublin: Field Day, 2008.

Lyons, F. S. L. *Culture and Anarchy in Ireland, 1890–1939*. Oxford: Oxford University Press, 1982.

McDonagh, O. *States of Mind: a Study of Anglo–Irish Conflict, 1780–1980*. London: Allen and Unwin, 1983.

Miller, D. W. *Church, State and Nation in Ireland 1898–1921*. Dublin: Gill and Macmillan, 1973.

O'Grady, S. *History of Ireland: The Heroic Period*, 2 vols. London: Longman, 1878.

Thompson, W. I. *The Imagination of an Insurrection: Dublin, Easter 1916*. Oxford: Oxford University Press, 1966.

Journals Devoted to Joyce

The oldest of the journals devoted to Joyce is the *James Joyce Quarterly*, University of Tulsa, Tulsa, OK 74104, USA. The *JJQ* was founded by Thomas F. Staley in 1963. For the *Wake* see *A Wake Newslitter* which ran from 1962 to 1984 (this is now available on a CD ROM published by Split Pea Press). See also:

James Joyce Broadsheet. The School of English, University of Leeds, Leeds LS2 9JT, UK.

James Joyce Literary Supplement. University of Miami, Coral Gables, FL 33124, USA.

Joyce Studies Annual, a yearly collection of essays on Joyce. P.O. Box 7219, University Station, The University of Texas, Austin, TX 78713, USA.

Index

Main entries are given in **bold** type.